Native Decatur

The earliest history of the Decatur, Georgia area
from its bedrock formation to the Creek wars

Native Decatur

The earliest history of the Decatur, Georgia area
from its bedrock formation to the Creek wars

Mark Pifer

Downriver Books

2017

First Printing: 2018

ISBN: 978-0-692-97437-7

Downriver Books
450 Clairemont Avenue
Decatur, GA 30030

Ordering Information:
Special discounts are available on quantity purchases by corporations, associations, educators, and others. For details, contact the publisher at the above listed address.
US trade bookstores and wholesalers: Please contact Downriver Books
Tel: (678) 237-3460; or email DownriverBooks@gmail.com.
Cover Art Map: Barker, William & Mathew, Carey (1795) "Georgia, from the Best Authorities", Library of Congress Geography and Map Division

First, to my family. I'm proud to be a figure in your history.
Second, to all who share an interest in preserving local history.

Contents

Maps, Photos, Lists and Illustrations

Acknowledgements

I'm extremely grateful for the generous help of many people in completing this book. First and foremost, I could not have finished it without the support, advice and editing hours of my wife Robin. I'd like to thank my children Ava and Sasha for coming with me on many trips to "look at a tree, a rock or a hole in the ground". They are great young historians and travel companions.

As anyone who wants to study local history does, I also got a great deal of invaluabl7e help from the DeKalb County Historical Society and from Fred Mobley, the DeKalb County Archivist. Please support the DeKalb County Historical Society, not only with money (which is preferred) but also by passing on any information you have about Decatur and the DeKalb County area including your stories, photos and by contributing your very valuable time.

Several other friends, family and well-wishers have given me very valuable advice about how to make this a better, more readable book. My good friend and fellow author Kerry Morris loves to talk about local history like I do and contributed several ideas including the creation of the book's illustrations. My parents, Larry and Janice, also gave me excellent advice and enthusiastic support that kept me grinding toward the finish line.

Foreword

History is as You Find It

There are two very good books about the history of the Decatur area already – "The Story of Decatur" by Caroline McKinney Clarke and "The History of DeKalb County" by Vivian Price. Every person who has any interest in the history of the Decatur area should have Vivian Price's book on their bookshelf as I do. It cannot be improved upon nor added to without inserting superfluous material.

In my desire to add something to this small collection, I've tried to create a book that can sit alongside these other two great books and complete the set. "The Story of Decatur" and "The History of DeKalb County" each focus primarily on the history of the area since its founding in the early 1800s, although each of them has a good but brief section about the area's prehistory. Therefore, I have focused on describing as much as possible about the prehistory of the area around Decatur before its founding. After all, there was a lot more years when things were happening there before 1823 than there were afterward.

I've also tried to assist your imagination in seeing the evidence of that prehistory as you walk around the city today. The area is rich with evidence of what people were doing a long time ago before Europeans arrived. Much of it is just a little hidden among the roads and buildings or covered by a layer of dirt or concrete. Once you have a sense of it though, it's all around you. I now can't drive anywhere in the area without noting several things that are still sitting there by the road (or the road itself) that were familiar to people long before there was an Atlanta or a Decatur.

History is always a work in progress. It needs to be intelligently debated. Don't rely on historians to render an opinion on everything you care about. It may not have been what they cared about. Do your own research. Develop your own opinions. Back them up and discuss them with people. Keep history alive by not letting it die. Allow these people who struggled through tough times and could have been misunderstood to continue telling us stories.

Significant Places to Decatur[1]

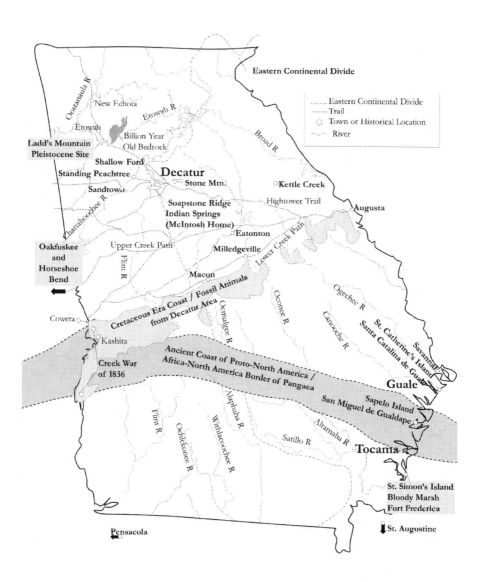

INTRODUCTION

The Land Under Your Feet Was Here a Lot Longer than the Town You Live In

You tell me. When did the history of an area begin? When the town was founded? A lot of things happened here, and there was a lot of people living here long before then. Was it when the Europeans arrived and put their names on things we use now? A lot of people called this home long before that. Was it when people first arrived? Is that when the history of a place begins? Before they arrived, how did everything else get here? The animals. The land. The water. The things that made it a place worth living. All those things must have been caused by something.

You, sitting in your home, are part of the history of the place where you live. Understanding how all of this came to be matters. Understanding how we fit with the world and how we have shaped this place and continue to shape it matters.

Before you start reading this book, I want you to do one thing, at least in your mind. Look down. Feel where you are. You're probably in a house or some other kind of building right now, but that's not what I mean. Think about the ground underneath you. The soil. The rocks beneath that. The lay of the hill you're on. The land. Are you on an upslope or a downslope? Walk outside if it's not too cold, and you're not too settled. You probably see houses. Or maybe you see office buildings. Trees. Roads. And other people, of course.

All those things. Those roads, buildings and grass. It's only been here for a blink of an eye. We get so used to seeing the town we live in. The buildings we made. The roads we made. They seem like they are the landscape. They're not of course. No matter how dense or how old the town is that you live in, it was created on top of something very ancient.

The slope of that hill over there may be that way for a reason. A straight road may take a meandering left turn for seemingly no reason. But more likely, there is a very good reason for that turn and someone a very long time ago figured that out when it was only a way to walk through the woods. A courthouse in the middle of town may look nice up on the hilltop where everyone can see it. Other people before us probably agreed that same hilltop was a useful spot and used it for other activities for a very long time. A shallow part of the stream has probably looked that way for thousands of years and made a nice spot to step across for much, much longer than you've been using it.

And if we draw the lens farther back and really look at the land, we can even see through eyes that are now millions of years old. That river. That mountain. That slab of granite jutting up out of the landscape. They were all there and looked just about the same as they do now long before the first human being arrived here. The signs are everywhere once you start looking around.

No matter how insignificant your town may seem in the history books, it was witness to eons of history. Millions of years of activity occurred here. Communities passed through or were created here thousands of years before we created ours. There have been eons of things being born and dying here. Countless beasts, huge ones and tiny ones, walked or slithered or flew or swam by here. Battles were fought here. Millions of footsteps have been taken here on this very spot where you stand or sit at this very moment. The fact we don't know exactly how it all happened makes those events no less significant to the history of this place and the many, many creatures who have passed by and thought of this place as their home.

As you look around, try to erase the buildings and the roads from your mind. It is much easier for us to do than we might think. The land around us and its features are still poking through the newer layers we have constructed on top of them. They are virtually unchanged from the way they've been for thousands of years or millions of years. All those thousands of passersby and homesteaders who have been here for such a long time before we left our mark left things behind for us to see and find.

Let's go look around at what was there and look for the signs that tell us.

Let's take a very close look at this one small place: Decatur, Georgia.

Decatur Prehistoric Trails Overlaid with Creeks and Roads

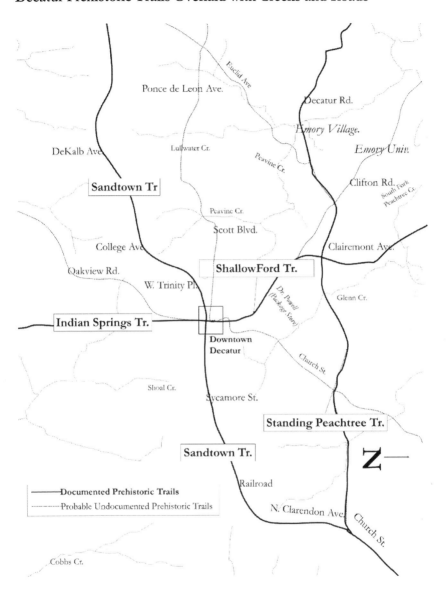

Early History Noteworthy to Decatur, Georgia

- **1,100MM years ago:** The first known supercontinent, Rodinia. Decatur is on a high mountainside.
- **325 to 250MM years ago:** Georgia collides with Africa during the formation of Pangaea and Decatur's bedrock.
- **300MM years ago:** First vertebrates emerge on the land in Decatur.
- **275MM years ago:** Magma creates the granite in Stone Mountain.
- **80MM years ago:** Decatur is a wet, swampy zone full of dinosaurs.
- **15MM years ago:** Erosion has exposed Stone Mountain.
- **5MM years ago:** Pleistocene animals like the giant sloth migrate up from South America across the Isthmus of Panama.
- **2.5MM to 12,000 years ago:** Pleistocene animals arrive in Decatur from the North after crossing through Beringia.
- **12,000 years ago:** Nomadic hunters arrive in Decatur following prey.
- **5,000 years ago:** The first known permanent homes are established in Decatur around the South River and Peachtree Creek.
- **4,000 years ago:** Soapstone from Decatur is traded all over the Southeast and far to the north.
- **1,800 years ago:** The Sandtown area near Decatur is first settled.
- **Circa 1034:** First settlers in Standing Peachtree.
- **1500 – 1800:** 90% of the native population dies due to contact.
- **1526:** Lucas Vazquez de Ayllon establishes the first European colony in North America on the Georgia coast.
- **1540:** De Soto makes a legendary trek through Georgia and makes note of an already growing health crisis among the Coweta Creek Indians.
- **1562:** Jean Ribault establishes Charles Fort near Savannah, the first fort in North America.
- **1565:** The Spanish capture and burn Fort Caroline and in its stead, establish St. Augustine.
- **Circa 1570:** Various Indian tribes coalesce into major groups including the Creeks and the Cherokees.
- **1586:** The English attack and burn St. Augustine.
- **1597:** The entrada of Pedro de Chozas passes through the area of Eatonton, probably the closest early Spanish expedition to Decatur.
- **1674:** Henry Woodward is the first known European to arrive in the Decatur area during a trading expedition fdown the Chattahoochee.
- **1680:** The English attack the Mission Santa Catalina de Guale on St. Catherine's Island. Artifacts of the Mission now reside in Decatur.
- **1732:** The Georgia colony is established by James Oglethorpe.
- **1739:** The War of Jenkins' Ear between Britain and Spain begins.
- **1742:** The Battle of Bloody Marsh between Georgia and the Spanish.

- **1750:** The initial ban on slavery in the Georgia colony is reversed.
- **1774:** Georgia sends no delegates to the First Continental Congress.
- **1775:** George Galphin secures the support or neutrality of many of the Creeks in the Southeast against the British.
- **July 20, 1775:** All five of the Georgia delegates arrive for the Second Continental Congress – two months after it began.
- **February 22, 1777:** Archibald Bulloch, Georgia's first executive leader, dies under very suspicious circumstances.
- **May 15, 1777:** Lachlan McIntosh kills Button Gwinnett in a duel.
- **1777-1778:** Georgia attempts three failed invasions of Florida.
- **1776:** Three Georgians sign the Declaration of Independence.
- **1778:** Archibald Campbell takes Savannah, then Augusta, making Georgia the only colony to return to the British during the Revolution.
- **1779:** The Battle of Kettle Creek preserves American control of the backcountry.
- **1779:** The Siege of Savannah fails to free it from the British.
- **1782:** Secret missions supporting the war occur in Standing Peachtree.
- **1787:** Four Georgia delegates attend the Second Constitutional Convention. Abraham Baldwin and William Few sign the original.
- **1788:** Decatur resident James McNeil is among those to ratify the new US Constitution
- **1790:** Alexander McGillivray signs the Treaty of New York, establishing the Creeks as a separate nation from the United States.
- **1795:** Decatur resident James McNeil is one of few to oppose the fraudulent Yazoo Land Act.
- **1813:** Beginning of the First Creek War, also called the Red Stick War.
- **1814:** The Battle of Horseshoe Bend ends the Red Stick War.
- **1821:** Land Lottery of 1821 distributes Decatur land gained from the First Treaty of Indian Springs.
- **1822:** DeKalb County is carved from Fayette, Henry and Gwinnett.
- **1823:** Land Lot 246 is chosen as the DeKalb County seat, Decatur.
- **1825:** Chief McIntosh is killed by Menawa for negotiating and signing the Second Treaty of Indian Springs.
- **1825:** A battle between Upper and Lower Creeks erupts in the Five Points area near Decatur leaving 50 dead.
- **Early 1836:** The Second Creek war. Six Decatur or DeKalb County residents are killed in the fighting.
- **Late 1836:** Nearly all Creeks and Menawa are forced to leave the South.

CHAPTER 1:
SETTING THE STAGE

A Billion Years Ago, Georgia Crashed into Eastern Europe

The Earth is believed to be around 4.5 billion years old.[2] During most of that time, the land that would become Decatur was located on a smaller North American continent called Laurentia or proto-North America that was often slowly colliding or drifting away from Eastern Europe (called Baltica).[3]

When continents collide (more accurately, the tectonic plates they ride on), a lot happens. As the two pieces of land come together, one will go high and the other will go low with a lot of violence happening in the middle. On the upper side, the land literally folds and mountains are raised. Down below, the intense pressure and heat melt the land and magma forms. Volcanoes rise. New rocks replace old ones.

This is the first piece of known history specific to the Decatur, Georgia area dating back a billion years ago.

About a billion years ago, the continent that the fusing together of North America and Eastern Europe created was called Rodinia.[4] The mountains that were thrown up were called the Grenville range. They stretched from Mexico up through Georgia, through Canada and all the way to Greenland as well as Scotland (which were all attached together at the time).[5]

This is the first piece of known history specific to the Decatur, Georgia area area.[6] We know it happened because the rocks that were created by this collision and made the roots of the Grenville range are still forming the bedrock of the Appalachian Mountains.

Scientists have been able to analyze their age and apply tectonic theory to piece together the story.[7]

[2] USGS Age of the Earth
[3] Gore, Pamela J. W. (2006), Geologic History of Georgia: Overview, New Georgia Encyclopedia
[4] Gore, Pamela J. W. (2006), Geologic History of Georgia: Overview, New Georgia Encyclopedia
[5] Corfu, F., Gasser, D. & Chew, D. M. (eds) New Perspectives on the Caledonides of Scandinavia and Related Areas. Geological Society, London, Special Publications, 390
[6] Gore, Pamela J. W. (2006), Geologic History of Georgia: Overview, New Georgia Encyclopedia
[7] Gore, Pamela J. W. (2006), Geologic History of Georgia: Overview, New Georgia Encyclopedia

The Forming of Rodinia 1 Billion Years Ago[8]

Unfortunately, none of these rocks are right in Decatur anymore because they were either eroded away or recreated as newer rocks by additional mountain building events. The billion-year-old Grenville rocks aren't far away though. There is a band of 1 billion-year-old gneiss that can easily be seen around 45 miles north of Decatur near Cartersville. If you exit I-75 at Route 20/Canton Highway and drive east, you are driving over a piece of the ancient continent of Rodinia and the Grenville range.[9]

---

[8] Sketch by the author using several sources
[9] Geology of the Greater Atlanta Area, Keith McConnell, Keith and Abrams, Charlotte; (1984), Geology of the Greater Atlanta Area, Department of Natural Resources Environmental Protection Division; Georgia Geologic Survey

This is the first time we know of when the continents came together into supercontinents, but it is very likely that it was not the first time it happened. When continents collide and form new continents and mountains, the rocks that were there are recycled into new ones.[10] The oldest rocks we have are most often the ones that were formed during latest crashing of continents or mountain building event ("orogeny" as it is called by geologists).

Rodinia began to break apart around 700 million years ago. As it did, the lowering of the mountains and the pulling apart of the land created a new ocean in between the continents called the Lapetus Sea – sometimes called the "proto-Atlantic" ocean.[11] Pulling continents apart creates lots of volcanic activity, almost as much as pushing them together. Eruptions at the bottom of the Laeptus Sea created not only volcanic or igneous rocks but deposited lots of minerals in the boiling, mineral-rich seabed. One of these minerals was gold. The gold that is still being mined in Dahlonega, Georgia was the result of the separation of Rodinia that created mineral rich vents and volcanoes under the Lapetus sea.

> **Georgia was still underneath this very warm, shallow sea making it an ideal habitat for early life.**

Over the history of Georgia, Decatur has risen into the mountains several times, and the land has twisted and spun to the point that the coast line was sometimes toward the east and sometimes to the south. Between 600 and 500 million years ago, Decatur lay near the equator, and the coastline was rotated due south.[12] Georgia was still underneath this very warm, shallow sea making it an ideal habitat for early life. The Lapetus Sea around Georgia was filled with different types of sponges, brachiopods and lots and lots of trilobites. These and several other species of this era have been recovered from the Coosa River and the Conasauga River in Murray and Gordon Counties.[13].

Bill Montante, a well-known geologist in Georgia, described the area in this period like this, "During the Cambrian (around 500 million years ago), what is now Georgia was on a long low sloping continental shelf (the beach was roughly where Iowa is today) of the Lapetus Sea."[14]

---

[10] USGS Age of the Earth
[11] Allmon, Warren et al. (2016) Geologic History of the Southeastern US: Reconstructing the Geologic Past, Paleontological Research Institution
[12] Allmon, Warren et al. (2016) Geologic History of the Southeastern US: Reconstructing the Geologic Past, Paleontological Research Institution
[13] An Aphelaspis Zone (Upper Cambrian, Paibian) Trilobite Faunule in the Central Conasauga River Valley, North Georgia USA. David R Schwimmer and William M. Montante. Southeastern Geology, V. 49, No. 1, June 2012, p. 31-41
[14] Georgia's Fossils. Georgiafossils.com

The Lapetus Sea then stopped widening, and the continents began to drift together again. A new set of mountains was thrown up between 490 and 460 million years ago (the Taconic Orogeny) and another continent-to-continent collision raised more mountains around 430 million years ago (the Acadian Orogeny). During each of these orogenies there were several periods of uplifting that created more mountains followed by long periods of erosion and separation.[15]

300 Million Years Ago, The Bedrock Under Downtown Decatur was Created

Finally, from 325 to 250 million years ago, the biggest event in the shaping of the world as we know it today occurred. Every piece of land on the planet drifted together into one enormous land mass. What is now called Georgia fused with what is now called Africa.[16]

Primitive life flourished in the ever shallower, warm Lapetus Sea and in the marshy wetlands that developed along the shifting coastline. When all the continents came together, they formed the great supercontinent of Pangaea (great name for a band by the way).[17]

As the Lapetus Sea slowly closed between Laurentia and Africa, more volcanoes rose in between the two colliding continents. These volcanoes stretched over Georgia and reached as far west as the location of today's Mississippi River.[18] Remnants of the lava spewed by these volcanoes can still be found in Northwest Georgia.[19]

South Georgia was fused into what is now the African countries of Senegal and Liberia.

Slowly, the ancient Lapetus Sea closed completely. South Georgia was fused into what is now the African countries of Senegal and Liberia. Think of it. You could have walked from Decatur to Senegal!

The pressure of the collision with Africa rippled through proto-North America for millions of years and created an entirely new landscape far to the north and west. The land folded. Mountains rose again. These mountains are

---

[15] Allmon, Warren et al. (2016) Geologic History of the Southeastern US: Reconstructing the Geologic Past, Paleontological Research Institution
[16] Allmon, Warren et al. (2016) Geologic History of the Southeastern US: Reconstructing the Geologic Past, Paleontological Research Institution
[17] US Geological Survey
[18] Gore, Pamela J. W. (2006), Geologic History of Georgia: Overview, New Georgia Encyclopedia
[19] USGS Age of the Earth

Decatur and Pangaea 300 Million Years Ago[20]

[20] Sketch by the author based on Image from page 29 of Collected reprints / Atlantic Oceanographic and Meteorological Laboratories [and] Pacific Oceanographic Laboratories (1968)

19

now called the Alleghenian Range (created by the Alleghenian Orogeny), and from them, our beloved Appalachian Mountains were finally born![21]

How do we know something as ridiculous as Pangaea existed? It happened hundreds of millions of years ago, and the evidence is spread across thousands of miles. One way we know is by comparing the rocks in multiple places to see how they are similar. Rocks in Georgia are very similar to ones you can find in Central Bohemia and Poland as well as those in Nova Scotia, North Africa and South America indicating that these places were connected at one time.[22]

Another interesting piece of evidence for Pangaea is the existence of fossils of a plant called glossopteris. Archaeologists believe its seeds were too large and heavy to have traveled on the wind or across an ocean. Yet, we find fossils of this plant in South America, Africa, Australia India and Antarctica indicating it once grew all the way across one great land mass.[23]

When continents collide, one of the more common types of rock that form is called gneiss. It contains quartz and feldspar (light colored minerals) along with dark-colored minerals (like biotite) giving it a speckled light and dark look. These ingredients to the rock make it very similar to granite, another rock created by magma activity in the area of Decatur. Though they are very similar, one way to differentiate between gneiss and granite is that gneiss will usually show strata (layer lines), while granite will not. Gneiss is a metamorphic rock formed when older rocks are morphed into different rocks. The type of gneiss is often identified with the name of the rock from which, it was formed.

Downtown Decatur sits directly on top of a huge block of biotite gneiss that was created by the collision of North America with Africa. [24] Unlike the rocks created by the Grenville event, you can take a walk in just about any part of downtown Decatur and see some of these roughly 300-million-year-old biotite gneiss rocks that were created when Africa collided with Georgia.[25]

The most beautiful outcrop of biotite gneiss I know of is at the corner of Clairemont Avenue and the I-85 off ramp. Hidden by weeds, next door to a body shop, covered with a disappointing amount of trash alongside an onramp, the best example of the rock upon which the city was built has rested for

---

[21] Gore, Pamela J. W. (2006), Geologic History of Georgia: Overview New Georgia Encyclopedia

[22] The Teacher Friendly Guide to the Earth Science of the Southeastern US; Robert M. Ross, Associate Director for Outreach; Don Duggan-Haas, Director of Teacher Programs; Paleontological Research Institution; January 2016

[23] The Teacher Friendly Guide to the Earth Science of the Southeastern US; Robert M. Ross, Associate Director for Outreach; Don Duggan-Haas, Director of Teacher Programs; Paleontological Research Institution; January 2016

[24] USGS Mineral Resources On-Line Spatial Data

[25] Gore, Pamela J. W. (2006), Geologic History of Georgia: Overview, New Georgia Encyclopedia

Mark Pifer

The Geology of Decatur[26]

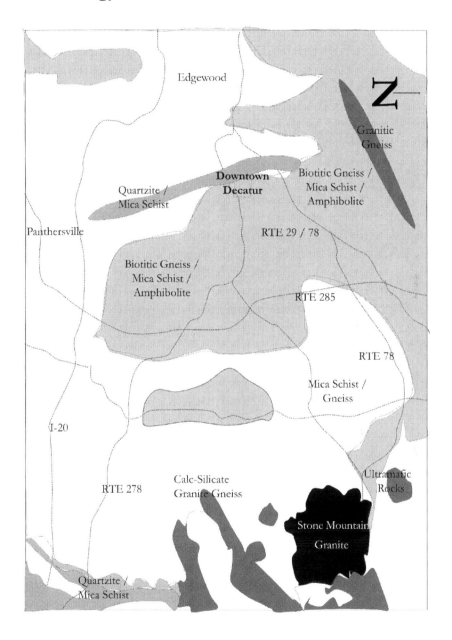

Edgewood

Granitic
Gneiss

Downtown
Decatur

Biotitic Gneiss /
Mica Schist /
Amphibolite

Quartzite /
Mica Schist

Panthersville

RTE 29 / 78

Biotitic Gneiss /
Mica Schist /
Amphibolite

RTE 285

RTE 78

Mica Schist /
Gneiss

I-20

Calc-Silicate
Granite Gneiss

Ultramafic
Rocks

RTE 278

Stone Mountain
Granite

Quartzite /
Mica Schist

[26] Geology of the Greater Atlanta Area, Keith McConnell, Keith and Abrams, Charlotte; (1984), Geology of the Greater Atlanta Area, Department of Natural Resources Environmental Protection Division; Georgia Geologic Survey

Decatur Bedrock in Glenn Creek Near the Decatur Cemetery[27]

300 million years. [28] If you walk along or in the streams, you are likely to come across other nice outcroppings of the town's bedrock. Farther from the downtown area, you will find other types of bedrock including granitic gneiss, quartzite and mica schist.

There is one spot downtown I can tell you about where you can see Decatur's bedrock that is much prettier than an I-85 off ramp (though with less impressive rocks) and much more reverent to the significance of 300-million-year-old rocks created by the formation of Pangaea. It is just below the Decatur Cemetery in Glenn Creek. If you enter the cemetery from Church Street, walk down the hill and take the fork in the trail that goes to your right with the pond on your left, from there, take the smaller trail on your right just before the bridge over the creek, and after a brief walk, you will get to a spot where there is a beautiful, tiny waterfall that cascades over Decatur's 300 million-year-old biotite gneiss bedrock.[29]

[27] Photo by the author
[28] Gore, Pamela J. W. (2006), Geologic History of Georgia: Overview, New Georgia Encyclopedia
[29] US Geological Survey

Mark Pifer

300 Million Years Ago, Decatur Rose above the Ocean for the Last Time and Became the Land

Slowly, around 300 million years ago, Decatur rose out of the ocean once again and for the most recent time to today (the last time was around 180 million years earlier during the Acadian Orogeny). The far northern parts of Georgia that are now the Smoky Mountains first crested the water around 320 million years ago.[30]

As the land continued to rise, Decatur became beachfront property. Tidal flats and muddy marshes formed. The first animals began to set foot or slither up onto the dry land.

At first, there were insects, then amphibians like eryops, that looked kind of like a cross between an alligator and a frog that could grow to 10 feet long and anapsids which were early versions of turtles.

The top predator of the time was the dimetrodon, a very early dinosaur. It looked like a large predatory lizard or a Komodo dragon but with a large sail on its back. They grew to 15 feet long and probably weighed around 500 pounds.[31] This period of pleasant, warm, marshy climate lasted until about 250 million years ago (called the end of the Permian epoch).

Around that time, the planet experienced the greatest mass extinction in the history of the world. There have been many periods of mass extinction in the history of our fragile planet, and it's often difficult to say just why they occurred. But the prevailing theory for why this one occurred is that there was a drastic change in the temperature of the planet. Exactly why that happened is uncertain. Nearly everything on Earth died. Ninety-five percent of all marine species and 70% of all land species disappeared.[32]

> Nearly everything on Earth died. 95% of all marine species and 70% of all land species disappeared.

---

[30] Gore, Pamela J. W. (2006), Geologic History of Georgia: Overview, New Georgia Encyclopedia

[31] A New Specied of Dimetrodon from the Lower Permian of Germany records first occurrence of genus outside of North America (PDF). Canadian Journal of Earth Sciences. 38 (5): 803–812. doi:10.1139/cjes-38-5-803

[32] Hoffman, Hillel J,(2000), The Permian Extinction—When Life Nearly Came to an End; R, National Geographic Magazine

Bedrock Outcropping Near Clairemont Avenue and I-85[33]

Stone Mountain and the Other Monodoks

Just a little bit after the creation of bedrock in Decatur, perhaps a few million years, two more areas of rock were created that would each play very significant roles in local history for thousands of years. These were Stone Mountain and Soapstone Ridge.

The collision of Georgia with Africa went on for a very, very long time, and there was constant movement and pressure in the ground. The rocks were metamorphosed again and again over millions of years. Sometimes magma being pushed up from below forced its way into the preexisting rocks, like the gneiss that underlies most of Decatur and formed chambers of new material. Scientists call this an intrusion. It's a very apt name I think. That's exactly what it is.

One such intrusion created an enormous chamber of magma that cooled deep underground and became granite. This huge block of granite would later become exposed on the surface and is now called Stone Mountain. Keep in mind, this was all happening deep underground at that time. It has often been mistakenly said that Stone Mountain was there on the landscape 300 million years ago. The rocks of Stone Mountain are indeed around 300 million years old. Stone Mountain itself did not emerge onto the landscape until about 15 million years ago, long after Pangaea broke apart. Millions of years of running water and other types of erosion wore away the softer rocks around the granite, and it was gradually exposed high above the surrounding area.[34]

This "island" of rock up above the landscape that was the result of an intrusion into the preexisting rocks is called a monodok. There are many of them in the Southeast.[35] Panola Mountain, Arabia Mountain, Kennesaw Mountain, Sweat Mountain, Pine Mountain, Sawnee Mountain and Stone Mountain are all examples of monodoks close to the Decatur area.[36]

A similar process of erosion exposed an area in southern Decatur around Panthersville. The heat and pressure of Pangaea created a large block of steatite, also called soapstone, that was slowly exposed at the surface, and it is now called Soapstone Ridge. Soapstone Ridge became very important to the Indians living in the Decatur area as far back as 4,000 years ago.[37]

---

[34] Atkins, Robert and Joyce, Lisa (1980), Geologic Guide to Stone Mountain Park, Georgia Department of Natural Resources, Environmental Protection Division and Georgia Geologic Survey
[35] Atkins, Robert and Joyce, Lisa (1980), Geologic Guide to Stone Mountain Park, Georgia Department of Natural Resources, Environmental Protection Division and Georgia Geologic Survey
[36] Atkins, Robert and Griffin (1977), Geologic Guide to Panola Mountain State Park, Georgia Department of Natural Resources, Environmental Protection Division and Georgia Geologic Survey
[37] Atkins, Robert and Griffin (1977), Geologic Guide to Panola Mountain State Park, Georgia Department of Natural Resources, Environmental Protection Division and Georgia Geologic Survey

A Large Part of Georgia Used to be Africa

The most incredible thing that has been discovered about the events that created our landscape in the Southeast has only recently begun to be understood.

For many years, scientists were curious about a magnetic anomaly deep beneath the surface that runs across Alabama and Georgia and out into the ocean off North Carolina called the Brunswick Anomaly. There have been several theories about its source. Many felt it might be an area of unusual volcanic activity. There is increasing evidence to support the theory that it is actually the border of North America and Africa.[38]

Pangaea remained as a supercontinent for less than 100 million years.[39] It started breaking up about 225 million years ago. The disassembly of a continent is almost as violent as when it is created. When continents join, they don't just touch together. They are forced into each other, and their land is welded together into a single thing. Pulling them apart is almost as violent as fusing them together. Volcanoes and magma form once more, and the rocks are melted and reformed into something new once again.[40]

Africa was so firmly welded into Georgia and Alabama that a huge piece of the African continent stayed connected. An enormous piece of the land that we now call Florida, Southern Georgia, Southern Alabama and the Bahamas is part of ancient Africa![41] It's mind boggling, but it's true. Florida and much of Georgia are bits of Africa, not North America.

Millions of Years of Pushing Up Rocks and Wearing Them Down Made Decatur's Hilly Landscape

As Pangaea drifted apart, the Appalachians remained. The bedrock became stable. The stage was now set for the creation of Decatur.

Unlike previous continental collisions that created new mountain ranges, the Appalachian Mountains have not yet been worn away. This is not only because they are not as old. It is also because there have been other uplifting events under the surface over long periods of time that continued to raise the Appalachian Mountains up as they were being worn down.

---

[38] Atkins, Robert and Joyce, Lisa (1980), Geologic Guide to Stone Mountain Park, Georgia Department of Natural Resources, Environmental Protection Division and Georgia Geologic Survey
[39] Atkins, Robert and Joyce, Lisa (1980), Geologic Guide to Stone Mountain Park, Georgia Department of Natural Resources, Environmental Protection Division and Georgia Geologic Survey
[40] Atkins, Robert and Griffin (1977), Geologic Guide to Panola Mountain State Park, Georgia Department of Natural Resources, Environmental Protection Division and Georgia Geologic Survey
[41] Atkins, Robert and Griffin (1977), Geologic Guide to Panola Mountain State Park, Georgia Department of Natural Resources, Environmental Protection Division and Georgia Geologic Survey

Magma underneath the current location of Decatur continued to well up and fall, lifting the ground and reforming parts of it into new rocks again and again for millions of years.[42]

The collision of Africa with North America created the Appalachian Mountains. As the ground was being uplifted in some places, and little cracks formed in other places (particularly once the continents began to pull apart) water found its way across the land and down into these crevices and rivers and streams formed in the paths of least resistance.[43] This process has been very thorough and steady for millions of years. A vast network of waterways formed including the Chattahoochee River and the South River. There is now an intricate network of very old, powerful streams running through the Decatur area including Nancy Creek, Peavine Creek, Barbashela Creek, Snapfinger Creek, Lullwater Creek, Glenn Creek, Peavine Creek and the historic and powerful Peachtree Creek.

All water that falls on Georgia will flow unless it has been blocked.

All the water that falls on Georgia will flow someplace unless it has been blocked by something we built. The state contains no major natural lakes.[44]

The combination of the initial rising of the land when Georgia collided with Africa, the continued periodic uplifting of some areas, the separation of the continents and then the long, slow effects of age and running water, all combined to create the rolling hilly landscape of Decatur and the character of the land we now know. These high, dry ridges interlaced with abundant, crystalline streams would attract animals of all kinds, followed by people, to the area for many thousands of years.

[42] Atkins, Robert and Joyce, Lisa (1980), Geologic Guide to Stone Mountain Park, Georgia Department of Natural Resources, Environmental Protection Division and Georgia Geologic Survey
[43] Gore, Pamela J. W. (2006), Geologic History of Georgia: Overview, New Georgia Encyclopedia
[44] Parker, Amanda K. (2004) Reservoirs, New Georgia Encyclopedia

Original Border of Africa and North America[45]

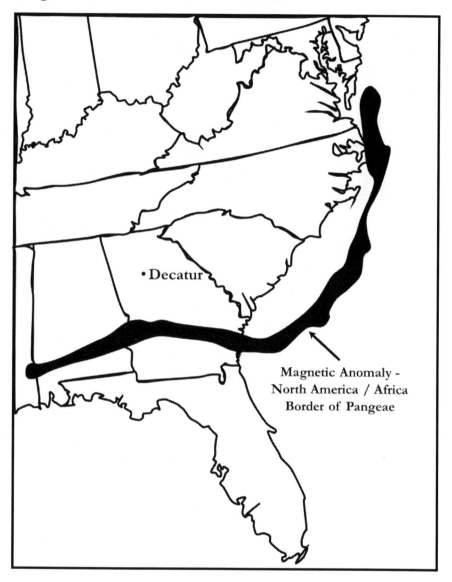

Magnetic Anomaly -
North America / Africa
Border of Pangeae

*Decatur

[45] Sketch by the author using Image taken from page 39 of 'US An Index to the United States of America and various sources describing the magnetic anomaly

Mark Pifer

Waterflow of Dekalb County Streams and Rivers[46]

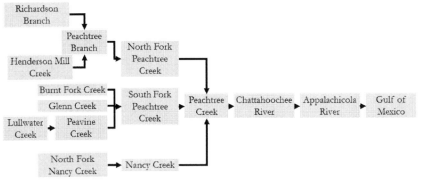

Eastern Continental Divide

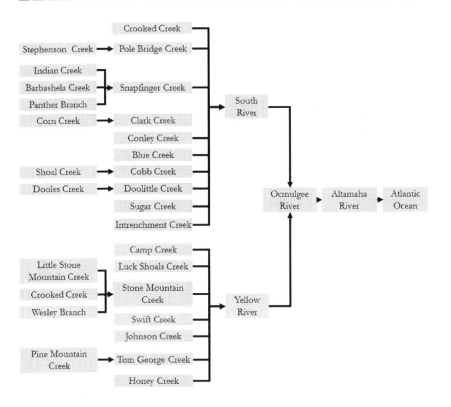

---

[46] Council, Evelyn (1982) Teacher's Guide to DeKalb County, Presented to the DeKalb Historical Society

CHAPTER 2:
DECATUR'S FIRST ANIMALS

80 Million Years Ago, Decatur was a Jungle Crawling with Dinosaurs

One hundred forty-five million years ago, Decatur was still at a much higher elevation than it is today on the side of the Appalachian Mountains that rose during the formation of the supercontinent Pangaea. This was the beginning of the Cretaceous period that lasted until 66 million years ago.

Sea Levels During the Cretaceous Period[47]

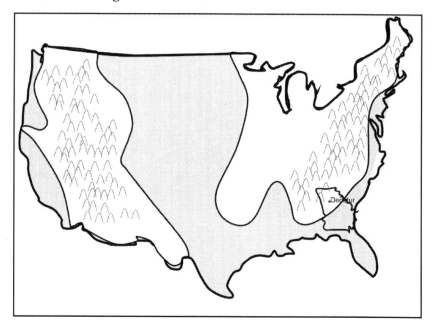

By the late Cretaceous, 80 million years ago, the Earth was much warmer than it is now. There weren't even any glaciers at the Earth's poles. As a result, sea levels were very high, as much as 850 feet higher than today.[48] The Atlantic coast was located where Macon is now.

---

[47] Sketch by the author from Image from page 211 of The American Journal of Science (1880)
[48] US Geological Survey

The mountains had worn much lower and land around Decatur had been smoothed into high foothills instead of mountainous peaks. Decatur had become a warm, wet sloping plain between the ocean and the mountains. It was an ideal haven for life to flourish and became crowded with dinosaurs.

Unfortunately, no fossils from this time period remain in Decatur. Any deposits of rock that would have dated back this far have all been worn away.[49] However, thanks to some very ingenious paleontologists, we do have the fossils of animals that lived in the Decatur area 80 million years ago that have been found in the Cretaceous deposits just south of Decatur at the border of the Piedmont and the Coastal Plain.

When some dinosaurs died, they were washed downstream into the creeks and rivers flowing through the area and eventually, their bodies came to rest in the shallow ocean that was covering what is now South Georgia. Cretaceous fossils have been found in Georgia in Hannahatchee Creek and in the Chattahoochee River[50] as well as in neighboring states like Alabama where the climate and landscape would have been identical to Decatur.[51]

From these fossils, we now know that the most common dinosaurs that lived in the Decatur area 80 million years ago were lophorhothons, a type of hadrosaur, and ornithomimids. Don't get the impression they were the only animals wandering this area. The lush forest in Decatur was teeming with sound and life. Giant insects were buzzing everywhere, little amphibians were crawling and croaking in the brush, and tiny mammals were scurrying around the dinosaurs' feet.

[49] Gore, Pamela J. W. (2006), Geologic History of Georgia: Overview, New Georgia Encyclopedia
[50] Schwimmer, David R. (1989) First dinosaur fossils from Georgia, with notes on additional Cretaceous vertebrates from the state, Columbus State University Press, Paper 463.
[51] (1996) Appalachiosaurus and The Dinosauria of Alabama; Originally posted 1996

Cretaceous Rocks and Fossils Found in the Southeast[52]

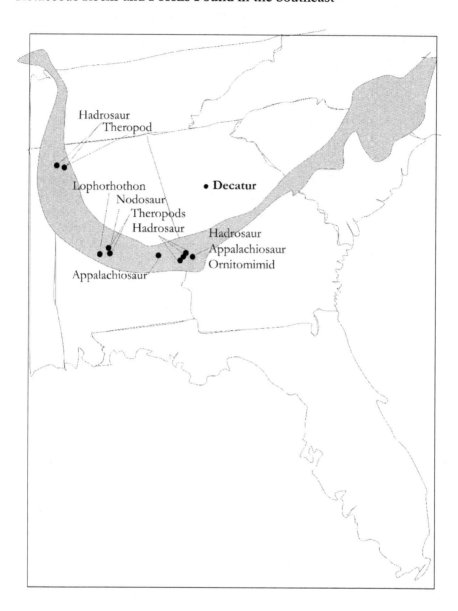

[52] Sketch by the author using; Schwimmer, David (1997) Late Cretaceous Dinosaurs in the Eastern USA; A Taphonomic and Biogeographic Model of Occurrences; Dinofest International

Decatur Lophorhothons (a.k.a., Duck Billed Dinosaurs)

The most common dinosaur residents of the Decatur area 80 million years ago were the hadrosaurs or duck-billed dinosaurs. The type of hadrosaur confirmed to have lived in middle Georgia is the lophorhothon.[53] Duck-billed dinosaurs are some of the most common in North America from this period and are by far the most common in the Eastern United States.[54]

Most Decatur residents have seen the three lophorhothons that still reside in the area in front the Fernbank Museum of Natural History.

They were well adapted to the tropical forests that covered Decatur back then. A full grown lophorhothon was eight feet tall, 15-feet-long from its nose to the tip of its tail and probably weighed around 5,000 pounds. [55] They probably had padded feet similar to a camel. Their large tails were too stiff to be waved around or used for swimming. This, as well as their sturdy bones and rapidly replaced teeth, suggest they spent most of their time on land but close to the water feeding on tough plants like leaves and ferns.[56]

The most interesting and debated trait of the hadrosaurs is their crest. It is not as prominent in lophorhothon as in other hadrosaurs, but the chamber at the top of the skull is still there. It was probably used for vocalization to warn of predators like appalachiosaurus and in other important circumstances to a hadrosaur such as attracting a mate. Hadrosaur nesting grounds have been discovered indicating that they would migrate together to have their young in a communal place. [57]

---

[53] Fernbank Information board

[54] Schwimmer, David R. (1997) Late Cretaceous Dinosaurs in the Eastern USA: A Taphonomic and Biogeographic Model of Occurrences, Dinofest International Symposium, Philadelphia: Academy of Natural Sciences), p. 203-11. & Schwimmer, David R., et al. (1993) Upper Cretaceous Dinosaurs from the Blufftown Formation in Western Georgia and Eastern Alabama, Journal of Paleontology 67 pg. 288-96

[55] Schwimmer, David R. (1997) Late Cretaceous Dinosaurs in the Eastern USA: A Taphonomic and Biogeographic Model of Occurrences, Dinofest International Symposium, Philadelphia: Academy of Natural Sciences), p. 203-11. & Schwimmer, David R., et al. (1993) Upper Cretaceous Dinosaurs from the Blufftown Formation in Western Georgia and Eastern Alabama, Journal of Paleontology 67 pg. 288-96

[56] Carroll, R.L (1988). Vertebrate Paleontology and Evolution. W.H. Freeman and Company, New York

[57] Carroll, R.L (1988). Vertebrate Paleontology and Evolution. W.H. Freeman and Company, New York

A Lophorhothon Mother and Baby in Decatur[58]

[58] Illustrations by Chulsan Um

Ornithomimids

Another common type of dinosaur in the Decatur area during the Cretaceous was the ornithomimid. Ornithomimid fossils have been found along with appalachiosaurus and lophorhothon in the Cretaceous deposits just south of Decatur.[59]

Ornithomimids were large, sleek looking dinosaurs with long powerful legs. The had a build that looks like it was made for running fast through the lush rain forests that covered Decatur 80 million years ago. They are often compared to ostriches. Scientists believe the ornithomimids could probably reach speeds exceeding 30 miles per hour.[60] The average ornithomimid ranged in size from around seven to 26 feet

> The name "ornithomimid" means "bird mimic", so named because of its many similarities to big, fast running birds like the emu that lives in the Lake Claire Land Trust a couple of miles from Decatur.

long, and adults weighed between 450 and 1,550 lbs.[61] Rocks have been found in the stomachs of many specimens suggesting they would swallow these to aid in the digestion of tough vegetation as some reptiles and birds do today.[62]

It is believed that ornithomimid belongs to the group of dinosaurs that gave rise to modern-day birds called the Coelurosauria group. Even the name "ornithomimid" means "bird mimic", so named because of its many similarities to the big running birds we have today like the emu that lives in the Lake Claire Land Trust near Decatur.[63]

[59] Schwimmer, David R. (1997) Late Cretaceous Dinosaurs in the Eastern USA: A Taphonomic and Biogeographic Model of Occurrences, Dinofest International Symposium, Philadelphia: Academy of Natural Sciences), p. 203-11
[60] Westfall, Andres (2015), Ornithomimids, Encyclopedia of Alabama
[61] Westfall, Andres (2015), Ornithomimids, Encyclopedia of Alabama
[62] Barrett, Paul M. (2005), The Diet of Ostrich Dinosaurs (Theropoda: Ornithomimosauria), Paleontology 48(2) pg.347-58
[63] Westfall, Andres (2015), Ornithomimids, Encyclopedia of Alabama

Ornithomimids Running Through Decatur's Forests[64]

---

[64] Illustrations by Chulsan Um

Appalchiosaurus[65]

Decatur's top, ferocious predator 80 million years ago, running through the tropical forests and striking fear into the hearts of the gentle lophorhothon or any ornithomimids it was able to catch unaware, was the appalachiosaurus.[66] Appalachiosaurus is the cousin of tyrannosaurus rex and the closer cousin of albertosaurus that was common in North America and on the western side of the United States.[67]

Albertosaurus and appalachiosaurus seem to have evolved independently when they were separated by the shallow ocean that covered the middle part of the present day United States.[68] One key difference between appalachiosaurus and its cousins albertosaurus and tyrannosaurus is that it had long forelimbs with large claws that it probably used to grasp its prey while making a kill, similar to how a lion holds tight with its claws when it takes down its prey.[69]

There is a very well-preserved specimen of appalachiosaurus in the McWane museum in Alabama. It is the oldest known specimen of any dinosaur in the tyrannosaurid family that has been found in North America – about 79 million years old.[70]

This premier specimen found in Alabama is 8.5 ft. tall and 23 feet long and weighed around 1,300 pounds, but it is not considered to have been fully grown. The adult appalachiosaurus was probably a third bigger than this one, perhaps 13 feet tall and 35 feet long, weighing 2,000 pounds, similar weight to an American Bison.[71]

---

[65] Carr, Thomas; Williamson, Thomas and Schwimmer, David (1997) A New Genus of Tyrannosauroid from the Late Cretaceous (Middle Campanian) Demopolis Formation of Alabama, Journal of Vertebrate Paleontology 25 (1) 118-143
[66] Schwimmer, David R. (1997) Late Cretaceous Dinosaurs in the Eastern USA: A Taphonomic and Biogeographic Model of Occurrences, Dinofest International Symposium, Philadelphia: Academy of Natural Sciences), p. 203-11..
[67] King, David (2009), Appalachiosaurus montgomeriensis, Encyclopedia of Alabama
[68] King, David (2009), Appalachiosaurus montgomeriensis, Encyclopedia of Alabama
[69] King, David (2009), Appalachiosaurus montgomeriensis, Encyclopedia of Alabama
[70] King, David (2009), Appalachiosaurus montgomeriensis, Encyclopedia of Alabama
[71] King, David (2009), Appalachiosaurus montgomeriensis, Encyclopedia of Alabama

An Appalchiosaurus Making a Meal of a Decatur Hadrosaur[72]

CHAPTER 3:
THE PEAK OF DECATUR WILDERNESS

After the Dinosaurs, Mammoths and Saber-Toothed Tigers Walked into Decatur

About 66 million years ago, at the end of the Cretaceous period, the dinosaurs disappeared in another mass extinction. This latest extinction was probably caused by a massive asteroid, or perhaps even multiple asteroids, that slammed into Earth throwing enough debris into the atmosphere to alter the climate of the entire planet for millions of years.[73]

This climate change led to changes in the vegetation available to the herbivores. The starving of the herbivores took away the food sources for the large predators. Nearly every animal on the planet bigger than a dog starved.[74]

Two of the only relatively large survivors of this cataclysm are still residing in Georgia today. These are the alligators and leatherback sea turtles.[75] Over the next epoch, reptiles, birds and particularly mammals inherited the Earth and Decatur.

The continents had separated and drifted into their current positions during the end of the Cretaceous period between 145.5 and 65.5 million years ago. Perhaps because it was still changing after the impact of the asteroid, or taking a rest from all that shuffling of continents and churning of magma, the Earth now entered a dramatic cooling phase.

During the Pleistocene period that began two and a half million years ago and lasted until around 12,000 years ago, there were several periods when the Earth cooled, and glaciers advanced far beyond the poles. The last period when this occurred began 300 thousand years ago and lasted until end of the Pleistocene epoch.[76]

[73] Gore, Pamela J. W. (2006), Geologic History of Georgia: Overview, New Georgia Encyclopedia
[74] Gore, Pamela J. W. (2006), Geologic History of Georgia: Overview, New Georgia Encyclopedia
[75] Cave, James; (2015), These 7 Animals Survived What Dinosaurs Couldn't, Huffington Post

For the next 50 million years, Decatur lay in the foothills of the Appalachian Mountains and experienced a long period of erosion. The rolling hills became smoother and covered in cool, hardwood and pine forests.[77]

As more water froze at the poles, oceans shrank. The much lower sea levels due to lower temperatures exposed a lot more of the land including two important land masses that connected North America to much of the rest of the world.

The first of these was the Isthmus of Panama that connected North and South America around four million years ago when the Andes Mountains were undergoing the last periods of being raised up. Animals that had been evolving in South America could now make their way up into North America including the armadillos, opossums and porcupines, common in the Piedmont today as well as some of the megafauna like giant ground sloths and glyptodonts (giant armadillos).[78]

> The number and diversity of animals living in Decatur peaked during the late Pleistocene period 20,000 years ago.

The other land mass exposed by the lower sea levels created a bridge between Siberia and North America and allowed animals to cross from Eurasia. It was called Beringia or often called the Bering Sea Land Bridge. This allowed several more well-known animals and megafauna to cross into North America like the mammoths and giant bison. Beringia was enormously important to human history because it allowed the first people to make their way into North America from Siberia.[79]

Unlike most of the rest of America, Georgia remained ice free through each ice age.[80] Decatur was nestled into the high, rolling foothills of the Appalachians.[81] Clear, cold streams and rivers rolled out of the mountains like they do farther north today. Evergreens and hardwoods covered the landscape interspersed with grassy meadows.[82] It was an ideal haven for animals between ice to the north and ocean to the south.

---

[76] Whites, Max E (2002) The Archaeology and History of the Native Georgia Tribes; University Press of Florida
[77] Gore, Pamela J. W. (2006), Geologic History of Georgia: Overview, New Georgia Encyclopedia
[78] O'Dea, Aaron et al. (2016), Formation of the Isthmus of Panama, Science Advances, Volume 2 (8).
[79] Whites, Max E (2002) The Archaeology and History of the Native Georgia Tribes; University Press of Florida
[80] Gore, Pamela J. W. (2006), Geologic History of Georgia: Overview, New Georgia Encyclopedia
[81] Gore, Pamela J. W. (2006), Geologic History of Georgia: Overview, New Georgia Encyclopedia
[82] Gore, Pamela J. W. (2006), Geologic History of Georgia: Overview, New Georgia Encyclopedia

The animals that arrived from the south through the Isthmus of Panama and from the north across Beringia all met in Decatur with the animals that had evolved in North America like the American mastodons, Yukon horses and Yukon camels and the animals that had survived the last extinction like the American alligators. Together, they formed perhaps the most diverse and astonishing ecosystem of species in the history of the world and Decatur was right in the middle of the zone where they all met.[83]

The most important paleontological find in Georgia is from Ladd's Mountain in Cartersville. With only about 50 miles separating Cartersville from Decatur north to south, we can logically conclude that the animals and environment in the two places were exactly alike. It has yielded a treasure trove of fossils from an environment teeming with all kinds of Pleistocene wildlife.[84]

The long-legged grazers were probably the first big animals to arrive in large numbers. There were bison, camels, horses, llamas, caribou,[85] moose, sheep, antelope, muskox, bison, small Yukon horses, short legged horses, large-headed llamas and, of course, deer.[86] Many people are surprised to learn that the first horses and the first camels to appear on Earth emerged in North America 30 to 50 million years ago. The traits that make a camel well suited as a desert beast of burden were adaptations that developed in the steppe-tundra of the Yukon where it originated.[87]

The cold but agreeable climate in Decatur and its abundant varieties of prey attracted an astonishing variety of predators. Every ice age super predator that fires our imagination today was present. Decatur didn't just host the smaller variety of saber-toothed cat. It also had the true, ferocious saber-toothed tigers, and those weren't the only big, predatory cats prowling the area. The American lion that once hunted the forests of Decatur was very like a modern African lion but much larger. There were also cougars, lynx, margays (now found mainly in South America), ocelots, jaguars and Fisher cats.

There was a wide variety of bears including black bears, brown bears and two extinct types of bear called the Florida cave bear and the giant short-faced bear. The giant short-faced bear that once walked the land of Decatur was the largest

[83] Whites, Max E (2002) The Archaeology and History of the Native Georgia Tribes; University Press of Florida
[84] See full reference in the appendices
[85] Confirmed to have lived in Georgia during the Pleistocene
[86] See full reference in the appendices
[87] Yukon Beringia Interpretive Center (2017) Government of Yukon, Dept. of Tourism and Culture

land predator to ever walk the Earth, much bigger than the mighty polar bear, today's largest land predator.[88]

Like it is today, Decatur was also a very dog-friendly place 20,000 years ago. There were red wolves, red foxes, gray wolves, gray foxes, coyotes and (fans of "Game of Thrones" will be happy to know) dire wolves running wild in Decatur.[89]

Among the true giants that arrived were mammoths, mastodon, giant bison, giant beavers, glyptodonts (giant armadillos) and giant ground sloths and (my favorite) the ferocious giant chipmunk. [90]

> **Dire wolves were once running wild in Decatur.**

---

[88] See full reference in the appendices
[89] Inferred to have lived in Georgia during the Pleistocene from their confirmed presence in neighboring states
[90] See full reference in the appendices

When Giant Chipmunks Ruled Decatur

The scientific name for the giant chipmunk is tamis aristus which means "Noblest Chipmunk", and so it was. It was about 30% larger than the current chipmunks residing in Decatur.

It's possible these earlier Pleistocene chipmunks stayed active throughout the year and forewent hibernation like our locals do today and therefore, had to gather more calories and grow bigger throughout the year.[91]

> **The Noblest Chipmunk was about 30% larger than its modern cousins still living in Decatur.**

---

[91] Ray, C. E. . (1965) A new chipmunk, Tamias aristus, from the Pleistocene of Georgia, Journal of Paleontology 39(5):1016-1022.

A Modern Chipmunk Greets the Ancient "Noblest Chipmunk"[92]

American Lions in Decatur

American lions were ferocious big cats that lived throughout most of North America during the Pleistocene. They closely resembled today's African lions but were about 25% bigger.[93] An adult American lion was about five feet long and stood four feet tall at the shoulder, weighing in at around 550 pounds.[94] They probably preyed mostly on deer, horses, camels and occasionally smaller mammoths or other large grazers. We know they preyed on giant bison because a bison carcass that was found frozen and preserved in Alaska shows all the signs of having been attacked and killed by American lions.[95]

There is also some evidence that Pleistocene hunters may have hunted and killed American lions. We know that they ate them because American lion bones have been found in the trash heaps of Pleistocene people.[96]

> There is some evidence that Pleistocene hunters hunted and killed American lions.

[93] Deméré, Tom (2009), SDNHM Fossil Field Guide: Panthera atrox
[94] Christiansen, Per, & Harris, John M. (2009). Craniomandibular Morphology and Phylogenetic Affinities of Panthera atrox: Implications for the Evolution and Paleobiology of the Lion Lineage. Journal of Vertebrate Paleontology. 29 (3): 934–945. doi:10.1671/039.029.0314
[95] Turner, Alan; Anton, Mauricio (1997). The Big Cats and Their Fossil Relatives.
[96] Turner, Alan; Anton, Mauricio (1997). The Big Cats and Their Fossil Relatives.

An American Lion Eyes Up a Modern African Lion[97]

Giant Bears in Decatur (also known as Arctodus).

The giant, short-faced bear was the largest mammalian predator known to have ever lived on Earth.[98] They are estimated to have weighed in at a hefty 3,500 pounds. For comparison, the modern polar bear, the biggest carnivore currently walking around planet Earth, weighs in at just 1,323 pounds, less than half the size of the Pleistocene beast. They stood about six feet off the ground at the shoulder. Standing up as bears can do, these giants would have stretched to about 11 feet tall.[99]

Despite its massive size, the bones of the giant short-faced bear were very light, and its toes were aligned forward, rather than inward like grizzlies and black bears, so giant short-faced bears did not waddle along as some modern bears do. They would have had a long, steady stride. They were built for long distance travel, but a giant short-faced bear could also probably move very quickly when it wanted to do so.[100]

There is also some evidence that they were tree climbers. They had an extra bone in the paw called "radial sesamoid" or false thumb. Panda bears have the same type of appendage that helps them grasp food and climb trees.[101]

The modern spectacled bear is the most similar species living today.[102] We can imagine some similarities. It may have been a bit shaggier than black bears or grizzly bears the way spectacled bears are today. Based on the shape of the mouth, the wear patterns of its teeth and comparison to similar bears today, most scientists theorize that the giant short-faced bear ate most things it came across including a wide variety of plants, animals and insects to sustain its enormous body.

> **The giant short faced bear was twice the size of a polar bear.**

It's easy to imagine a giant short-faced bear appearing at a fresh kill made by saber-toothed cats, American lions or dire wolves and using its size to take over the meal. Similar standoffs often happen today between grizzly bears and wolves.

---

[98] Dell'Amore, Christine (2011), Biggest Bear Ever Found – 'It Blew My Mind,' Experts Say, National Geographic News
[99] San Diego Zoo, (2009) Short Faced Bear, Arctodus; San Diego Zoo Global
[100] San Diego Zoo, (2009) Short Faced Bear, Arctodus; San Diego Zoo Global
[101] San Diego Zoo, (2009) Short Faced Bear, Arctodus; San Diego Zoo Global 2009
[102] San Diego Zoo, (2009) Short Faced Bear, Arctodus; San Diego Zoo Global

A Giant Short-Faced Bear Encounters a Modern Black Bear[103]

---

[103] Illustrations by Chulsan Um

Dire Wolves in Decatur

The ancient dire wolf looked very much like a modern gray wolf but was much larger. They are the largest canine to have ever existed on our planet. Modern wolves average about 88 pounds. By comparison, dire wolves were around 133 pounds.[104]

Dire wolves were quite common during the Pleistocene. They ranged right across North America and down into South America.[105] Nearly 4,000 dire wolf fossils have been found in the La Brea Tar Pits in Los Angeles.[106] They would have been familiar with our modern gray wolves since the two of them coexisted and shared their range together about 12,000

> Dire wolves coexisted with modern gray wolves.

years ago. So far, there's no evidence of there having been dire wolf / gray wolf hybrids though. [107]

Like gray wolves, dire wolves were pack hunters and worked cooperatively to bring down their food. The larger size of the dire wolf probably put it at a disadvantage to gray wolves for long term survival though. Gray wolves are legendary distance runners that wear down their prey mainly by outlasting it on the run and tiring it out. Dire wolves were ambush hunters, more like lions, that specialized in surprising the slower, plant-eating species of the Pleistocene. [108]

Dire wolves were also extremely tough and more often, took on larger prey than gray wolves. Many fossils found in La Brea show evidence of broken bones and damaged skulls when the wolf survived a serious wound and healed.[109] Their primary prey was probably the mammoths, mastodons, giant sloths and giant bison. When these slower moving animals started becoming rare, so did dire wolves, while the leaner, faster gray wolves were better able to adapt to the more common, leaner prey.[110]

[104] Switek, Brian (2016), Dire Wolves Were Real, Scientific American
[105] Dykens, Margartet and Gillette, Lynett, (2017) Dire Wolf, San Diego Natural History Museum
[106] Switek, Brian (2016), Dire Wolves Were Real, Scientific American
[107] Dykens, Margartet and Gillette, Lynett, (2017) Dire Wolf, San Diego Natural History Museum
[108] Dykens, Margartet and Gillette, Lynett, (2017) Dire Wolf, San Diego Natural History Museum
[109] Dykens, Margartet and Gillette, Lynett, (2017) Dire Wolf, San Diego Natural History Museum
[110] Dykens, Margartet and Gillette, Lynett, (2017) Dire Wolf, San Diego Natural History Museum

A Dire Wolf Sizing Up a Modern Gray Wolf[111]

[111] Illustrations by Chulsan Um

CHAPTER 4:
DECATUR'S FIRST PEOPLE

12,000 Years Ago, People Arrived to Hunt Mammoths in Decatur

The exact period that human beings followed the animals across the Bering Sea land bridge (called Beringia)[112] and down into North America and into Georgia is a subject of debate. By around 14,000 years ago, human beings were certainly living in North America[113] and made their way into Georgia and the Decatur area by about 12,000 years ago.[114]

There is some limited evidence that people may have arrived in the Southeast much earlier. Sixteen-thousand-year-old spear points have been found in South Carolina. Without more examples, it's hard to know exactly how these older points came to be there or draw broader conclusions about them.[115]

It's obvious from their ability to survive a trip on foot across frozen continents, that these first people were astonishingly brave and effective hunters and travelers. They needed to remain always on the move and follow their food to survive. They probably never took time to build permanent homes. They probably only encountered other people a few times a year when there was a good reason to all be in one place, such as nut or shellfish harvesting.[116] They may have established some more permanent spots to act as base camps, but most nights were spent camping out in the open. Shelter was probably made of animal hides and brush or by simply curling up into a shallow pit to get underneath the wind.[117]

They mostly lived in small groups of around 20 people. That's about the number that could be fed by a typical hunting trip. Their favorite meals were the big mammals like mammoths, mastodons, bison, ground sloths, giant armadillos, tapirs, horses, wild pigs and caribou.[118]

---

[112] Jackson, Edwin L. and Stakes, Mary E. (2004) The Georgia Studies Book: Our State and the Nation; University of Georgia, Carl Vinson Institute of Government, Chapter 4
[113] Jackson, Edwin L. and Stakes, Mary E. (2004) The Georgia Studies Book: Our State and the Nation; University of Georgia, Carl Vinson Institute of Government, Chapter 4
[114] Whites, Max E (2002) The Archaeology and History of the Native Georgia Tribes; University Press of Florida
[115] Whites, Max E (2002) The Archaeology and History of the Native Georgia Tribes; University Press of Florida
[116] Stanyard, William, A Technical Summary of Georgia Prehistory, TRC Garrow Associates
[117] Jackson, Edwin L. and Stakes, Mary E. (2004) The Georgia Studies Book: Our State and the Nation; University of Georgia, Carl Vinson Institute of Government, Chapter 4
[118] Stanyard, William, A Technical Summary of Georgia Prehistory, TRC Garrow Associates

Nearly everything they used to survive was drawn from the animals they followed. Skins, bones, antlers, teeth, sinew, intestines, hooves and anything else that could be used provided clothing, protection and tools.

More than anything else, survival depended on having a good supply of well-made spears and the skill to use them effectively. It is mainly through these spear points (often called Clovis points because of where they were first found in Clovis, NM) that we have been able to date the arrival of these earliest Americans. They have been found all over the continent. Most Clovis points date back around 13,000 years or so.

> **Pleistocene spear points have been found all over the Southeast, including around Lake Allatoona and Lake Lanier.**

Pleistocene spear points have also been found all over the Southeastern US, including around Lake Allatoona and Lake Lanier. Of course, neither lake existed during the Pleistocene. They were created when the Chattahoochee river and the Etowah river were dammed in the 1940s and '50s. Spear points revealed on the shores of these lakes were uncovered by the rising and lowering water levels and are evidence that Pleistocene points could be found along any river or major creek bank in Georgia.[119] Many Clovis points have been found in Florida where the natural springs and sandy soil make the conditions excellent for preservation and exposure of ancient artifacts.

They would make them by knapping a piece of stone, preferably made of flint or chert.[120] Knapping is essentially where you bang two pieces of rock together at an angle so that flakes or chips of rock fly off the one you are trying to sharpen. Done with a skilled hand, you end up with a point that sort of resembles a leaf, a little more rounded at one end and coming to a point at the other, and all along the edges, it runs in a rippling pattern. These ripples are where the edges were formed, and they were extremely sharp. Even now, most of these 12,000-year-old spear points can cut you if you run one across your finger.

Many artifacts left by Pleistocene people have been found very close to the remains of ancient animals. Mastodon bones and Pleistocene horse bones have been found showing signs of cut marks from butchering. A sharpened

[119] Whatley, John S., (2002) An Overview of Georgia Projectile Points And Selected Cutting Tools, Early Georgia, The Society For Georgia Archaeology, Volume 30, Number 1, P.24
[120] Whites, Max E (2002) The Archaeology and History of the Native Georgia Tribes; University Press of Florida

Decatur's First People Hunting Giant Bison Near Stone Mountain[121]

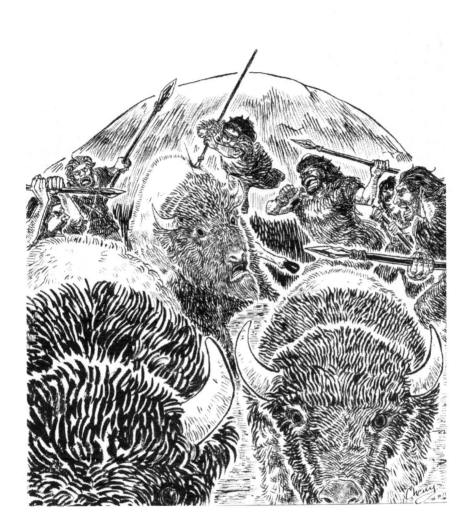

wooden stake has been found piercing an ancient tortoise shell. A sharpened stone point was also once found embedded in the skull of an ancient bison. These provide us some direct evidence of the Clovis hunters' methods and diet for survival.[122]

Attached to a long straight pole, these points were extremely lethal to whatever the early hunters stabbed with them. They would make a large, jagged wound and cause profuse bleeding. A hunter could stab an animal once and then just keep track of it until bleeding made the animal too weak to run or fight back. Cane was a commonly used resource for spear shafts and the sharp points were attached with animal sinew.[123]

> Few of these early Decatur residents lived past 40 years old.

They had no system of writing. That's certainly not because they weren't capable of abstract thought. It's probably because they didn't have time for it. They were too busy focusing on more immediate needs like not dying. Survival was as much as they could handle and just doing that was certainly not a guaranteed accomplishment.

They were just as intelligent as people today. Their brains functioned just like ours do now. The fact they were able to survive in this harsh world is a testament to their intelligence and amazing tenacity. They lived and raised children in a very cold world using only what they were able to produce with their own hands from what they found in the landscape.[124] The mortality rate was very high. Few of these early Decatur residents lived past 40 years old. Most died before they reached 30 years of age.[125]

We don't know about a religion they might have followed for certain. It is theorized to have been based on animism, the belief that all things, the sky, the wind, the animals, the water and all other things are imbued with a conscious spirit that can be influenced using magic.[126]

The one thing we do know from the limited art they left behind is that the animals surrounding them were a central part of their thoughts and interest. No art has been found in Georgia yet, but the British Museum houses a beautiful carving found in Europe that depicts two swimming reindeer made

---

[122] Whites, Max E (2002) The Archaeology and History of the Native Georgia Tribes; University Press of Florida.
[123] Jackson, Edwin L. and Stakes, Mary E. (2004) The Georgia Studies Book: Our State and the Nation; University of Georgia, Carl Vinson Institute of Government, Chapter 4
[124] Bednarik, Robert (2014), Pleistocene Paleoart of the Americas, International Federation of Rock Art Organizations
[125] Jackson, Edwin L. and Stakes, Mary E. (2004) The Georgia Studies Book: Our State and the Nation; University of Georgia, Carl Vinson Institute of Government, Chapter 4
[126] Dickens, Roy Jr. and McKinley, James (1979), Frontiers in the Soil: The Archaeology of Georgia

from a mammoth tusk.[127] An engraving that appears to be a mammoth has also been found on a bone fragment found in Vero Beach, Fl.

Pleistocene era sites have been found in several parts of Georgia. The closest known sites to Decatur are in Barnett Shoals near Athens; in the Ocmulgee National Monument near Macon; and on Horse Leg Mountain near Rome.[128] There is no reason we would not find artifacts closer to Decatur though. We just need to keep looking in places they are likely to be such as alongside the South River or Peachtree Creek.

10,000 Years Ago, the People of America Began to Settle
(The Paleoindian Period: 12,000 to 10,000 years ago)

The culture of the people who had come to occupy the Decatur area began changing immediately upon their arrival about 12,000 years ago. It had to because they were immediately forced to deal with some very new circumstances. The world was rapidly warming up, and Decatur was developing into the mild climate we enjoy now. Even more impactful, most of the game they hunted was rapidly disappearing.[129]

There is a long-standing, fervent debate about the true cause for the disappearance of most of the big animals during the Pleistocene. There is no question that climate change played a primary role. As it changed, the food sources it provided also changed. Big wooly animals that arrived during the cold Pleistocene were unprepared to survive in a warmer environment.[130]

However, many paleontologists also believe that the skill of these ancient hunters and their lethal spears was a major catalyst that brought about this latest mass extinction. After a vast array of amazing animals had flourished throughout the Americas for over 100,000 years, almost all the large animals like mammoths, mastodons and giant sloths all began dying off at the very same time people arrived. This happened simultaneously across the entire continents of North and South America.[131]

While the circumstantial evidence is there, scientists on the other side of the debate argue that not enough direct evidence has been found that Pleistocene people hunted the big animals on a scale that would have killed them all off. The importance of hunting large animals may be overestimated in the diet of these ancient people and the changes in the environment may be entirely to blame.[132]

[127] Trustees of the British Museum (2017)
[128] Whites, Max E (2002) The Archaeology and History of the Native Georgia Tribes; University Press of Florida
[129] Examining the Extinction of the Pleistocene Megfauna; Gibbons, Robin; Anthropological Sciences; (2004)
[130] Balter, Michael (2014) What Killed the Great Beasts of North America, Science
[131] Balter, Michael (2014) What Killed the Great Beasts of North America, Science

I wonder what it was like for those early hunters when they could see the mammoths and mastodons were disappearing, and with them, the big saber toothed cats and American lions. For a culture in which these large animals played a huge role for the human beings, as prey, undoubtedly as predators and as meaningful symbols, this must have been a very frightening thing to experience.[133] It seems clear to me from the limited art they left behind that those animals were at least awe striking to them and were probably held sacred. I can't believe these early people didn't see them as something more than food or competition. They would have revered them and loved them. The predators as well as the prey. The big super predators must have been terrifying, of course, but I think the people who watched them must have also looked at them with the same admiration and wonder we give to impressive predators today. Pleistocene people would of course have recognized that they too, were predators. It's hard to imagine a hunter would not have felt the natural human desire to want to believe in some way of influencing the environment and the animals and introduce something like a religion.

> They became excellent fishermen and created dams to trap trout, bluegill, and bass in the Chattahoochee and the South River.

Did they realize the animals were disappearing, at least partially by their own hand? Or did they think there might be some more mystical reason for the animals disappearing? Did they think some sort of malevolent spirit might be taking them away? Did they worry they might be next?

The Paleoindians Adjust to a Changing World

As society adjusted to the changing environment, the people began to act in more similar ways to how we think of Indians in America. They stopped moving around as much as they had before, building more permanent homes using wooden posts and thatch[134]

Their diet became much more varied. They hunted everything people hunt in Georgia today and some things we don't, including turkey, bear, opossum, raccoon, ducks, muskrat, beaver and turtles. Basically, anything that moved.

They also became excellent fishermen and created dams to trap trout, bluegill and bass in the Chattahoochee and the South River.[135] This method of fishing

---

[132] Stanyard, William, A Technical Summary of Georgia Prehistory, TRC Garrow Associates
[133] Koch, Paul; Barnozky, Anthony (2006) Late Quarternary Extinctions: State of the Debate; The Annual Review of Ecology, Evolution and Systematics;
[134] Jackson, Edwin L. and Stakes, Mary E. (2004) The Georgia Studies Book: Our State and the Nation; University of Georgia, Carl Vinson Institute of Government, Chapter 4
[135] Price, Vivian (1997) History of DeKalb County, Georgia, 1822-1900; Wolfe Pub. Co.

remained unchanged for many thousands of years. In the exhibits of this book, you can read a listing of where many of the later historical fish weirs can still be seen in the rivers near Decatur.

Getting up close enough to stick a deer with a spear is not as easy as sneaking up near a giant ground sloth (I'm guessing here, but I'd bet that's true). Deer spook easily, and they run fast. There was a problem that needed a technological advancement – developing a weapon that could be used to kill a smaller animal from a greater distance away. The first innovation these ancient hunters made was to change their spear points. Instead of smooth, leaf-shaped points meant to be thrust into the animal and then removed, they added barbs that would keep the spear point lodged in the animal and weaken it over a longer period after it may have run away. Archaeologists now call these newer types of points Dalton points.[136]

These newer spear points were an improvement. The problem of getting closer to a very skittish deer remained. The paleo-Indians made another innovation that improved on the issue of distance to the animal with the invention of the atlatl. It's a stick about the length of your forearm that has one end of it fitted with a kind of hook

If you go to one of the dog parks in Oakhurst, Glenn Creek, or Adair Park, you will see people still basically using atlatls to get more distance into their throw today.

into which the end of the spear is knocked. Hunters used it with great success to multiply the force of their throwing arm and send a spear much farther.[137] A person can hurl a spear around 70 yards. With an atlatl, a person can easily hurl a spear over 150 yards with good accuracy.[138]

If you go to one of the dog parks in Oakhurst, Glenn Creek, or Adair Park, you will see people still basically using atlatls to get more distance into their throw today. The long sticks people use to throw a tennis ball for their dog work on exactly the same principle.

With the help of the atlatl, deer hunting became a tent pole of their entire culture, a skill that would later be prized by the Europeans then, over-exploited to the point it became one of the core reasons for the collapse Indian society.

[136] Whites, Max E (2002) The Archaeology and History of the Native Georgia Tribes; University Press of Florida
[137] Jackson, Edwin L. and Stakes, Mary E. (2004) The Georgia Studies Book: Our State and the Nation; University of Georgia, Carl Vinson Institute of Government, Chapter 4
[138] Price, Vivian (1997) History of DeKalb County, Georgia, 1822-1900; Wolfe Pub. Co.

A last big change in their world that must have had an impact on their culture was that there were no more continents to be discovered. Europe, Asia, Africa and now North America and South America were all occupied by human beings. Unlike the past, whichever direction they walked, they knew they would find other people. It's hard to imagine that there was a large part of human history and in Georgia, when that was not the case, but it's a fact. Imagine travelling through the Georgia woods where you are the first to ever lay human eyes on everything you're seeing.

CHAPTER 5:
DECATUR'S OLDEST INTACT HOMES

Decatur's 4,000-Year-Old Quarries
(The Archaic Period: 10,000 to 3,000 years ago)

The oldest residential sites identified so far in Decatur date back to when people were still adjusting to a more settled way of life 4,000 years ago. Many of these people arrived to take advantage of the unique uses of soapstone that became apparent around this time, and Decatur was the best source of this stone in the Southeast.[139] Slabs from Soapstone Ridge were being traded widely in the Southeast as far as Louisiana and even to the Great Lakes[140].

Just like Stone Mountain, the rocks that comprise Soapstone Ridge were pushed into place deep below the surface during the assembly of Pangaea 300 million years ago. Then, over the next 250 million years or so, the land was pulled apart and worn down by water and the soapstone was uncovered and remained as a high hill on the surface.[141]

> Visiting this park, you can take a walk through the woods and peruse the handiwork of people who lived in Decatur 4,000 years ago.

Soapstone, also called steatite, has several unique qualities that made it useful. First, it is very resistant to erosion because it is non-porous. Water can't get down inside of it, freeze and break it apart. Despite its resistance to water erosion and the acids and alkalis that normally break down stone, it is soft and very workable. It can be easily carved into shapes. Being nonporous means it will also hold water. Last, most important, soapstone can be heated to be very hot and unlike most stones, it won't crack. These characteristics together made it ideal for use as material for cooking vessels and smoking pipes.[142]

With this innovation, the first major manufacturing zone in the region was born. Soapstone Ridge, in the vicinity of Flat Shoals Road, the South River and

[139] Whites, Max E (2002) The Archaeology and History of the Native Georgia Tribes; University Press of Florida
[140] Worth, Dr. John Fall; (2000) The First Georgians, -- The Late Archaic Period (3000 BC – 1000 BC) – Fernbank Quarterly
[141] Price, Vivian (1997) History of DeKalb County, Georgia, 1822-1900; Wolfe Pub. Co.
[142] Price, Vivian (1997) History of DeKalb County, Georgia, 1822-1900; Wolfe Pub. Co.

Route 285 is registered as a National Historic Site[143]. It has the highest density of prehistoric soapstone quarries among any area in the Southeastern United States including many intact and understudied sites.[144]

Bowl Scars in Fork Creek Mountain Park[145]

Some of these sites can be visited today, like the quarry in Decatur's Fork Creek Mountain Park. Visiting this little park, you can take a walk through the woods and peruse the handiwork of people who lived in Decatur 4,000 years ago,[146] still lying out on the ground as if the masons just walked away from their work.

The first common use the Indians found for Soapstone was to make "cooking stones." These were usually hand-sized pieces of soapstone with a hole carved out of the middle. In order to cook with it, a person would collect some water with other foods or herbs to make a stew in a small pit in the ground. The pit may have been lined with an animal skin or intestine to hold the water while the stone was heated in a fire. Once it was hot, a

---

[143] Elliott, Daniel T. (1986) The Live Oak Soapstone Quarry, Georgia Waste Management,
[144] Elliott, Daniel T. (1986) The Live Oak Soapstone Quarry, Georgia Waste, A Division of Waste Management,
[145] A bowl scar is a rounded-out depression where a bowl form has been removed. Photo by the author
[146] Whites, Max E (2002) The Archaeology and History of the Native Georgia Tribes; University Press of Florida

A Scene Along the South River in Decatur 4,000 Years Ago[147],[148]

---

[147] Illustrations by Chulsan Um
[148] Note: The man depicted on the right above is a portrait of Chulsan Um, my illustrator.

Unfinished Bowl Form in Fork Creek Mountain Park[149]

stick was poked through the hole in the stone to pick it up and put it into the water and heat up the stew. In addition to cooking stones, soapstone was later carved by archaic people to make atlatl weights, smoking pipes, gaming stones, ornaments and bowls of many shapes and sizes.[150]

The most common use of soapstone was in making bowls before the invention of pottery. Most of what you'll see in quarries on Soapstone Ridge is evidence of bowl making. To understand what you're seeing as you look at a soapstone quarry or at my pictures from one of the many quarries around Decatur, you must understand just a little bit about the method for making bowls from soapstone. The mason would first locate a convenient bulge in the rocks where they see a nice shape for a bowl. They would then chip away at the bulge until it resembled a sort of mushroom (the bottom of the bowl would be facing outward). The mason would then wedge branches or saplings into the gap to snap it away from the main rock.

A round depression would then be left on the larger boulder where the bowl form had been removed called a "bowl scar". Once removed, the pre-form would then be brought to the campsite to be further chipped and smoothed

---

[149] Photo by the Author
[150] Price, Vivian (1997) History of DeKalb County, Georgia, 1822-1900; Wolfe Pub. Co.

Several Unfinished Bowl Forms in Fork Creek Mountain Park[151]

---

[151] Photo by the author

into a bowl. Working a pre-form into an actual bowl would take around 20 hours of labor.[152] These soapstone bowls were evidently very prized family possessions to the owners. Soapstone bowls have been placed with the deceased in many archaic burial sites.[153]

Thankfully for us and archeologists, the bowl making process was far from flawless. At each step, many pre-forms or bowls would break incorrectly or fail to meet with the mason's standards in some other way. The fragments were then discarded on the ground as trash and left for us to find thousands of years later.

Potential Human Petroglyph Near the Dekalb County Landfill[154]

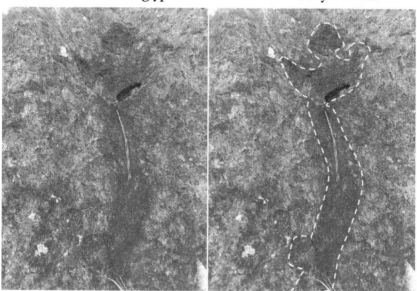

What are the Petroglyphs in Georgia?

I hope it goes without saying that if you should go to take a look and see something you think is a piece of a bowl there on the ground, please leave it there and allow others to enjoy the significance of the place and appreciate how lucky we are to have it.

One of the mysteries of local archaeology are the petroglyphs that have been found in the Southeast. No one is quite sure what they represent, if anything.[155] They are usually lines, dots and circles. Some of them resemble animals like bears, turkey, deer, or even human shapes.

---

[152] The Live Oak Quarry: Soapstone Ridge, Georgia, Prepared for Waste Management of North America, Inc.
[153] Records in the DeKalb County Historical Society
[154] Photo by the author
[155] Whites, Max E (2002) The Archaeology and History of the Native Georgia Tribes; University Press of Florida

We do know with some certainty that these were not created as part of a religious ritual, and they are not a written language. One plausible explanation was provided by a Cherokee that creation of these petroglyphs was simply a way to pass the time while sitting and waiting for something. Often, they were created by hunters waiting for game to pass by.[156] A boulder located in Track Rock Gap in Blairsville is covered with petroglyphs, and it's easy to imagine a hunter sitting there many times, whiling away the hours making pictures in the rock.

I believe I may have identified one petroglyph in Decatur located near the Live Oak Quarry on the grounds of the Dekalb County Landfill. It's very hard to say. I make no definitive claims. You can judge for yourself (see above). I would not be surprised to find more petroglyphs along the South River in the Soapstone Ridge area. We know there were people carving on these rocks for a long, long time.

> I would not be surprised to find more petroglyphs along the South River in the Soapstone Ridge area of Decatur.

[156] Whites, Max E (2002) The Archaeology and History of the Native Georgia Tribes; University Press of Florida

2,000 Years Ago, Most People Near Decatur Lived Along the Chattahoochee
(The Woodland Period: 3,000 years to 1,100 years ago)

During the next two thousand years, people living in the Southeast went through a long period of population growth, and several innovations occurred that had important effects on human history. Residence of Indians living right in Decatur probably peaked around 1,500 years ago. There were people living along every waterway in the area.

Living sites have been located along the North Fork and the South Fork of Peachtree Creek, along Snapfinger Creek, Sugar Creek and the South River.[157] They are most common in the delta where two creeks or a creek and a river reach a confluence. The largest concentration of small camps and villages has been found along each fork of Peachtree Creek along today's Clairemont Avenue between I-85 and the VA hospital. There were also several small settlements of people in the Redan area along Barbashela Creek and Snapfinger Creek.[158] Prehistoric people also inhabited at least five separate campsites spread across 8,000 acres along Stone Mountain Creek. [159]

The first of these major innovations had a direct impact on the people living in Decatur. This was the invention of pottery. Ceramic pots made far superior cooking vessels, to the heavy soapstone bowls being created in Decatur.[160]

There was a loose but active trading network operating in the Southeast, which saw frequent travel through Decatur.

The earliest use of pottery in Georgia dates to around 5,000 years ago on the coast.[161] The practice then spread over Georgia and became more common by 3,000 years ago and led to the gradual phasing out of soapstone bowls.[162]

The methods and patterns of creating pottery are now the keystone element to identifying groups and time periods. Each village had a different style that it used in making its pottery and these styles developed over time. We can now identify who lived in a certain place and when, by comparing their pottery. As time wore on and the Indians developed more skill, pottery became more

[157] Price, Vivian (1997) History of DeKalb County, Georgia, 1822-1900; Wolfe Pub. Co.
[158] Price, Vivian (1997) History of DeKalb County, Georgia, 1822-1900; Wolfe Pub. Co.
[159] Price, Vivian (1997) History of DeKalb County, Georgia, 1822-1900; Wolfe Pub. Co.
[160] Thomas J. Pluckhahn, (2003), Tampa, New Georgia Encyclopedia; Woodland Period: Overview
[161] Dickens, Roy Jr. and McKinley, James (1979), Frontiers in the Soil: The Archaeology of Georgia
[162] Whites, Max E (2002) The Archaeology and History of the Native Georgia Tribes; University Press of Florida

intricate and beautiful as well. Stamps appearing on pottery began to include animal forms and intricate geometric designs.[163]

As pottery gradually replaced soapstone bowls, some limited quarrying continued on Soapstone Ridge but at much smaller production levels. It was still used to make ornamentation, and it continued to be the preferred material for making smoking pipes all the way up into the colonial period. So, there were undoubtedly Indians frequenting the area all the way up to removal in the 1830s and 1840s.[164]

People were also gradually becoming less spread out. They developed more permanent and sophisticated homes that grew into larger settlements than ever before. Many villages began to support 50 people or so.[165] Most of the people that had been living in the Decatur area to be near the soapstone moved farther away but stayed nearby along the major waterways.[166]

Living sites dating back to this period 2,000 years ago have been identified around Stone Mountain, at the confluence of the North and South Forks of Peachtree Creek, along Nancy Creek, and near the point Peachtree Creek flows into the Chattahoochee (where the settlement of Standing Peachtree was later built).[167]

There was a loose but active trading network operating in the Southeast, which saw frequent travel along the major trails running through Decatur. Marine shells from Georgia's coastal areas reached the Midwest in return for exotic stones and copper that returned to the South.[168] Copper and exotic stones were also coming back from the Midwest. Semi-precious and useful stones like soapstone, quartz and mica were traveling out of the Decatur area south to the coast and north into the mountains.[169]

Cultivation of crops also became more sophisticated and important.[170] No direct evidence has yet been found in Georgia. In neighboring areas, we know that Indians were cultivating sumpweed, goosefoot, maygrass, knotweed, sunflower and eventually corn around 3,000 years ago.[171] Corn would become a central part of Indian culture with both deep practical and deep religious significance.[172]

---

[163] Thomas J. Pluckhahn, (2003), Tampa, New Georgia Encyclopedia; Woodland Period: Overview
[164] Price, Vivian (1997) History of DeKalb County, Georgia, 1822-1900; Wolfe Pub. Co.
[165] Thomas J. Pluckhahn, (2003), Tampa, New Georgia Encyclopedia; Woodland Period: Overview
[166] Price, Vivian (1997) History of DeKalb County, Georgia, 1822-1900; Wolfe Pub. Co.
[167] Price, Vivian (1997) History of DeKalb County, Georgia, 1822-1900; Wolfe Pub. Co.
[168] Thomas J. Pluckhahn, (2003), Tampa, New Georgia Encyclopedia; Woodland Period: Overview
[169] Thomas J. Pluckhahn, (2003), Tampa, New Georgia Encyclopedia; Woodland Period: Overview
[170] Thomas J. Pluckhahn, (2003), Tampa, New Georgia Encyclopedia; Woodland Period: Overview
[171] Thomas J. Pluckhahn, (2003), Tampa, New Georgia Encyclopedia; Woodland Period: Overview
[172] Thomas J. Pluckhahn, (2003), Tampa, New Georgia Encyclopedia; Woodland Period: Overview

Along with a more settled town life, a more organized social structure, clearly defined religious beliefs, burial customs and ritualism also appeared around this time.[173] Rock mounds like the ones near Eatonton, were created around 1,800 years ago and reflect these developing beliefs.[174] Eagles must have been an important cultural symbol. The rock mound in Eatonton is in the shape of an eagle and the Ocmulgee mounds in Macon also include an altar in the shape of an eagle.[175]

One of the best known symbols of Indian life in Georgia also began to appear on the landscape about 2,000 years ago when mound construction began. Mounds constructed during this time were small compared to ones that would be created later. They were mostly used as burial mounds, but some were probably used as stages from which town leaders would address the residents.[176] The Kolomoki site in Southwest Georgia dates to this early mound building period. This site is unique in that seven of the eight mounds that were created there have been preserved.[177] The landscape of Georgia was once littered with mound sites but most have sadly been destroyed by development.

> Semi-precious and useful stones like soapstone, quartz, and mica were traveling out of the Decatur area south to the coast and north into the mountains.

In addition to making better pottery and growing lots of corn, the Indians started hunting using the bow and arrow in the Southeast around 2,000 years ago.[178] The projectile points from this period are smaller and triangular shaped compared to earlier ones.[179] This invention was probably the most impactful innovation since they learned to grow crops. It not only vastly expanded their ability to hunt but also sharpened a more sinister ability -- their capacity for war.

Success led to large population growth. This, in turn, created scarcity and competition for resources like food. Groups became more independent and borders more defined. A more complicated hierarchical system started to

[173] Price, Vivian (1997) History of DeKalb County, Georgia, 1822-1900; Wolfe Pub. Co.
[174] Thomas J. Pluckhahn, (2003), Tampa, New Georgia Encyclopedia; Woodland Period: Overview
[175] Whites, Max E (2002) The Archaeology and History of the Native Georgia Tribes; University Press of Florida
[176] Price, Vivian (1997) History of DeKalb County, Georgia, 1822-1900; Wolfe Pub. Co.
[177] Thomas J. Pluckhahn, (2003), Tampa, New Georgia Encyclopedia; Woodland Period: Overview
[178] Whites, Max E (2002) The Archaeology and History of the Native Georgia Tribes; University Press of Florida
[179] Thomas J. Pluckhahn, (2003), Tampa, New Georgia Encyclopedia; Woodland Period: Overview

emerge to manage and distribute resources.[180] Towns began to defend their borders, and when possible, plunder another group's resources.

The Indians began to fortify their towns against attack around 1,100 years ago.[181] Many towns from this period include ditches and palisades made from wooden posts.[182] Trade also seems to have sharply decreased. Shells and other ornaments disappeared from the artifacts found dating from this time. Cultivation of corn became more prevalent and took on greater symbolic importance in the culture. [183] Mound construction declined for a while, further indicating there may have been unrest between groups.[184] Warfare and cultivation of corn became two of the central tent poles of Indian culture during the next cultural period.[185]

1,000 Years Ago, People Were Building Mounds Along the Chattahoochee
(The Mississippian Period: 1,100 years ago to 1541)

Between 1,100 years ago and 1541, the native culture of the Southeast developed into what many people picture when they imagine Indian life in Georgia. Native society reached its peak in terms of religion, art and customs. Southeastern people fully turned to a town-based, agricultural way of life. With it, they also turned to a more ceremonial way of life, which centered around the huge, flat-topped mounds they were now constructing, like the Etowah Mounds near Cartersville.[186] This span of time is called the Mississippian period by anthropologists.

At the center of each village, there was a courtyard where the residents gathered for religious ceremonies and social gatherings. If the village contained any mounds, they would be located in the plaza. Houses surrounded the plaza, and farther out, some villages contained defensive structures like a palisade.[187] Villages with more than one mound were the capitals of their areas and ruled over a network of other villages.[188] Larger chiefdoms were loosely organized together to connect other smaller chiefdoms. The vast chiefdom of Coosa in today's Gordon and Murray counties, included seven different smaller chiefdoms.[189]

[180] Whites, Max E (2002) The Archaeology and History of the Native Georgia Tribes; University Press of Florida
[181] Thomas J. Pluckhahn, (2003), Tampa, New Georgia Encyclopedia; Woodland Period: Overview
[182] Thomas J. Pluckhahn, (2003), Tampa, New Georgia Encyclopedia; Woodland Period: Overview
[183] Thomas J. Pluckhahn, (2003), Tampa, New Georgia Encyclopedia; Woodland Period: Overview
[184] Thomas J. Pluckhahn, (2003), Tampa, New Georgia Encyclopedia; Woodland Period: Overview
[185] Thomas J. Pluckhahn, (2003), Tampa, New Georgia Encyclopedia; Woodland Period: Overview
[186] Whites, Max E (2002) The Archaeology and History of the Native Georgia Tribes; University Press of Florida
[187] King, Adam, (2002) Mississippian Period: Overview, New Georgia Encyclopedia
[188] King, Adam, (2002) Mississippian Period: Overview, New Georgia Encyclopedia
[189] King, Adam, (2002) Mississippian Period: Overview, New Georgia Encyclopedia

The largest villages now contained a few hundred residents. It is estimated that the Etowah sites and other scattered villages up and down the river may have represented a total population of 15,000 people.[190]

On the surface at least, there are several similarities between Mississippian Indians of the Southeast and other recognizable groups found farther to the south, such as the Mayans. First, there is the similarity of the mounds to Native American pyramids like Chichen Itza. Before I saw one of these mounds in person, I

To the Indians who built them, the mounds were a symbol of the Earth itself and the chief who stood atop one could change the inner workings of the Earth.

was picturing something like a cairn or a burial mound. Pictures just don't do them justice. Standing in front of one feels much more like you're visiting a pyramid than something someone would call a mound. Some of them are ten stories high. Most mounds were rectangle or oval-shaped with a flat top. There is no question you are looking at a very important structure that took a long time to build. To think they were built by hand, one load of dirt after another, is incredible.[191]

Second, like Mayan chiefs, the Mississippian chiefs amassed enormous power and held dominion over a strictly ranked society.[192] Chiefs in both regions were given a much more elite lifestyle than the rest of the group.[193] They lived in the biggest house in the village. They commanded many slaves who were captured from other chiefdoms. They were covered in very ornate jewelry and ornaments. They were even sometimes carried on a litter held up by slaves. Every luxury the group could provide was given to the chief.[194]

The people of the Natchez region in Louisiana believed that their chief had descended directly out of the Sun. The chief was revered as a direct connection to the spiritual world – not a military leader. To the Indians who built them, the mounds were a symbol of the Earth itself. The chief who stood atop one could perform rituals that changed the inner workings of the Earth and kept the tribe safe. It was believed he could ensure important events to occur like the rising of the sun, the warming of Springtime and the periodic flooding of

[190] Whites, Max E (2002) The Archaeology and History of the Native Georgia Tribes; University Press of Florida
[191] King, Adam, (2002) Mississippian Period: Overview, New Georgia Encyclopedia
[192] King, Adam, (2002) Mississippian Period: Overview, New Georgia Encyclopedia
[193] King, Adam, (2002) Mississippian Period: Overview, New Georgia Encyclopedia
[194] King, Adam, (2002) Mississippian Period: Overview, New Georgia Encyclopedia

the river to soak the crops.[195] Standing atop a giant mound, a chief could make his people feel the dominance he commanded over the Earth.[196]

One of the chief's primary duties was the ushering of souls into the afterlife. Extensive artifacts have been found associated with burial such as figurines, ornaments, pipes, pottery and other cherished items.[197] The art the people created during this time may have been their most impressive achievement and was almost always associated with religion.[198] Pieces are normally recovered from burial zones where they were placed with chiefs and religious leaders.[199] The most common pieces were gorgets, cups, intricately detailed bowls, pendants, figurines, pipes, beads and effigy celts made out of pottery, stone or shell.[200] They also hammered copper into thin sheets that could be shaped, cut into images, or engraved with designs depicting mythological beings or events.[201]

Natchez Chief Great Sun Being Carried on a Litter[202]

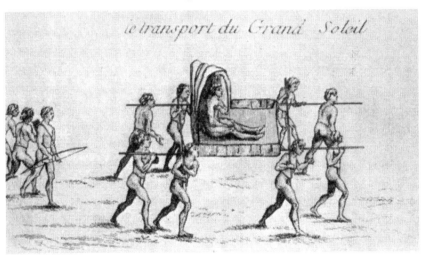

The primary responsibility for the non-elite members of the village was to grow food. Large villages were always located alongside a river and plants were intentionally placed in the flood plain so the crops would be flooded from time to time.[203] Apart from corn, they grew beans, squash, sunflowers, goosefoot

[195] King, Adam, (2002) Mississippian Period: Overview, New Georgia Encyclopedia
[196] King, Adam, (2002) Mississippian Period: Overview, New Georgia Encyclopedia
[197] Whites, Max E (2002) The Archaeology and History of the Native Georgia Tribes, University Press of Florida
[198] King, Adam, (2002) Mississippian Period: Overview, New Georgia Encyclopedia
[199] King, Adam, (2002) Mississippian Period: Overview, New Georgia Encyclopedia
[200] King, Adam, (2002) Mississippian Period: Overview, New Georgia Encyclopedia
[201] King, Adam, (2002) Mississippian Period: Overview, New Georgia Encyclopedia
[202] Natchez chief (Great Sun) carried on square litter, drawing by LePage Du Pratz 1758.
[203] King, Adam, (2002) Mississippian Period: Overview, New Georgia Encyclopedia

and sumpweed, among other plants. They also continued to gather nuts and fruits and to hunt and fish.[204]

Their homes were made by weaving together posts that were set in ditches or holes and often covered with clay or daub. The roofs were covered with thatch, with a hole left in the middle for smoke to escape. The longest walls of the house were usually around 12 or 15 feet long.[205] The fireplace was placed at the center of the house. Members of the household would sleep on low benches placed around the walls.

Even though they had many similar characteristics like mound building, there were several distinct cultures coexisting in Georgia. The two largest ones have been named the Lamar culture and the Hopewell culture.

Lamar takes its name from a site about three miles from the Macon Plateau. It contained a village surrounded by a wooden palisade 3,560 feet long. It's located in the middle of a swamp that was probably an island surrounded by water at the time people lived there. Houses were square and constructed of wattle and daub. It seems to have been created as a refuge to which to retreat if an attack were to come from the outside.[206]

The earliest site of the Hopewell culture in Georgia is the Mandeville site on the Chattahoochee River in Clay County near Dawson.[207] The Hopewell culture occurred first in the Ohio River valley and then expanded into areas now within much of the United States and in Georgia.[208]

Other nearby transitional cultures included the Averett culture along the lower part of the Chattahoochee River and the Cartersville culture in the upper Piedmont that includes the Etowah Mounds.[209]

[204] Whites, Max E (2002) The Archaeology and History of the Native Georgia Tribes; University Press of Florida
[205] Whites, Max E (2002) The Archaeology and History of the Native Georgia Tribes; University Press of Florida
[206] Whites, Max E (2002) The Archaeology and History of the Native Georgia Tribes; University Press of Florida
[207] Whites, Max E (2002) The Archaeology and History of the Native Georgia Tribes; University Press of Florida
[208] Whites, Max E (2002) The Archaeology and History of the Native Georgia Tribes; University Press of Florida
[209] Whites, Max E (2002) The Archaeology and History of the Native Georgia Tribes; University Press of Florida

A Scene Along the Chattahoochee Near Decatur 3,000 Years Ago[210]

---

[210] Illustrations by Chulsan Um

Most people in Georgia are familiar with the best-known mounds at the Etowah site near Cartersville and the Ocmulgee Mounds near Macon. The landscape around Decatur was once littered with small villages and major mound sites that have been lost.[211]

Anyone living in Decatur at that time would have been part of the chiefdom of those residing along the Chattahoochee on the current property of Six Flags Over Georgia (also in the vicinity of the later Creek village of Sandtown). This location was probably part of the same chiefdom as the Etowah mounds, part of the Cartersville cultural expression.[212] However, the mound site closer to Decatur predated the Etowah mounds by around 800 years. The oldest mounds at the Etowah site dated back to around 1,000 AD whereas the oldest portions of the Six Flags site date to 200

> The mound site closer to Decatur predated the Etowah mounds by around 800 years.

AD. There were several mounds located at this site and it could have been the capitol of the region. The site was tragically bulldozed when the amusement park was constructed in 1967, and it was never studied. We lost vast amounts of information about a very significant site to Decatur's prehistory.[213]

Apart from the sites in the vicinity of Six Flags Over Georgia associated with the later Creek village of Sandtown, there were mounds and other structures at the site of the village of Standing Peachtree where the Atlanta Waterworks pumping station is now located.[214] Standing Peachtree was first occupied around 1,000 AD and remained occupied into the 19th century, probably all the way up to Creek Removal and the Cherokee Trail of Tears. People were also still residing in Decatur along the north banks of the South River between 1,700 and 1,500 years ago.[215]

Two other major mound sites are now submerged beneath nearby lakes. The Woodstock site, just east of the Etowah Indian Mounds was located along the Etowah River and is now submerged beneath Lake Allatoona. The Summerour site that was along the Chattahoochee is now under Lake Lanier. There was also once a stone wall at the top of Stone Mountain that was probably another ceremonial structure made by the people of the

[211] King, Adam, (2002) Mississippian Period: Overview, New Georgia Encyclopedia
[212] Stanyard, William (2000) A Technical Summary of Georgia Prehistory, TRC Garrow Associates
[213] Kelly, Arthur and Meier, Larry. (1969) A Pre-Agricultural Village Site in Fulton County, Georgia, Bulletin No. 11; Proceeding of the Southeastern Archaeological Conference
[214] Trotti, Louis Haygood (1952), DeKalb County Georgia, The DeKalb Historical Society's Year Book - 1952
[215] Price, Vivian (1997) History of DeKalb County, Georgia, 1822-1900; Wolfe Pub. Co.

Hopewell culture.[216] It was disassembled by visitors to Stone Mountain after the arrival of settlers to the area.

A little farther away, near Columbus, is the Annawakee Mound site. It was probably a town connected to Chattahoochee village, located farther south. It was first identified in 1938 and revisited in 1975 before being destroyed by the landowner.[217] The Singer Moye site in Stewart County also contains several well-preserved mounds.[218] There is a Leake mound site in Bartow County about 56 miles north of Decatur. [219]

> Two other major mound sites are now submerged beneath Lake Alatoona and Lake Lanier.

Contact between the Europeans and the Indians marked the end of the prehistoric era and the beginning of the historical era in North America. Trade between the Indians in the Southeast and the Europeans at the coast began around 1513 and kicked off the rapid decline of the native culture. Among the many cultures like Hopewell and Cartersville that had appeared earlier, a single cultural tradition started to pervade most of Georgia that was derived from the Lamar culture.[220]

[216] Whites, Max E (2002) The Archaeology and History of the Native Georgia Tribes; University Press of Florida
[217] Woodliff, Dylan (2013) Revisiting Anneewakee Creek, The Society for Georgia Archaeology
[218] King, Adam, (2002) Mississippian Period: Overview, New Georgia Encyclopedia
[219] Woodliff, Dylan (2013) Revisiting Anneewakee Creek, The Society for Georgia Archaeology
[220] Whites, Max E (2002) The Archaeology and History of the Native Georgia Tribes; University Press of Florida

CHAPTER 6:
DECATUR'S WEB OF PREHISORIC TRAILS

Decatur's Major Roads Were Built Overtop of Several Prehistoric Indian Trails

If I were to pick a point in history when the current character of the city of Decatur was first defined by its residents, I would say it is around 5,000 years ago when we know that trade was occurring between the people living in the Decatur area and other groups far away on the coast,[221] down in Louisiana, and far up to the north.[222] A distinguishing characteristic of Decatur that has really remained consistent through most of its known and confirmed history of human habitation is that it has passed trade up and down the Southeast.

> The oldest human-made elements in Decatur that are still clearly visible on the landscape are the ancient Indian trails.

In the modern era, it grew out of the railroads. In the past it grew out of the network of Indian trails. The oldest human-made elements in Decatur that are still clearly visible on the landscape are trails that traverse the rolling ridges between the Savannah River and the ocean to the south and east and the Chattahoochee River and the mountains to the north and west. Even today, Decatur is laid out on a network of ancient trails that have become the major roads of the city.[223]

The trails took full advantage of a key part of what makes Decatur stand out on the landscape: Its position atop the Eastern Continental Divide – the border on which water either trickles down to the Atlantic or to the Gulf of Mexico.

At first glance, this seems like simply another of the many neat little pieces of trivia that make Decatur interesting. However, if you think back and consider the reasons Decatur ended up in this location and then follow those reasons forward, it's easy to see that it is really no coincidence that the city center is straddling the Eastern Continental Divide.[224]

---

[221] Whites, Max E (2002) The Archaeology and History of the Native Georgia Tribes; University Press of Florida
[222] Price, Vivian (1997) History of DeKalb County, Georgia, 1822-1900; Wolfe Pub. Co.
[223] Price, Vivian (1997) History of DeKalb County, Georgia, 1822-1900; Wolfe Pub. Co.
[224] See accompanying maps

> ## There is no coincidence that Decatur is straddling the Eastern Continental Divide.

The Indians that constructed the trails in the area were masters at surveying the smoothest, driest routes to walk on. To travel north and south in the Southeast, the best route possible would have been the Eastern Continental Divide. Water trickles away on each side of it, and the trail stays navigable. These commonly used trails naturally became an ideal place for trade. Someone was always going to eventually pass by, and a trading post was eventually put on the intersection of the Sandtown Trail and the Shallowford Trail that is now Clairemont Avenue. Later, the same high point at the intersection of these trails was chosen for the location of the county seat of DeKalb County and the courthouse.

I can't help but feel there is one more reason why the intersection of the Sandtown Trail and the Shallowford Trail made a pleasing choice for the location of the county seat. Above all, these trails were important routes for commerce. It was only natural that a trading post should eventually crop up smack on top of the intersection of the two trails, but a courthouse is another thing entirely. It occurred to me as I was reading about the Metropolitan Cathedral in Mexico City. Before there was Mexico City, there was Tenochtitlan, the capital city of the Aztec empire. As the Spanish displaced the Aztecs and established their own capital city on top of the older one, they chose the location for what would become the largest cathedral in the Americas on the site of the Templo Mayor, one of the Aztec's main religious temples. Buildings are obviously very clear societal symbols, and often their locations are chosen to send very clear messages. Imagine the message being sent to anyone by the Americans now settling the area, especially to an Indian travelling these trails to or from the frontier who comes upon a courthouse where there had once only been a crossroad (even though it was just a small log building at the time). It was a physical reminder making a clear statement. "We are here now. We are not leaving. This is ours."

Sandtown Trail (Sycamore Street/College Avenue/DeKalb Avenue)

Before there was Decatur or Atlanta, the largest and oldest settlement in this area was Sandtown, and if you wanted to get there you needed to take the Sandtown Trail. The trail runs west from Stone Mountain along the ridge where the Georgia Railroad is now (also the location of the old Stone Mountain wagon road).[225] It then enters the area of Decatur along Sycamore Street and then passes out on Atlanta Avenue and follows the location of the

---

[225] Hudgins, Carl T. (1952) Collection of the DeKalb Historical Society, The Year Book – 1952

railroad and Eastern Continental Divide – College Avenue to DeKalb Avenue to La France Street to Decatur Street to Five Points in Atlanta. [226]

At Five Points, the trail turns down what is now Whitehall Street to Mitchell Street to Forsyth Street along Peters and Whitehall Streets along Cascade Avenue, then Cascade Road and then to Sandtown right around the point where Wilson Creek and Utoy Creek enter the Chattahoochee near Buzzard's Roost Island.[227]

The Sandtown Trail runs right over the top of the Eastern Continental Divide. When surveyors came to lay the railroad many years later, they made no corrections in its course as the best, most gradual, and dry route to the river. As it runs east from Stone Mountain through the area in Decatur and all the way to the Chattahoochee River, the Sandtown Trail crosses only one stream known once as Tanyard Branch now Peavine Creek."[228] One has to wonder if whoever constructed the original trail was aware of how well placed it was and that it represents such a significant ridge for the entire southeast region. The Sandtown Trail was also called the Echota Trail. It may have been more commonly known by that name to people living farther away from the area. The trail eventually reaches Echota in North Georgia, the capital of the Cherokee Nation.[229]

> As it runs east from Stone Mountain through Decatur and all the way to the Chattahoochee River, the Sandtown Trail crosses only one stream.

Shallowford Trail (Clairemont Avenue and Lavista Road)
Another very important location that was a common waypoint for people passing through Decatur, usually headed into Cherokee territory, was the shallow ford in the Chattahoochee.

From the old DeKalb courthouse, the Shallowford Trail runs north on Clairemont Avenue, a slight right onto to Lavista Road, then a slight left onto Oakgrove Road until it becomes Briarcliff Road. There, it finally gets back to its original name form the settlement era of Shallowford Road. It then runs over Peachtree Creek, crosses Peachtree Road between Chamblee and Doraville and then reaches the Chattahoochee at the old Shallow Ford around

[226] Hudgins, Carl T. (1952) Collection of the DeKalb Historical Society, The Year Book – 1952 (with some updates to current Street names)
[227] Hudgins, Carl T. (1952) Collection of the DeKalb Historical Society, The Year Book – 1952
[228] McKinney Clarke, Caroline (1973) The Story of Decatur 1823-1899; Higgins-Macarthur/Longing & Porter
[229] Hudgins, Carl T. (1952) Collection of the DeKalb Historical Society, The Year Book – 1952

two miles south of Roswell, where it intersects with the Hightower/Etowah trail.[230]

There is some confusion over where the trail passes to after this point. The best authority on the topic, Carl Hudgins, believed the trail leaves Shallowford Road where it intersects with Buford Highway, crosses over that road and passes northward toward the foot of the hill there. It then turns to the right and crosses Peachtree Trail at the Presbyterian Cemetery north of Chamblee. It then coincides with Peachtree Road, and in land lot 334 of the 18th land district, it turns to the left some and runs toward what is now Chamblee Dunwoody Road. From there, it passes through Dunwoody and meets up with the Hightower/Etowah trail east of Roswell Road.[231]

South of the courthouse, the trail was called the Indian Springs Trail because it leads to the Indian Springs plantation owned by the chief of the Lower Creeks, William McIntosh. It runs along what is now McDonough Street and at some point, probably overlaps with Candler Road. [232]

Standing Peachtree Trail (Rockbridge Road and Nelson's Ferry Road)
Apart from Sandtown, the other major Indian town that predated Decatur was Standing Peachtree. Standing Peachtree, located at the confluence of Peachtree Creek and the Chattahoochee River, was first occupied between 1034 and 1154, almost 400 years before the first Europeans set foot on the America continent[233]

The Standing Peachtree Trail runs from Stone Mountain out along Rockbridge Road and Nelson's Ferry Road through DeKalb County. In what is now Fulton County, it runs along Rock Springs Road to Montgomery Ferry Road, to Collier Road and skirts the edge of what is now Piedmont Park.[234]

This trail was used as a well-traveled stagecoach route between Decatur and Marietta as was described by Mrs. Willis Carlisle.[235]

---

[230] Hudgins, Carl T. (1952) Collection of the DeKalb Historical Society, The Year Book – 1952
[231] Hudgins, Carl T. (1952) Collection of the DeKalb Historical Society, The Year Book – 1952
[232] Price, Vivian (1997) History of DeKalb County, Georgia, 1822-1900; Wolfe Pub. Co.
[233] Price, Vivian (1997) History of DeKalb County, Georgia, 1822-1900; Wolfe Pub. Co.
[234] Hudgins, Carl T. (1952) Collection of the DeKalb Historical Society, The Year Book – 1952; Hemperley, Mario R., (1989), Historic Indian Trails of Georgia, The Gard Cluyb of Georgia, pg. 30-31 Goff, Dr. John H., Collection, Georgia Dept. of Archives and History
[235] I'm a bit confused by the reference in the Standing Peachtree – Stone Mountain Trail to Nelson Ferry Road. The obvious path from Stone Mountain to Standing Peachtree seems to correspond perfectly to Rockbridge Road and the other roads referenced above with the addition of Decatur Road. But the section of Nelson's Ferry Road that persists in Decatur seems to be off the path. I've chosen not to show this section in my map and instead continue my supposed Standing Peachtree – Stone Mountain path along Decatur Road where it seems to make the most sense. But this may be inconsistent with what was intended by the Marion Hemperley, the author and historian from whom I gathered this information. I have not thus far found any historical changes in the location of Nelson's Ferry Road that might explain this.

Decatur Prehistoric Indian Trails Overlaid with Modern Roads[236]

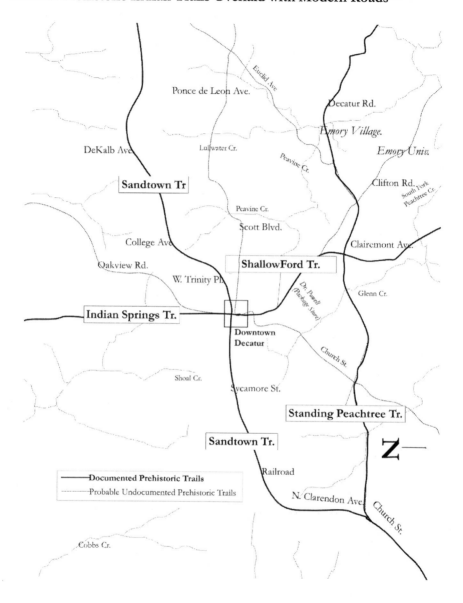

[236] Hudgins, Carl T. (1952) Collection of the DeKalb Historical Society, The Year Book – 1952; Hemperley, Mario R., (1989), Historic Indian Trails of Georgia, The Gard Club of Georgia, pg. 30-31 Goff, Dr. John H., Collection, Georgia Dept. of Archives and History

"The stage from Decatur to Marietta passed every other day and was driven by Tom Shivers. Formerly the stage road between these two towns went west from Decatur, passing by what is today Piedmont Park, along the Echota trail (the name "Echota" was often applied to the whole network of trails that lead into Cherokee territory), crossing Peachtree Road to Montgomery Ferry which, was at Standing Peachtree, then northwest to Marietta. But now that a prospective railroad was being centered at Terminus, the road had been changed."[237]

Hightower / Etowah Trail (The eastern border of DeKalb County)

The most historically important trail in the region is the Hightower Trail. After people began to settle the area and as treaties were establishing the division of land between the Creeks to the south and Cherokees to the north, the Hightower Trail was often used to define the boundary.[238]

With only two exceptions, we now call these trails by the names given to them by English speaking settlers. The Hightower Trail is (sort of) one of

these exceptions and the other is the Echota. Several early maps use the name "Hightower" interchangeably with the word "Etowah" when referring to the River and other landmarks. The word is derived from the Cherokee

Several early maps use the name "Hightower" interchangeably with the word "Etowah".

word "Ita-Wa." Although it is most commonly called the Hightower, the more proper name for the trail is the Etowah Trail.

Unlike some of the other trails, it's easy to locate where much of the Hightower Trail is relative to Decatur because it forms the northern boundary between DeKalb County and Gwinnett County.[239] It descends into the Decatur region from the Etowah river in the north. It then crosses the Chattahoochee River at the Shallow Ford located two miles south of Roswell.[240] A section of the old trail crosses Roswell Road just south of the river and is still called the "Hightower Trail".[241]

From there, it runs a meandering route following the DeKalb County border along Dunwoody Club Road, part of Winter's Chapel Road, along the southern border of Graves Park and across the Heritage Golf Links. It then crosses

---

[237] Mrs. Willis Carlisle in Bulletin number 13 page 116 volume 3, Atlanta Historical Society.
[238] Historical markers
[239] Hudgins, Carl T. (1952) Collection of the DeKalb Historical Society, The Year Book – 1952
[240] Hudgins, Carl T. (1952) Collection of the DeKalb Historical Society, The Year Book – 1952
[241] Hudgins, Carl T. (1952) Collection of the DeKalb Historical Society, The Year Book – 1952 with some corrections to modern names.

Lawrenceville Road just northeast of Tucker. It then passes on to a small part of Old Tucker Road and on to Stone Mountain. It crosses the Yellow River at the old rock bridge, now Rockbridge Road and passes on to a section that still bears the name just southeast of there. From there, the trail passes High Shoals on the Apalachee River and goes on toward Augusta.[242] Along its course, there are historical markers in several places, including the point at which it crosses Lawrenceville Highway and Peachtree Road just north of Doraville. [243]

Soapstone Ridge Trail (Bouldercrest Road and Flat Shoals Road)
There is another important trail that passes through Decatur and leads from Soapstone Ridge to Five Points in Atlanta. It runs along Bouldercrest Road and Flat Shoals Road and connects with the Stone Mountain-Sandtown Trail somewhere before reaching Five Points. On the plaque attached to the old DeKalb County courthouse, it is marked as the Sandtown Trail but should be distinguished from the Stone-Mountain – Sandtown Trail that runs along Rockbridge Road.

Fayetteville Trail (Panthersville Road and Fayetteville Road)
There is almost certainly another trail that runs from the Soapstone Ridge area of Decatur to Fayetteville though, there is no known documentation of it. An 1864 map of Georgia shown on page 72[244] shows a road that runs in this direction and most of these roads were indeed created along Indian trails.[245]

The likely course of this one is along Panthersville Road to Bouldercrest Rd. then on to Mt. Zion Blvd and then Fayetteville Road.

The Stone Mountain Walkup Trail
There is one trail that has almost certainly been in constant use longer than any of the others and is still in daily use today. We know that is was being used long before the Creeks came here. It almost undoubtedly has been used since the first human beings set foot in the Southeast. This is the one that ascends the western slope of Stone Mountain. Stone Mountain was exposed above the landscape about 15 million years ago and has looked almost

> The Stone Mountain trail has been used continually since the first human beings set foot in the Southeast.

the same during all that time as it looks today. If you were the first hunter to

[242] Hudgins, Carl T. (1952) Collection of the DeKalb Historical Society, The Year Book – 1952
[243] Hudgins, Carl T. (1952) Collection of the DeKalb Historical Society, The Year Book – 1952
[244] Price, Vivian (1997) History of DeKalb County, Georgia, 1822-1900; Wolfe Pub. Co.
[245] Price, Vivian (1997) History of DeKalb County, Georgia, 1822-1900; Wolfe Pub. Co.

venture into new hunting grounds and noticed that giant rock rising above the trees, visible from miles away, would you be able to resist approaching it and walking to the top? I certainly would want to do that.

Peachtree to Sandtown Trail
Another trail runs down the banks of the Chattahoochee to take travelers between the two Indian towns of Standing Peachtree and Sandtown.[246]

Stone Mountain Trail Intersection
Several principal trails meet at Stone Mountain. It was a popular meeting and waypoint for people in the area as long as there have been people living in the area for obvious reasons. It's easy to see and locate from a long way off.[247]

Peachtree Trail (Peachtree Road)
Another of the easiest trails to locate in the area of Atlanta, like the Hightower/Etowah trail is the Peachtree Trail. This is because it is now called Peachtree Road. This trail forks in Buckhead with one fork running through what is now Atlanta following Peachtree Road and the other following Paces Ferry Road and Moores Mill Road to the location of the old town of Standing Peachtree where Peachtree Creek meets the Chattahoochee.[248] The Peachtree Trail passes through DeKalb County along the high ground where the Southern Railway to Washington is now located.[249]

Five Points - Standing Peachtree Trail (Marietta Street)
Another smaller trail is known to have existed that left Five Points over the ridge where Marietta Street is now located and passed to Standing Peachtree.[250]

[246] Price, Vivian (1997) History of DeKalb County, Georgia, 1822-1900; Wolfe Pub. Co.
[247] Price, Vivian (1997) History of DeKalb County, Georgia, 1822-1900; Wolfe Pub. Co.
[248] Hudgins, Carl T. (1952) Collection of the DeKalb Historical Society, The Year Book – 1952
[249] Hudgins, Carl T. (1952) Collection of the DeKalb Historical Society, The Year Book – 1952
[250] Hudgins, Carl T. (1952) Collection of the DeKalb Historical Society, The Year Book – 1952

How Old are the Decatur Trails?

How old do you think the trails upon which our roads in Decatur were built really are? Normally, the creation of the trails is thought to have happened somewhere around the creation of sophisticated trading in the Southeast. We know that soapstone slabs from Soapstone Ridge were being traded widely in the Southeast as far back as 4,000 years ago and were getting as far as Louisiana and even to the Great Lakes[251]. Then, the trails came into heavy use in the 1800s when trade with the British was passing along these routes between larger towns like Augusta and the Indian territories. To get that soapstone from Decatur to Louisiana, people loaded canoes on the South River and paddled south. They must have been using trails to get back north. Most of these trails must be at least 4,000 years old, almost certainly older.

We also know that people were walking up and down the Southeast long before that for thousands of years. We can presume they were using some types of trails but, what if it goes back even farther? Animals create trails. Not just humans. If you've spent a fair amount of time in the woods, especially around rivers, you have seen that there will normally be rough trails through the brush created by animals finding the path of least resistance to get to the water or some other resource – a "game trail." Then, when people come along and need a trail in the same area, the natural thing to do is to use the game trail. It's better than bushwhacking through the thorns and poison ivy, and it usually leads some place. Taking another jump, we know that large mammals arrived in North America around hundreds of thousands of years ago. Big animals and the kind that migrate over long distances like caribou and bison, the kind that leave a trail. Maybe the trails we have in Decatur are more than 100,000 years old. Just a wild thought.

---

[251] Worth, Dr. John Fall; the First Georgians, -- The Late Archaic Period (3000 BC – 1000 BC) – Fernbank Quarterly

1864 Map of DeKalb County and Decatur[252]

The map below shows the early roads coming out of Decatur. Many of these early roads were established on top of older Indian trails and help to confirm their location. The map also shows the location of the county's land lots including number 246 that was chosen as the location of the County seat (and later as the name of the restaurant on East Ponce de Leon Avenue).

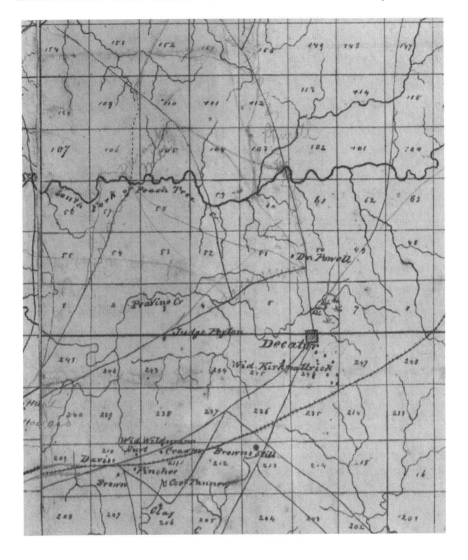

[252] Top. Engr. Office, Dept. of the Cumberlnad (1864) Dekalb and Fulton County, Ga.: compiled for the use of the topographical engineers, Library of Congress Geography and Map Division

CHAPTER 7:
EUROPEANS ARRIVE IN DECATUR

As Empires Raced to Claim America, Six Nations Laid Claim to Decatur

As the native culture, centered around their larger villages and towering ceremonial mounds, continued to flourish at the interior of Georgia, they were slowly becoming aware of the crisis unfolding at the coast and on the nearby islands in the Caribbean. Europeans were quickly increasing efforts to extract profits from the new land they had found and each nation was fighting to claim a piece. By my count, there have been six different nations that laid claim, or tried to lay claim, to the land of Decatur during modern, historical times: The Creeks, the Portuguese, the Spanish, the French, the British and finally the Americans.[253]

The race for the most legitimate European claim to America began in 1492 when Christopher Columbus came within sight of the coast. As most know, he was not the first European to reach North America, and America was not "discovered" by Europeans. Leif Eriksson, a Viking, journeyed to North America from Greenland about 500 years before Columbus. Long before that, people crossed over the Bering Sea Land Bridge from Eurasia and were truly the first people to discover the continent.

A Swiss mapmaker labeled the New World with Amerigo Vespucci's name. Other mapmakers followed his labeling, and the land became mistakenly known as "America."

However interesting, this point is irrelevant in the context of the European race for land ownership. Leif Ericson didn't make a claim to North America on behalf of the Vikings as a state. Columbus had traveled to North America thinking it was Asia, but when he made that mistake, he was sailing under the flag of Spain, sponsored by King Ferdinand and Queen Isabella with the specific objective of finding and claiming new land on their behalf. Therefore,

---

[253] Jackson, Edwin L. and Stakes, Mary E. (2004) The Georgia Studies Book: Our State and the Nation; University of Georgia, Carl Vinson Institute of Government, Chapter 5

during the Age of Discovery when European nations were aggressively exploring the rest of the world, Spain felt it had the most legitimate claim to the region.[254]

Columbus believed America was part of East India and called the inhabitants "Indians". An Italian businessman who accompanied him on a later voyage named Amerigo Vespucci believed it was not Asia but a new world. The name stuck, and people started referring to America as the New World. For reasons that are unknown today, a Swiss mapmaker later labeled the New World with Amerigo Vespucci's name. Other mapmakers followed his labeling, and the land became mistakenly known as "America."[255]

Until Columbus passed by North America, the Portuguese had been the clear leaders in the race to fill in the edges of the maps. They had explored much of Africa and were searching for an eastbound route to Asia when Columbus ventured out on his westward attempt. After Spain's new success, tension rose between the two countries. Both Spain and Portugal were Catholic countries, so Pope Alexander VI felt it was his duty to

> And that's the story of why they speak Portuguese in Brazil, but they speak Spanish in most of the rest of South America

keep peace between his church members. The Pope issued a decree in 1493 that there would be a "Line of Demarcation" from north to south about 400 miles west of the Azore islands. Portugal would have claim to everything east of the line, and Spain would have claim to everything west of the line.[256]

They didn't know it at the time, but the placement of this line gave all of North and South America to Spain. Even though no one knew what lay farther west at the time, Portugal protested the placement of the Line of Demarcation. The two countries then agreed in 1494 to move the line 700 miles farther to the west in the Treaty of Tordesillas. The movement of the line only added a small piece of eastern South America to Portugal's claims. This small piece of South America is what we now call Brazil. And that's the story of why they speak Portuguese in Brazil, but they speak Spanish in the rest of South America. [257]

[254] Jackson, Edwin L. and Stakes, Mary E. (2004) The Georgia Studies Book: Our State and the Nation; University of Georgia, Carl Vinson Institute of Government, Chapter 5
[255] Jackson, Edwin L. and Stakes, Mary E. (2004) The Georgia Studies Book: Our State and the Nation; University of Georgia, Carl Vinson Institute of Government, Chapter 5
[256] Jackson, Edwin L. and Stakes, Mary E. (2004) The Georgia Studies Book: Our State and the Nation; University of Georgia, Carl Vinson Institute of Government, Chapter 5
[257] Jackson, Edwin L. and Stakes, Mary E. (2004) The Georgia Studies Book: Our State and the Nation; University of Georgia, Carl Vinson Institute of Government, Chapter 5

Who Was the First European to Set Foot in Georgia?

Most people with an interest in state history are aware that the first Europeans to ever set foot in what is now Georgia were the Spanish, not the British, but who was the first explorer to do so?

Many might guess that the first Spaniard to visit Georgia was Ponce de Leon because he is well known to have explored Florida in search of the Fountain of Youth and some of the major roads in Decatur and Atlanta bear his name. Juan Ponce de Leon landed near what is now St. Augustine in April of 1513. He made landing during the Easter season and named it for the holiday, "Pascua, Florida" or "Feast of Flowers." The Spanish territory of La Florida would later include the area that is Florida, Georgia, South Carolina, Alabama and Mississippi. However, Ponce de Leon probably never actually set foot in what is now Georgia.[258]

Another common guess as to who was the first European to reach Georgia is Hernando de Soto. He was the first to explore the interior land of America and made a legendary trek through the Southeast and through much of Georgia in 1540, but he was not the first Spanish explorer to reach Georgia.

The first European positively confirmed to have ever laid eyes on Georgia (at least that has been definitively documented) was a man named Pedro de Quejos. He passed close to the Georgia coast in 1521 while searching for Indians to enslave.[259] It's possible that the Englishman John Cabot got as far south as Georgia in 1497, but that can't be confirmed.[260]

The first European to finally set foot in what is now Georgia was a man named Lucas Vazquez de Ayllon. His landing and the calamities that followed it are associated with several firsts in American history of which few people are aware. Vazquez de Ayllon was a wealthy nobleman who arrived in Hispaniola (the island that was later called Haiti and the Dominican Republic) in 1504 to serve as a judge and build his fortune. He did well for himself there by acquiring large landholdings in Puerta Plata, now part of the Dominican Republic and exploiting the local Indians as slaves.[261]

Very soon after the Spanish arrived and began establishing plantations in the Caribbean, they needed more slaves than were available close to Hispaniola. Vazquez de Ayllon, and others began venturing farther out and raiding nearby islands like the Bahamas to capture Indians and bring them back for sale. They

---

[258] Jackson, Edwin L. and Stakes, Mary E. (2004) The Georgia Studies Book: Our State and the Nation; University of Georgia, Carl Vinson Institute of Government, Chapter 5

[259] Allen, Logan (1997) A New World Disclosed, Volume 1, University of Nebraska Press

[260] Jackson, Edwin L. and Stakes, Mary E. (2004) The Georgia Studies Book: Our State and the Nation; University of Georgia, Carl Vinson Institute of Government, Chapter 5

[261] Allen, Logan (1997) A New World Disclosed, Volume 1, University of Nebraska Press

soon began looking beyond the islands to mainland North America. Soon after that, Vazquez de Ayllon began to envision a prosperous colony on the American mainland.[262]

In July 1526, Vazquez de Ayllon received support to start the first colony that would ever be attempted in North America. He left Hispaniola with six ships and about 600 colonists including a few women, several African slaves and three Dominican friars.[263] With that, another first in American history was achieved when the first native African people set

> In July 1526, Lucas Vazquez de Ayllon started the first colony that would ever be attempted in North America.

foot in North America (albeit not by their free will).[264] In addition to all these people, Vazquez de Ayllon brought 89 horses, probably the first ones to reach Georgia since the extinction of Native American horses at the end of the Pleistocene epoch.

The convoy first landed in South Carolina where associates of Vazquez de Ayllon had visited earlier and reported a beautiful country full of Indians. This was when the first of the expedition's disasters occurred. Vazquez de Ayllon's flagship, the Captiva, ran aground and sank with most of its food supply and equipment. After consolidating onto the remaining ships, they found the area too sandy and swampy for the colony and continued farther south until they found a more promising looking location near Sapelo Island in Georgia.[265] There, they founded the colony of San Miguel de Gualdape some 200 years before Oglethorpe, the founder of the Georgia colony, would arrive in the same area. [266]

The colonists' troubles then worsened. The weather turned exceptionally cold for the Georgia coast in mid-summer. They were next attacked by local Indians. As the colonists grew cold and hungry, paranoia and distrust grew. Fights broke out among them, and there was eventually even murder.

Finally, there was a revolt by the African slaves. The slaves that arrived with Vazquez de Ayllon were the first Africans to ever set foot in North America and the only ones from the expedition who remained in America. They burned several of the buildings and ran into the forest where it is likely that they joined

[262] Allen, Logan (1997) A New World Disclosed, Volume 1, University of Nebraska Press
[263] Allen, Logan (1997) A New World Disclosed, Volume 1, University of Nebraska Press
[264] Jackson, Edwin L. and Stakes, Mary E. (2004) The Georgia Studies Book: Our State and the Nation; University of Georgia, Carl Vinson Institute of Government, Chapter 5, pg 100
[265] Allen, Logan (1997) A New World Disclosed, Volume 1, University of Nebraska Press
[266] Worth, John E. (2003), Spanish Exploration, New Georgia Encyclopedia

the local Indians. It's possible that the descendants of these first African arrivals in the United States are still in Georgia or perhaps in Oklahoma where the Creeks were eventually forced to relocate.[267]

Inevitably, after their food had faltered, disease broke out and killed many of the colonists and Vazquez de Ayllon himself on October 18, 1526. The remaining colonists continued as best they could but disbanded the colony before the winter of 1526. In the end, San Miguel de Gualdape lasted only a few months. Of the 600 colonists that had landed to begin the colony, only about 150 returned to Hispaniola.[268]

Who Was the First European to Reach Decatur?

We now know who the first Spanish explorer was to come within sight of Georgia and who the first to land in Georgia was, but who was the first European to reach Decatur? Unfortunately, that's not absolutely clear, but there is one person who seems very likely to have been the first.

Hernando de Soto was the first to reach the interior of Georgia away from the coast. He passed through Georgia and met with many of the Creeks including the Cowetas, the group known to have lived in the Decatur area. The eastward route he took on the lower part of his looping journey down from the mountains is not completely clear. It is generally agreed he did not pass through the Decatur area specifically.[269]

Another entrada (march to the interior) into Georgia like de Soto's was made by Tristan de Luna in 1560. This one followed a similar route to de Soto passing north of Decatur.[270]

Juan Pardo made another set of entradas between 1566 and 1568. There are some persistent legends that Juan Pardo visited Stone Mountain in 1567 because he wrote of a place he called "Crystal Mountain."[271]. It is all but certain

> The Indians spoke of a mountain in the neighboring region to the west that was "very high, shining when the sun set like fire", believed to be a reference to Stone Mountain.

[267] Jackson, Edwin L. and Stakes, Mary E. (2004) The Georgia Studies Book: Our State and the Nation; University of Georgia, Carl Vinson Institute of Government, Chapter 5, pg 100
[268] Hudson, Charles (1994) The Forgotten Centuries: Indians and Europeans in the American South: 1521 – 1704, University of Georgia Press
[269] DeKalb County Historical Society Year Book (1952)
[270] Southeast Archeological Center, The Creeks
[271] DeKalb County Historical Society Year Book (1952)

that he was in North Carolina during this expedition when he found a place he called Crystal Mountain. He seems to have been a long way from Georgia, so it's very unlikely this legend is true.[272]

It doesn't appear that any of the early Spanish explorers reached Decatur but one of them came very close. This was Pedro de Chozas who passed through the interior of Georgia in 1597. He led a small group of Spaniards that reached as far as Eatonton, Georgia in the chiefdom of Ocute. Gaspar de Salas, the only soldier of the expedition, made note that the Indians spoke of a mountain in the neighboring region to the west that was "very high, shining when the sun set like fire." They also told the Spanish that a "short haired people" lived on the other side of the mountain. The mountain to which the Indians referred seems to be in the right location and distance from Eatonton to have been Stone Mountain, and the short haired people may refer to Indians living along the Chattahoochee.[273]or it may refer to Indians who lived around the Dog River who were part of the Lamar culture that inhabited the Chattahoochee drainage area in the later 16th century.[274]

The best current evidence is that the first European to set foot on the soil of Decatur was probably an Englishman, not a Spaniard, by the name of Henry Woodward. He was already a very successful trader from South Carolina who had strong relationships with the Indians farther north. In 1674, he ventured into the backcountry and made direct contact with Indians in Middle and Southern Georgia. He established contact with many of the Creek villages along the middle and upper Chattahoochee using several Creek guides to lead him into the wilderness. In many of these villages, it was the first contact any European had made with that specific group. While travelling from village to village, Woodward certainly used the major trails in the area and would have used the trails that passed right across the high point where downtown Decatur is now located.

> The first European to finally set foot on the soil of Decatur was probably an Englishman, not a Spaniard, by the name of Henry Woodward.

While exploring and introducing himself to the Indians, he got word that a group of 250 Spanish soldiers were searching for him in the woods to prevent the English from securing relationships with the Creeks in the area. Instead of

[272] Pratter, Chester (1987) The Route of Juan Pardo's Explorations in the Interior Southeast, 1566-1568; Institute of Archaeology and Anthropology, South Carolina
[273] David Freedman (1986) Carved in Stone, The History of Stone Mountain, Mercer University Press
[274] Southeast Archeological Center, The Creeks

fleeing, Woodward nailed a note to a tree along one of the major trails in which he taunted the Spanish to catch him if they could. He then continued his journey and met with several more Creek villages but never met with the Spanish face-to-face.

By the time he made his way back to Charles Town, he was so loaded with deerskins that he had to pay 150 Creek men and boys to carry his cargo. Other traders followed Woodward's example of going directly to the Creeks to secure relationships, and English trade with the Creeks living near the Chattahoochee skyrocketed.[275]

With a gap of 77 years between the time Pedro de Chozas reached Eatonton and the time Henry Woodward made contact with the Creeks along the Chattahoochee, more research is obviously needed to confirm he was the first European to reach Decatur. I plan to continue searching for documentation of an earlier visitor.

The First Military Fort in the United States Was in Georgia

While the Spanish were establishing their presence in the Southeast, France was making its own claims in the region. In 1524, Giovanni Verrazano sailed under a French flag looking for a westward route to Asia. He came ashore somewhere around South Carolina and then sailed north to Nova Scotia. France used this trip as the primary basis of their claim to the Southeast.[276]

French efforts to establish themselves in Georgia then increased dramatically during the 1560s. In 1562, Jean Ribault established the settlement of Port Royal, just north of Savannah and constructed the first military fort in North America, which he called Charles Fort. However, lack of food and illness caused the French to soon abandon Port Royal.[277]

Two years later, the French tried again to establish a military fort to defend their claims to the Southeast with the construction of Fort Caroline at the mouth of the St. John's River. The fort was again destined to spend little time under French control. It was sacked by the Spanish in September 1565. In its place, Pedro Menéndez de Avilés founded St. Augustine, today the oldest surviving city in the United States.[278]

---

[275] DeKalb County Historical Society Year Book (1952)
[276] Jackson, Edwin L. and Stakes, Mary E. (2004) The Georgia Studies Book: Our State and the Nation; University of Georgia, Carl Vinson Institute of Government, Chapter 5
[277] Jackson, Edwin L. and Stakes, Mary E. (2004) The Georgia Studies Book: Our State and the Nation; University of Georgia, Carl Vinson Institute of Government, Chapter 5
[278] Jackson, Edwin L. and Stakes, Mary E. (2004) The Georgia Studies Book: Our State and the Nation; University of Georgia, Carl Vinson Institute of Government, Chapter 5

France established its own colony in 1682 in the Mississippi valley that they called "Louisiana" for King Louis XIV. The French were working their way east along the Gulf Coast trying to claim all the Southeast.[279]

The English Set Out to Take the Southeast from the Spanish in 1586

During the first part of the 16th century, Spanish dominance of trade in the New World continued to grow. It had control of vast coastal territories from Florida down through Central America and much of South America. As Spain accumulated vast wealth in the New World, England increased its efforts. The English declared that the Pope's decree in 1493 that divided the world outside Europe between the Portuguese and the Spanish was an illegitimate claim. Spain argued that in addition to the Pope's decree, they were the first to arrive in several areas of the New World and, therefore, had the "Right of First Discovery" of the Southeast. After Columbus passed by America, Spain had dramatically increased its voyages to the New World and sent explorers to sight and claim (most claims were made by the first ships to pass and observe a piece of land) ever expanding pieces of the map.[280]

The first explorer to sail under an English flag and make a major exploration of the New World was the Italian, John Cabot (Giovanni Cabotto). In 1497, he sailed along much of the coast from Nova Scotia and may have gotten as far south as Georgia. England used this voyage to counter Spanish claims of First Discovery to all this coastline.[281]

When words failed to resolve the argument, England took a more direct approach to disrupting Spanish claims. In 1586, Sir Francis Drake attacked and burned St. Augustine. The English once again asserted the explorations of John Cabot. England now claimed nearly all the North American coast north of La Florida.[282] However, the border of La Florida at this time was well north of present day Florida and still included all of Georgia.[283]

The Juanillo Rebellion

As the turn of the 16th century approached, the Spanish were awakened to the fact that England was not the only power threatening their hold on the

---

[279] Jackson, Edwin L. and Stakes, Mary E. (2004) The Georgia Studies Book: Our State and the Nation; University of Georgia, Carl Vinson Institute of Government, Chapter 5
[280] Jackson, Edwin L. and Stakes, Mary E. (2004) The Georgia Studies Book: Our State and the Nation; University of Georgia, Carl Vinson Institute of Government, Chapter 5
[281] Jackson, Edwin L. and Stakes, Mary E. (2004) The Georgia Studies Book: Our State and the Nation; University of Georgia, Carl Vinson Institute of Government, Chapter 5
[282] Jackson, Edwin L. and Stakes, Mary E. (2004) The Georgia Studies Book: Our State and the Nation; University of Georgia, Carl Vinson Institute of Government, Chapter 5
[283] Jackson, Edwin L. and Stakes, Mary E. (2004) The Georgia Studies Book: Our State and the Nation; University of Georgia, Carl Vinson Institute of Government, Chapter 5

Southeast when the Indians began killing all of their Spanish friars. Spain had chosen a different strategy to protect their control of the Southeast when dealing with the native population as opposed to how they chose to deal with other Europeans. They used missions instead of forts and tried to convert the Indians to become Catholic, thereby, in their view, also fulfilling a spiritual mission to deliver new souls to the church.

Under the mission system, the Spanish divided the Georgia coast into two territories and named them for the two large Indian tribes in the area who they were trying to convert, Guale and Mocama (refer to the map at the beginning of the book). Guale lay to the north including the land between the Savannah and the Altamaha Rivers. Mocama lied between

> The Spanish were awakened to the fact that England was not the only power threatening their hold on the Southeast when the Indians began killing Spanish friars.

the Altamaha and St. Mary's River.[284] Eighteen missions were established, beginning in 1568, in what is now Georgia, 13 on the coast and five along rivers more to the interior.[285]

As would happen several times in colonial history, the Europeans overreached in their early efforts to control the native population. Don Juanillo was a Guale Indian who was in line to become chief. He had been baptized as a Catholic but also had two wives in the tradition of the Guale. The local Spanish friars were struggling for power in the Guale community and trying to enforce Catholic principles. In a bold maneuver in September 1597, they publicly declared that Don Juanillo was unfit to be chief as a bigamist and named another Indian who they decided was a more fitting chief.[286]

Don Juanillo was furious. He responded by gathering a group of followers and killing the Franciscan friar Pedro de Corpa at the Tolomato mission. He then called on other chiefs in Guale to rise up and overthrow the missions and return to traditional Indian customs. Many of them did.

The violence was finally squelched with the help of Indians in Mocama who had remained allied with the Spanish. The Spanish mission system was now in

[284] Jackson, Edwin L. and Stakes, Mary E. (2004) The Georgia Studies Book: Our State and the Nation; University of Georgia, Carl Vinson Institute of Government, Chapter 5
[285] Jackson, Edwin L. and Stakes, Mary E. (2004) The Georgia Studies Book: Our State and the Nation; University of Georgia, Carl Vinson Institute of Government, Chapter 5
[286] Jackson, Edwin L. and Stakes, Mary E. (2004) The Georgia Studies Book: Our State and the Nation; University of Georgia, Carl Vinson Institute of Government, Chapter 5

shambles because of the rebellion, and Spanish confidence was seriously shaken. Nearly all the Spanish churches in Guale were burned. Five Spanish friars were killed. Only one of the friars present at the time survived, Francisco Davilla.[287] The Spanish managed to reestablish the mission system in 1605, and it was not fully dismantled in Georgia until 1702.[288]

The South Carolina Colony is Established Including the Land of Present-Day Georgia

During the next hundred years, England colonized most of the East Coast of North America. At first, the British concentrated mainly on the colonies north of Virginia. In 1663, King Charles II issued a charter for England's sixth colony, Carolina.

The initial southern boundary of Carolina was said to be at the 31st parallel, just north of where Georgia's southern boundary is today. Later, in 1665, England declared that boundary to be as far down as the 29th parallel, 60 miles south of St. Augustine. For a short period of time, Decatur was part of Carolina. England again used the voyage of John Cabot as their justification for this claim against Spain.[289]

The British began evicting people from the Spanish missions in what they now claimed as British territory in 1680. English officers, supported by Indian allies, raided the Mission of Santa Catalina de Guale on St. Catherine's Island. The English attack was repulsed, and the Spanish retained control of the mission. However, fearing another attack, they abandoned Santa Catalina de Guale and retreated to Sapelo Island.[290]

Artifacts from Santa Catalina de Guale are now housed in Decatur at the Fernbank Museum of Natural History.

At first, the Spanish continued missionary work at Sapelo Island but then retreated farther south to St. Augustine four years later. By 1702, Spain had withdrawn from the current area of Georgia but continued to declare the land to belong to Spain. Artifacts from Santa Catalina de Guale are now housed in Decatur at the Fernbank Museum of Natural History.[291]

---

[287] Jackson, Edwin L. and Stakes, Mary E. (2004) The Georgia Studies Book: Our State and the Nation; University of Georgia, Carl Vinson Institute of Government, Chapter 5

[288] Millier, Fr. Don Pedro de Corpa and Companions, Franciscan Media

[289] Jackson, Edwin L. and Stakes, Mary E. (2004) The Georgia Studies Book: Our State and the Nation; University of Georgia, Carl Vinson Institute of Government, Chapter 5

[290] Jackson, Edwin L. and Stakes, Mary E. (2004) The Georgia Studies Book: Our State and the Nation; University of Georgia, Carl Vinson Institute of Government, Chapter 5

[291] Jackson, Edwin L. and Stakes, Mary E. (2004) The Georgia Studies Book: Our State and the Nation; University of Georgia, Carl Vinson Institute of Government, Chapter 5

Spanish officials encouraged slaves in the colonies to escape to La Florida where they would be given freedom as a way to continue to destabilize the British. Many slaves did so. Florida continued to be a haven for escape for escaped slaves even long after it came under British rule, first by joining the Spanish and later by joining Indians who opposed the Americans. The Spanish Fort Mose was established in 1738 north of St. Augustine and was entirely garrisoned by escaped slaves from the British colonies to the north.[292]

The Spanish would not officially relinquish all of La Florida to the English until the end of the French and Indian War in 1763. Its claims were now severely diminished and England had established the stronger claim to most of the Southeast.[293]

---

[292] Jackson, Edwin L. and Stakes, Mary E. (2004) The Georgia Studies Book: Our State and the Nation; University of Georgia, Carl Vinson Institute of Government, Chapter 5
[293] Jackson, Edwin L. and Stakes, Mary E. (2004) The Georgia Studies Book: Our State and the Nation; University of Georgia, Carl Vinson Institute of Government, Chapter 6

CHAPTER 8:
THE NATIVE APOCALYPSE BEGINS

The Arrival of the Indian Apocalypse in Georgia[294]

The old cannon in the Decatur City Square is something nearly all residents have seen many times. It sits near the southeast corner of the old courthouse pointing roughly off into the southeast, mounted onto a large stone inscribed with the phrase "Relic of the Indian War of 1836."

It has been a cherished item belonging to the town for many years. After its service in the Creek War of 1836, it was often rolled out and fired during local celebrations and weddings. When General Sherman, and his army passed through Decatur during the Civil War, residents took the care to bury it and avoid it being confiscated by the Union.[295] It was placed in its current location by the Decatur Chapter of the Daughters of the Confederacy in 1906.[296]

Every time I visit the Decatur City Square, I have to go over and take a look at the cannon for a few moments. I have to touch it and think about where it's been and with whom it's been. This cannon represents so much more than a relic of the city. It would have been more appropriate to set it on the west side of the old courthouse facing west because it both literally and figuratively was used to drive the people who had been living in this area in that direction, all the way to Oklahoma where most of the Creek Nation now resides.

> "This country, according to what the Indians stated, had been very populous, but it had been decimated shortly before by a pestilence." ~ Hernando de Soto (1540)

I don't know exactly where the cannon came from or who forged it. I wish I did. The story of how it became a part of local history began when the first European made contact around 1513, 27 years before when most people think Europe made contact with the Indians during Hernando de Soto's famous march through the interior or Georgia.[297][298] By 1540, the results of that initial contact already had devastating effects across Georgia and the rest of the Southeast.

---

[294] Photo on previous page by the author
[295] Collections of the DeKalb Historical Society, Year Book, 1952 – Excerpt from a story in the AJC by Winifred L. Moore.
[296] Price, Vivian (1997) History of DeKalb County, Georgia, 1822-1900; Wolfe Pub. Co.
[297] Price, Vivian (1997) History of DeKalb County, Georgia, 1822-1900; Wolfe Pub. Co.
[298] Etheridge, Robbie; (2003) Creek Country, University of North Carolina Press

The first and most deadly rider of the Native American apocalypse in Georgia was disease.[299] The Indians had lived for thousands of years completely isolated from Europe. As a result, they had not developed natural immunities to many of the common diseases introduced by the Europeans and by the domestic animals they brought with them.

More than half of the native population of the Southeast, and conceivably as much as 90% perished from diseases like measles, smallpox and cholera that were brought by the Europeans.[300] The few survivors of towns that were infected went to live with connected groups and continued the spread of these new diseases.

Even during his early trek through Georgia, as the first person to reach the interior of the Southeast in 1540, Hernando de Soto, made note of the growing devastation among the Indians.[301]

"The inhabitants are brown of skin, well-formed and proportioned. They are more civilized than any people in all the territories of Florida, wearing clothes and shoes. This country, according to what the Indians stated, had been very populous, but it had been decimated shortly before by a pestilence."[302]

Epidemics continued to sweep through the Native American population from Georgia and decimate their numbers as late as 1783.

The second rider of the Indian apocalypse was in some ways even more tragic than the rampant deadly diseases because the Indians took an active role in creating their own misery. This was slavery. The Indians already practiced a form of slavery prior to European contact by capturing members of other groups who were forced to become slaves, but slaves were not bought and sold until the arrival of Europeans. This practice began with the Spanish and accelerated with the arrival of the British in the New World.[303]

The European process for acquiring Indian slaves created a vicious cycle that greatly accelerated the collapse of the societal structure by which the Indians previously lived and kept balance with each other. The circle would begin when a group of European traders would give guns to a group of Indians on credit. That group would then use those guns to raid another group of unarmed Indians and deliver them back to the traders as slaves to pay off the credit.[304] Any Indians who had escaped among the enslaved group would then need to

---

[299] Etheridge, Robbie; (2003) Creek Country, University of North Carolina Press
[300] Price, Vivian (1997) History of DeKalb County, Georgia, 1822-1900; Wolfe Pub. Co., pg. 26
[301] Etheridge, Robbie; (2003) Creek Country, University of North Carolina Press
[302] Swanton, John R. (1922) Early History of the Creek Indians and Their Neighbors; Smithsonian Institution Bureau of American Ethnology; Bulletin 73; Washington Government Printing Office
[303] Etheridge, Robbie; (2003) Creek Country, University of North Carolina Press
[304] King, Adam, (2002) Mississippian Period: Overview, New Georgia Encyclopedia

contact another group of traders to acquire more guns to defend themselves from further raids, and the only way to get guns was to prey upon another weaker group and trade more Indian slaves. This cycle not only accelerated their own demise, but it destroyed any hope the Indians would have of confronting the Europeans on equal ground as a nation.[305]

The Iroquois were the first Indians to take part in the slave trade for the British in Carolina during the early part of the 1600s.[306] Traders from Jamestown began supporting slave raids by Indians across most of the Piedmont.[307]

By the late 1600s, the slave raids had arrived in the Southeast. Iroquois raids from the North reached into current regions of Alabama, Georgia, Tennessee, Florida, Kentucky, Arkansas and Louisiana. Most of the Iroquois raids preyed on unarmed groups of Cherokees.[308] In response, there was a general migration of Indians in Georgia out of the mountains and down to the south and west toward the Decatur area and the Chattahoochee and away from the Iroquois.[309]

Most Indian slaves were sent to work plantations in the West Indies. They were also being sent to Virginia, South Carolina, Louisiana and New England.

The last rider of the apocalypse was commerce. As more and more Europeans found their way to

> The remaining artifacts of this time in native history have all the signs of a cultural collapse.

America, the primary livelihood of most Southeastern Indians shifted from subsistence hunting and farming to commercial hunting and slave trading. Other professions emerged for Indians that hadn't existed before like guide, translator, postal rider, or hired soldier as well as horse thief, prostitute, or slave catcher. This shift to commercial hunting and trading also led to the decimation of the white-tailed deer population in the South and the eventual shift of American and European interests from deerskins to farming.[310]

The shift toward a trade-based livelihood also led to financial debts, another new concept for the Indian. Rising debts with the European traders led to the Yamasee War and later contributed greatly to the pressure the Indians felt to sell their land for money to pay off their debts.[311]

---

[305] Etheridge, Robbie; (2003) Creek Country, University of North Carolina Press
[306] Ethridge, Robbie (2002), English Trade in Deerskins and Indian Slaves, New Georgia Encyclopedia
[307] Ethridge, Robbie (2002), English Trade in Deerskins and Indian Slaves, New Georgia Encyclopedia
[308] Ethridge, Robbie (2002), English Trade in Deerskins and Indian Slaves, New Georgia Encyclopedia
[309] Ethridge, Robbie (2002), English Trade in Deerskins and Indian Slaves, New Georgia Encyclopedia
[310] Etheridge, Robbie; (2003) Creek Country, University of North Carolina Press
[311] Etheridge, Robbie; (2003) Creek Country, University of North Carolina Press

The remaining native, cultural artifacts of the early 18th century have all the signs of a cultural collapse.[312] Mound building stopped entirely. The creation of art and religious or ritualistic material completely disappeared. The intricate items with which people had been buried in past years were gone.[313]

The Gathering of the Creeks

In order to gather together their remaining strength to both protect themselves and have a stronger attacking force, the remaining Indian populations joined into loosely allied groups that are often collectively referred to as the "coalescent groups." The term "coalescent groups" is an accurate and important one because it conveys the point that these were not tribes or nations, though they are often referred to using both terms. They were collections of tribes who all agreed to act together as a unit to gather strength. Each of the groups that joined the coalescent groups (or "confederacy" as is often used in reference to the Creeks) had a distinct history and character and did not necessarily see eye-to-eye with other groups in the confederacy.[314]

> The Creek Confederacy, though generally cooperative, was far from a unified "tribe" or "nation."

The coalescent groups joined according to past connections like heritage, language, location or economic interest. For example, many moved closer to the European trading locations like Pensacola, St. Augustine and Charles Town, to both trade and be less vulnerable to other Indian slave raiders.[315]

In the case of the Creeks, who came to occupy nearly all Middle and Southern Georgia (including Decatur), they were loosely bound together by a common basic language, Muskogean. The Muskogean language consists of two different dialects; Creek and Seminole.[316]

The name "Creeks" was not created by the Indians as a reference to themselves. Creeks themselves did not have a specific word to refer to the overall group. They later used this term invented by the English or collectively called themselves the Muskogeans. In the beginning, they referred to each other most often using the name of a specific band or the name of the town

---

312 Etheridge, Robbie; (2003) Creek Country, University of North Carolina Press
313 Etheridge, Robbie; (2003) Creek Country, University of North Carolina Press
314 Swanton, John R. (1922) Early History of the Creek Indians and Their Neighbors; Smithsonian Institution Bureau of American Ethnology; Bulletin 73; Washington Government Printing Office
315 Etheridge, Robbie; (2003) Creek Country, University of North Carolina Press
316 Etheridge, Robbie; (2003) Creek Country, University of North Carolina Press

where a group lived. The term was created by the English and most likely comes from a shortening of a phrase used to refer to "the Indians living along Ocheese Creek." "Ocheese" is the Muskogean word for the Ocmulgee River.[317] The English living nearby began referring to all Indians who spoke the same language as simply, the Creeks.

There are 12 original larger bodies of the Creek Confederacy whose origins could theoretically be traced: Kashita, Coweta, Coosa, Abihka, Wakoki, Eufaula, Hilibi, Atasi, Kolomi, Tukabahchee, Pakana and Okchai.[318] At the time the Europeans arrived, these 12 were splintered into 47 different, independent groups who lived in three major provinces. These provinces were the Abihka, who lived around the middle Coosa River in Northern Alabama; the Tallapoosa who came from the Tallapoosa River in what is now Central Alabama; and the Apalachicola, who came from the lower Chattahoochee River and its tributaries and creeks in Georgia.[319]

The two largest groups by far among the Creeks were the Cowetas and the Kashitas.[320] According to oral history, "The Kashita and Coweta both came from the west 'as one people' but, in time, those dwelling toward the west came to be called the Kashita and those to the east the Coweta."[321] The Creeks who lived in the Decatur area

The Creeks who lived in the Decatur area were part of the Coweta group of the Lower Creeks.

were part of the Coweta group of the Lower Creeks.[322] There is also some evidence of a connection between the Creeks in the Decatur area and the Hilibi group of Creeks. The Hilibis are believed to be the origin of the name for the village of Sandtown.[323]

The Cowetas were viewed by many of the Lower Creeks and certainly by the English and later the Americans, to be the primary leaders of the Lower Creek Indians and at times, the whole Creek Confederacy.[324] This point of whether the Cowetas were the leading group among all the Creeks and could speak on

[317] Swanton, John R. (1922) Early History of the Creek Indians and Their Neighbors; Smithsonian Institution Bureau of American Ethnology; Bulletin 73; Washington Government Printing Office
[318] Swanton, John R. (1922) Early History of the Creek Indians and Their Neighbors; Smithsonian Institution Bureau of American Ethnology; Bulletin 73; Washington Government Printing Office
[319] Price, Vivian (1997) History of DeKalb County, Georgia, 1822-1900; Wolfe Pub. Co.
[320] Swanton, John R. (1922) Early History of the Creek Indians and Their Neighbors; Smithsonian Institution Bureau of American Ethnology; Bulletin 73; Washington Government Printing Office
[321] Swanton, John R. (1922) Early History of the Creek Indians and Their Neighbors; Smithsonian Institution Bureau of American Ethnology; Bulletin 73; Washington Government Printing Office
[322] 1755 map in the appendices
[323] Price, Vivian (1997) History of DeKalb County, Georgia, 1822-1900; Wolfe Pub. Co.
[324] Swanton, John R. (1922) Early History of the Creek Indians and Their Neighbors; Smithsonian Institution Bureau of American Ethnology; Bulletin 73; Washington Government Printing Office

behalf of the entire confederacy later became a crucial area of disagreement among the Creeks and would eventually lead to tragedy.

The Cowetas were also probably the first Indians to ever make contact with Europeans. Ever since the time DeSoto passed through large portions of the Georgian Piedmont, many scholars believe that the "Chisi" (Also referred to as the "Ichsis" or "Achese"), who chroniclers of the de Soto journey reported meeting in 1540, were part of the Coweta group. The word "Ochisis" (Otci'si) in Muskogean, as spoken by the Hititchi people, means "Coweta."[325]

The location of the major towns of the Cowetas on older maps drifts among the upper regions of the Chattahoochee, Coosa, Flint and Ocmulgee Rivers during the late 1600s and early 1700s. This is partly because of the incomplete information and understanding of the inner workings of the confederacy in those days but also because many of the Cowetas shifted their location at different times to avoid a conflict with one of the other groups or more often, to occupy a better location for trade with the British, the French or the Spanish.[326]

> The Cowetas were also probably the first Indians to ever make contact with Europeans

Some groups tried to avoid joining the larger, coalescent groups as they were forming. Sadly, this strategy most often failed completely. For example, the Apalachees did their best to avoid other groups and confined themselves to North Florida, away from the Creeks and tried to re-establish their traditional customs prior to European contact.[327] In 1704, the English funded and armed the Creeks in a slave raid to North Florida, and the Apalachees were completely obliterated.[328]

The Cherokees continued shifting to the south away from Iroquois slave raids through the 1700s and started appearing more regularly in the Decatur area looking to settle on land that was occupied by the Creeks.[329] Eventually, the Cherokees took over Standing Peachtree from the Creeks, the old village at the confluence of Peachtree Creek and the Chattahoochee near Decatur. The Creeks continued to occupy Sandtown and Buzzard's Roost a few miles downriver.[330]

---

[325] Swanton, John R. (1922) Early History of the Creek Indians and Their Neighbors; Smithsonian Institution Bureau of American Ethnology; Bulletin 73; Washington Government Printing Office
[326] Swanton, John R. (1922) Early History of the Creek Indians and Their Neighbors; Smithsonian Institution Bureau of American Ethnology; Bulletin 73; Washington Government Printing Office
[327] Etheridge, Robbie; (2003) Creek Country, University of North Carolina Press
[328] Etheridge, Robbie; (2003) Creek Country, University of North Carolina Press
[329] Ethridge, Robbie (2002), English Trade in Deerskins and Indian Slaves, New Georgia Encyclopedia
[330] Swanton, John R. (1922) Early History of the Creek Indians and Their Neighbors; Smithsonian Institution Bureau of

Trade with the Indians was an extremely lucrative practice. Many of the early traders who secured agreements with a chief that could speak for a large group of Indians became extremely wealthy. As one tactic in securing these relationships, many of the traders took Indian wives and fathered lots of children who would grow up to have dual membership in both the Indian world and the European one.

This gave rise to a new class of elite members of Indian society who were half Indian and half European. These people of blended heritage gained a special status among the Indians for a few reasons. Probably the most important reason was that they were often sent for a formal education. There was also a prejudice in the European society that saw these lighter skinned Indians as more trustworthy or intelligent. After spending time in white society and using connections through their father, these offspring were also used as ambassadors to the Europeans from among the Indians, and many of them became famous historical figures.[331] Notable people of blended Creek heritage discussed in this book include Mary Musgrove, Alexander McGillivray, Menawa and William McIntosh. Interestingly, these people each had Scottish heritage from a father blended with the Creek heritage of their mother.

Political factors made the Southeast particularly lucrative for the Creeks in Middle Georgia during the colonial period. For a while, many of them began to prosper in this new system. During the 17th and 18th centuries, the land was claimed by multiple European nations. England claimed most of the East Coast. Spain controlled Florida. Each of them had loose, overlapping claims in the territory that is now Georgia. The French laid claim to Louisiana and areas farther to the west, with aspirations to spread farther east.[332] As a result, the Indians had multiple potential customers to whom they could sell their deerskins and slaves.

Under these conditions, the Creeks and the Europeans met on equal ground for a short period of time. Each tried to get an advantage over the other and believed they had the greater negotiating power in the relationship.[333] By 1704, the Carolina and Virginia traders had created a thriving network with all the Creeks along the Chattahoochee. Commerce flowed fast and heavy along the Hightower Trail and the Shallowford Trail running through Decatur.

In 1715, Indians Nearly Destroyed the South Carolina Colony
As Indian wealth accumulated among some, the pursuit of more power and status intensified. Resentment began to creep in among the Indians and

American Ethnology; Bulletin 73; Washington Government Printing Office
[331] Etheridge, Robbie; (2003) Creek Country, University of North Carolina Press
[332] Etheridge, Robbie; (2003) Creek Country, University of North Carolina Press
[333] Etheridge, Robbie; (2003) Creek Country, University of North Carolina Press/

between the Indians and the British.[334] Some Indians who commanded large groups became very powerful and fought for advantage over one another.

Most of the trade in the Southeast was controlled by the Creeks and the Yamasee Indians.[335] Hundreds of thousands of deerskins were shipped out of Charles Town, Savannah, Mobile, Pensacola and New Orleans during the 18th century.[336] The Yamasee Indians, trading on credit, began to accumulate significant debts with the British in South Carolina (Carolina was split into North and South in 1663). As those debts rose, the Yamasee could not pay the bill. The British were unwilling to extend further credit to the Yamasee until the debt was paid with the delivery of more deerskins or slaves. In 1715, the Yamasee decided to rid themselves of the British in their territory once and for all. Their cousins, the Creeks, joined them, and together they killed all the British traders and nearly all the settlers in the backcountry of the South Carolina colony. The conflict became known as the Yamasee War.[337]

> **The Creeks that had allied with the Yamasee returned to the Chattahoochee and became known as the "Lower Creeks."**

In the aftermath of the war, the main body of Creeks reestablished trade with the British, but the Yamasee aligned themselves with the Spanish out of St. Augustine and Pensacola.[338] A branch of the Yamasee who had been involved with the conflict chose to break apart from the others and settle in the bluffs near the Savannah River. These were the Yamacraw, led by Tomochichi, who would become close allies and advisors to the Georgia colonists and James Oglethorpe.[339]

After the Yamasee war, the final grouping of the five major Indian alliances in the Southeast was firmly established. These were the Cherokees, the Chickasaws, the Choctaws, the Catawbas and the Creeks. The Creeks that had allied with the Yamasee returned to the Chattahoochee and became known as the "Lower Creeks." The two provinces that had originated in Alabama became known as the "Upper Creeks."

The largest part of the Coweta group settled on the western bank of the Chattahoochee, north of the town called Chattahoochee. This town was said to have been settled earlier than 1715 by a branch of the Coweta to open trade

[334] Price, Vivian (1997) History of DeKalb County, Georgia, 1822-1900; Wolfe Pub. Co.
[335] Sweet, Julie Anne, (2006), Yamacraw Indians, New Georgia Encyclopedia
[336] Etheridge, Robbie; (2003) Creek Country, University of North Carolina Press pg. 9
[337] Sweet, Julie Anne, (2006), Yamacraw Indians, New Georgia Encyclopedia
[338] Sweet, Julie Anne, (2006), Yamacraw Indians, New Georgia Encyclopedia
[339] Sweet, Julie Anne, (2006), Yamacraw Indians, New Georgia Encyclopedia

with the Spaniards. Chattahoochee may have been made up of several settlements. It was located about 65 miles south of Decatur on the Chattahoochee in present day Heard County and remained an active Creek settlement until sometime around 1800.[340]

> Britain also decided to further settle and protect South Carolina by establishing a new southernmost colony.

The Yamasee War had shocked and terrified the British. South Carolina came very close to collapsing because of the conflict. It was two years before peace and relative stability could be established again in the young colony. [341]

The conflict failed to reestablish equal footing for the Indians in their relationship with the British, but it did cause the British to rethink their approach to slavery. They decided it might be easier and more profitable to use the Indian population as a source of deerskins, rather than slaves. Importing African slaves became more reliable than capturing more slaves in the New World while the demand for deerskins in England continued to grow.[342]

The British also decided to further settle and protect South Carolina by establishing a new southernmost colony to act as a buffer to the Spanish and further fortify the region deeper into Creek territory.[343]

---

[340] Swanton, John R. (1922) Early History of the Creek Indians and Their Neighbors; Smithsonian Institution Bureau of American Ethnology; Bulletin 73; Washington Government Printing Office
[341] Sweet, Julie Anne, (2006), Yamacraw Indians, New Georgia Encyclopedia
[342] Etheridge, Robbie; (2003) Creek Country, University of North Carolina Press
[343] Cobb, James C. and Inscoe, John C. (2009), Georgia History: Overview, New Georgia Encyclopedia

CHAPTER 9:
COLONIAL GEORGIA

Georgia Became the 13th British Colony in 1732

Once England announced it was going to fund a new colony that would act as a southern buffer between South Carolina and Florida as well as between the colonies and the Creeks, several proposals were brought to British Parliament. The first one that showed promise was made in 1717 by Sir Robert Montgomery. He called the land "the most delightful country in the universe."[344]

"It abounds with rivers, woods and meadows. Its gentle hills are full of mines, lead, copper, iron and even some of silver. 'Tis beautiful with odoriferous plants, green all the year. Pine, cedar, cypress, oak, elm, ash or walnut with innumerable other sorts, both fruit or timber trees, grow everywhere so pleasantly, that though they meet at the top and shade the traveler, they are, at the same time so distant in their bodies and so free from underwood or bushes, that the deer and other game, which feed in droves among these forests, may be often seen near half a mile between them."[345]

However, Montgomery couldn't raise the funds to launch his plan.[346] Another proposal for a new colony was devised by Jean Pierre Purry of Switzerland in 1724. This also failed, but he had planned to name the new colony either "Georgine" or "Georgia." The name stuck. Future proposals adopted it. Thus, at least in name, Georgia was born. [347]

Finally, the colony was established in 1732 at the urging of James Oglethorpe. Oglethorpe was a member of British Parliament who had worked to provide opportunity for British subjects imprisoned for having accumulated too much debt during a time when jobs were scarce in England. Among the primary reasons stated in the proclamation by King George II for the establishment of Georgia was to create a home for the "worthy poor of England." The original charter named James Oglethorpe and 20 other British gentlemen as the colony's Trustees. They oversaw Georgia for the next 20 years.

---

[344] Jackson, Edwin L. and Stakes, Mary E. (2004) The Georgia Studies Book: Our State and the Nation; University of Georgia, Carl Vinson Institute of Government, Chapter 5
[345] Sir Robert Montgomery (1717) Proposal to Create a Colony called the Margavate of Azilla
[346] Jackson, Edwin L. and Stakes, Mary E. (2004) The Georgia Studies Book: Our State and the Nation; University of Georgia, Carl Vinson Institute of Government, Chapter 5
[347] Jackson, Edwin L. and Stakes, Mary E. (2004) The Georgia Studies Book: Our State and the Nation; University of Georgia, Carl Vinson Institute of Government, Chapter 5

The colonists landed and began the colony on Yamacraw Bluff on February 12, 1733 and founded the city of Savannah.[348] The founding of the Georgia colony was very late by comparison to the other colonies. It was founded more than 50 years after the 12th colony, Pennsylvania, founded in 1681.[349]

The Wisdom of James Oglethorpe

James Oglethorpe was a very noble and wise man. Above all, his talent seems to have been in bringing together various groups of people and inspiring them to contribute the utmost of their talents. He was also very cognizant of the value of the unique backgrounds and talents of the many types of people who arrived in Georgia that he could use to build a strong, well-rounded community.

Probably his most impressive and important maneuver was the effort Oglethorpe put into immediately establishing friendly and profitable relationships with the nearby Indians. On May 21, 1733, he met with chiefs of the Lower Creeks and entered into an agreement to peacefully exchange goods. The British would have the right to settle on lands that the Creeks were not using, and the Creeks agreed they would not trouble the settlers. Oglethorpe also agreed to pay restitution for any trouble the new settlers would give the Indians as a way of discouraging any retaliation for future conflicts between the settlers and the Indians that he knew would be unavoidable. Both parties agreed to "keep the talk in their heads as long as the sun shines and the water runs."[350] Adding to his good reputation in the annals of history, James Oglethorpe also took pains to honor these agreements he had made with the Creeks.

Oglethorpe's closest ally among the Indians and the person who had brokered the meeting with the Lower Creeks was Tomochichi. He was a leader of the Yammacraw group that had split away from the Yamasee Indians after their war with the British in South Carolina. He became an important person in the history of Georgia and a great help to the British in establishing the colony. Tomochichi accompanied Oglethorpe when he returned to England in 1734 to brief the trustees on the status of the colony.[351] After Oglethorpe and Tomochichi met with Parliament, it was decided that the colony must begin to focus on its primary military purpose to protect the border from the Spanish.[352]

---

[348] Jackson, Edwin (2003), James Oglethorpe, New Georgia Encyclopedia

[349] Cobb, James C. and Inscoe, John C. (2009), Georgia History: Overview, New Georgia Encyclopedia

[350] Franklin M. Garrett (1969) Atlanta and Environs: A Chronicle of Its People and Events, Volume 1; University of Georgia Press, pg. 2

[351] Jackson, Edwin L. and Stakes, Mary E. (2004) The Georgia Studies Book: Our State and the Nation; University of Georgia, Carl Vinson Institute of Government, Chapter 6

[352] Jackson, Edwin L. and Stakes, Mary E. (2004) The Georgia Studies Book: Our State and the Nation; University of Georgia, Carl Vinson Institute of Government, Chapter 6

Parliament sent 150 Scottish Highlanders to Georgia to begin the construction of a military fort, Fort Frederica, in 1735. Oglethorpe also brought 257 more colonists back with him.[353] He also used these additional resources to establish Fort St. Simon's on the south end of the island.

Remnants of Fort Frederica[354]

These Highlanders had a reputation for being excellent fighters, extremely tough in withstanding harsh conditions and aggressively self-reliant people. Oglethorpe did another very smart thing to gain their cooperation. Knowing the strong feelings of independence among the Scots, he allowed them to found another town, Darien and another fort, Fort King George, a few miles from Frederica. This meant Oglethorpe now had a third fort to add to the chain he planned to establish along with Fort Frederica and Fort St. Simon's. It also gave him the trust and loyalty of the Scots.

In Frederica, Oglethorpe assembled people from Salzburg to establish farms and skilled laborers from the debtor's prisons to establish a utopian structure for the fort and accompanying town. Georgia represented a second chance for these people that they didn't plan to squander, and their loyalty and devotion to Oglethorpe was extremely strong.

---

[353] Jackson, Edwin L. and Stakes, Mary E. (2004) The Georgia Studies Book: Our State and the Nation; University of Georgia, Carl Vinson Institute of Government, Chapter 6
[354] Photo by the author

Another important figure in the success of Fort Frederica who deserves mention in this story is Mary Musgrove. Her father was a Scot trader named Edward Griffin and her mother was a high-born member of the Yamacraw tribe. Mary lived with the Yamacraw for the first 10 years of her life but left to receive an education in South Carolina. She married an English trader named John Musgrove and they started a trading post on the Savannah River. For many years, Mary acted as a guide, translator, ambassador and negotiator between Oglethorpe and the Creeks.[355]

The War of Jenkins' Ear and the Battle of Bloody Marsh

The Spanish objected to the construction of Fort Frederica and its connected nearby forts as a clear sign the British were going to seek to settle disputes over the border through military means rather than negotiation. Oglethorpe worked out a treaty with the Spanish governor of La Florida, Francisco Dal Moral Sanchez, but the relationship was still very tense. Rumors circulated that Spain was assembling an invasion force in Hispaniola with designs on taking Georgia. Oglethorpe returned to Britain and appealed to Parliament for greater funding and more troops.[356]

In response, Oglethorpe was given the rank of Colonel in the British Army and 600 more soldiers were sent back to the colony with him in October 1736. He was also put in command of all British forces in Georgia and South Carolina.[357]

After tensions had been rising for years, Britain declared war on Spain in 1739 and kicked off the War of Jenkins' Ear. The unusual name for this war has interesting origins. The primary driver of the conflict was the dispute over land between the British and the Spanish that centered on Georgia. However, it was also driven by the age of piracy and privateering. Both powers were

> Jenkins returned to England and presented his severed ear to Parliament.

frequently capturing ships laden with treasure on their way to and from Hispaniola, the New World or Europe. During one of these incidents, a Spanish privateering captain captured the ship of British captain Robert Jenkins.[358]

[355] Frank, Andrew (2002), Mary Musgrove (ca. 1700 – ca. 1763), New Georgia Encyclopedia
[356] Jackson, Edwin L. and Stakes, Mary E. (2004) The Georgia Studies Book: Our State and the Nation; University of Georgia, Carl Vinson Institute of Government, Chapter 6
[357] Jackson, Edwin L. and Stakes, Mary E. (2004) The Georgia Studies Book: Our State and the Nation; University of Georgia, Carl Vinson Institute of Government, Chapter 6
[358] Sweet, Julie Anne (2013) War of Jenkins' Ear, New Georgia Encyclopedia

Jenkins may have been smuggling goods out of the Spanish colonies in violation of the Treaty of Utrecht which was signed at the end of the War of Spanish Succession. It stipulated a quota on the amount of goods that the British could trade directly with the rich Spanish colonies. The terms of the treaty were frequently violated. As retribution for the offense, the Spanish captain cut off Jenkins' ear and presented it to him. Jenkins returned to England and presented his severed ear to Parliament pickled in a jar. The outrage over the story of the ear became a loud rallying cry heard all over England to launch a war with Spain.[359]

The Siege of St. Augustine

Back in Georgia, after war had been declared, Oglethorpe anticipated that the Spanish would soon attack. He set out to execute a preemptive strike on St. Augustine, the main Spanish stronghold. As they headed south to St. Augustine, the British troops came across two other Spanish forts to the north. The first was Fort Diego which, they caught unaware early in the day and captured.

The second was Fort Mose, an unusual fort in American history. It was a Spanish fort garrisoned by escaped slaves from the colonies. Upon arriving, Oglethorpe found Fort Mose abandoned. Knowing the British were approaching, the defenders had fallen back to the larger fort at St. Augustine. Oglethorpe left 300 soldiers at Fort Mose and proceeded on to St. Augustine. He then brought his small army farther south and deployed batteries on the island of Santa Anastasia near St. Augustine. While a British squadron blockaded the port, Oglethorpe bombarded the town for 27 days.[360]

On June 26, 1740, Spanish soldiers and some of the militia returned and launched a surprise attack on the British that Oglethorpe had left garrisoning Fort Mose. Sixty-eight of Oglethorpe's men were killed and another 34 were taken prisoner.[361]

A group of Spanish ships managed to get through the blockade in the port of St. Augustine. Oglethorpe lost any chance of starving the Spanish out. An attack was planned. The British squadron would attack the fleet, and Oglethorpe would attack with his army on land. However, threat of hurricanes caused British Commodore Pearce, commanding the squadron, to cancel his attack by sea. Oglethorpe was finally forced to abandon the siege on July 20, 1740. He returned to Savannah, leaving his artillery behind on Santa Anastasia. The Siege of St. Augustine was a failure.[362]

---

[359] Sweet, Julie Anne (2013) War of Jenkins' Ear, New Georgia Encyclopedia
[360] Jackson, Edwin L. and Stakes, Mary E. (2004) The Georgia Studies Book: Our State and the Nation; University of Georgia, Carl Vinson Institute of Government, Chapter 6
[361] Jackson, Edwin L. and Stakes, Mary E. (2004) The Georgia Studies Book: Our State and the Nation; University of Georgia, Carl Vinson Institute of Government, Chapter 6

The Battle of Bloody Marsh

A year after the failed siege of St. Augustine, rumors of a Spanish invading army assembling in Hispaniola were proven true. The Spanish set out with around 5,000 soldiers ready to deliver Georgia to Spain through force. Oglethorpe had only about 1,000 soldiers and militia to defend the island against the much greater number of Spanish soldiers. The Spanish landed on the southern tip of St. Simons Island and quickly took over Fort St. Simons to use as their base.[363]

On July 7, 1742, a small Spanish force marched up from the south to survey Fort Frederica and plan a Spanish attack. They were spotted by some of Oglethorpe's scouts, probably his Creek Indian allies, just a mile from the fort. Hearing that the Spanish were headed toward the main fort, Oglethorpe reacted with bitter anger. He very quickly assembled a group of Scottish Highlanders, Rangers and Creek Indians and flew out of the fort. The Spanish were completely taken by surprise as the Indians and Scots descended upon them with Oglethorpe in the lead on horseback and engaged them in a bitter battle at close range.[364] The Spanish line quickly broke and retreated leaving 12 Spanish soldiers dead or wounded.[365]

While the Highlanders and some British Rangers and Creek allies stayed behind to prepare for a new Spanish assault, Oglethorpe then rode back to the fort to gather reinforcements, leaving several of his men stationed among the brush and swamps. A few miles from the fort, his Scottish Highlanders lay in hiding along a narrow path through the marsh when the Spanish reappeared in the afternoon with a much larger force of several hundred Spanish soldiers. The Rangers, Scottish Highlanders and Creeks were well positioned in the heavy

> Oglethorpe mounted a horse and galloped out with reinforcements wading directly into the battle himself.

---

[362] Fort Matanzas National Monument Florida, Description of the 1740 Siege

[363] Sweet, Julie Anne (2003); The Battle of Bloody March, New Georgia Encyclopedia

[364] Sweet, Julie Anne (2003); The Battle of Bloody Marsh, New Georgia Encyclopedia

[365] Jackson, Edwin L. and Stakes, Mary E. (2004) The Georgia Studies Book: Our State and the Nation; University of Georgia, Carl Vinson Institute of Government, Chapter 6

Oglethorpe's Scottish Highlanders in the Battle of Bloody Marsh[366]

---

[366] Illustrations by Chulsan Um

brush around the swamp. The two forces met across a marshy area and exchanged fire for several hours with little result. Early in the battle, the British Rangers broke and began to retreat to the fort but most were retrieved and repositioned by one of the British Regular officers. Though they far outnumbered the British, the Spanish never advanced across the marsh, largely because the thick smoke of musket fire and the guerrilla tactics employed by the Highlanders and Indians prevented the Spanish from being able to assess the size of the British forces. The Spanish were forced to retreat once they ran out of ammunition. They then gave up the invasion and left the island defeated on July 13, 1741.[367]

The confrontation later became known as the Battle of Bloody Marsh. In the end, it had few casualties. It had far more important symbolic effects than direct ones. Oglethorpe had redeemed himself as an effective military

leader after his failure in St. Augustine. Back in England, he was hailed as a hero, and his troops in Georgia shared this enthusiasm. They were impressed with the direct role he had taken in the fighting. The Spanish, on the other hand, were demoralized and reluctant to recommit themselves to taking Georgia.[368]

In 1743, Oglethorpe went back to England covered in glory. Sadly, he never returned to the colony he had founded and defended, after this last departure.[369]

In 1752, rule of the colony shifted from a non-governmental Board of Trustees based in London to a royally appointed set of governors.[370] With this shift, Oglethorpe officially lost control of the colony he had founded.

Slavery Arrived Much Later in Georgia than Any of the Other Colonies

Ironically in comparison to its later position in the Civil War, Georgia was the last colony to allow slavery. For the first 18 years the colony existed, slavery was outlawed even though the other colonies had allowed the practice since 1607.

One of the noble principles upon which Oglethorpe established the colony was as a path

> The early Georgia colony also banned rum, Catholics and lawyers.

---

[367] Jackson, Edwin L. and Stakes, Mary E. (2004) The Georgia Studies Book: Our State and the Nation; University of Georgia, Carl Vinson Institute of Government, Chapter 6
[368] Sweet, Julie Anne (2003); The Battle of Bloody March, New Georgia Encyclopedia
[369] Jackson, Edwin L. and Stakes, Mary E. (2004) The Georgia Studies Book: Our State and the Nation; University of Georgia, Carl Vinson Institute of Government, Chapter 6
[370] Cobb, James C. and Inscoe, John C. (2009), Georgia History: Overview, New Georgia Encyclopedia

to redemption for the many poor citizens flooding the debtor's prisons in England. Many of the laws established in the early colony were also designed to prevent the creation of an elite class of land owners. Colonists were restricted in the quantity of land they could purchase in Georgia. The ability to acquire vastly more land than other members of the colony was limited. Therefore, slavery was inconsistent with these principles.

The early Georgia colony also banned rum, Catholics and lawyers. Jewish people did not have explicit permission to join the colony, but they were permitted to stay after arriving in 1733.[371] Rum was eventually legalized in 1742.

By 1733, the slave population of the rest of the colonies was around 90,000 people. As the colony grew and tried to compete commercially with the other colonies, especially South Carolina, the Georgia colonists put more and more pressure on Oglethorpe and the other trustees to repeal the slavery ban. Many of the colonists argued that slavery was necessary to compete with the labor forces of the Carolina and Virginia colonies.

By 1750, after Oglethorpe's influence over the colony had begun to decline, the slavery ban was lifted. Slavery in Georgia then grew rapidly.

By 1773, there were already 15,000 slaves in the colony and 18,000 free colonists.[372] By the time of the revolution, about half of Georgia's population were black slaves.[373]

[371] Cobb, James C. and Inscoe, John C. (2009), Georgia History: Overview, New Georgia Encyclopedia
[372] Jackson, Edwin L. and Stakes, Mary E. (2004) The Georgia Studies Book: Our State and the Nation; University of Georgia, Carl Vinson Institute of Government, Chapter 6
[373] Jockley, Timothy (2004), Slavery in Revolutionary Georgia, New Georgia Encyclopedia

CHAPTER 10:
REVOLUTIONARY GEORGIA

The Backcountry and the Important Role of Traders in the Revolution

In the decades prior to the Revolutionary War, both the French and the Spanish concentrated their efforts in America farther to the north while fighting the French and Indian War that began in 1756. As a result of the treaty ending that war in 1763, Georgia's western border was reduced from the Pacific Ocean to the Mississippi River. More importantly, the Spanish, who had supported France in the war, had to give up La Florida. France had to relinquish its claim to all land east of the Mississippi except for New Orleans.

Both countries would later gain back some of their claims after they supported the Americans in the Revolutionary War. Spain would regain Florida from 1783 to 1821 but the Georgia border remained in dispute. After years of border disputes with America, the Spanish finally ceded the land when they could no longer protect and fortify it. France regained Louisiana from the Spanish in a secret treaty in 1800 and then finally sold it to the United States in 1803 under the Louisiana Purchase.[374]

During the Revolutionary War, the action in Georgia mainly shifted toward the coast near Savannah where the new state government and legislature was being formed. Decatur was part of what commonly was referred to as the "backcountry". There were dramas unfolding in the backcountry as the British and Americans each tried to gain an upper hand by securing the support of the Creeks and the Cherokees. The attention of most of the central players of the revolution was focused farther east than Decatur. Nevertheless, the arguments, decisions and fights occurring there were the rising action in how Decatur would become established and who the eventual settlers in Decatur would be.

While soldiers and politicians were fighting the war with the British mainly in Savannah and along the coast, the securing of the deeper backcountry of Georgia largely became the responsibility of fur traders. They had the closest relationships with the Indians which often extended into kinship. Most of the traders travelling in the backcountry had been British loyalists, in no small part because their trading businesses relied on Britain as a primary customer.

---

[374] Franklin M. Garrett; (1969) Atlanta and Environs: A Chronicle of Its People and Events, Volume 1; University of Georgia Press

Their task as trader-diplomat was to persuade the Indians to support their side of the conflict. By tradition, the Creeks were loyal to the British with whom they had healthy trading relationships. The Cowetas of the Lower Creeks, the group that occupied the Decatur area, was persuaded not to take part in the war, largely due to the efforts of the trader George Galphin.[375] The Upper Creeks supported and cooperated with the British in several engagements, especially in Florida, but they still did not fully, openly deploy their numbers as British allies.

Among the Americans and the British, the Georgia woods were often used as a hiding place for whichever party was currently out of control. When Augusta was taken by the Whigs, many of the Tories would take to the forest and the reverse would happen when a region changed hands again. Brigands and raiders patrolled the trails for any parties that could be caught and robbed to supply one side or the other.[376]

The Decatur area played an important role in establishing this support in the backcountry, as is made clear through a handful of letters and stories from this period. It is one of many areas of study in local history that deserves more attention. Standing Peachtree and other areas around Decatur were active with intrigue and maneuvering between different bands of Indians and soldiers. This becomes evident from two documents from the later Revolutionary war period that mention Standing Peachtree as well as several names that figure prominently in the history of this area: William McIntosh, Elijah Clarke and Gen. Andrew Pickens.

In August of 1782, a note was written making payment to a Mr. John Brandon for his "secret service" in travelling to Standing Peachtree to meet with the Indians there. This was probably a trip to secure their support or neutrality in the war or to begin preparing a relationship with the Indians in the new United States.[377]

The second document is letter written from John Marten on May 27, 1782 asking Gen. Andrew Pickens for support in August (sic; probably referring to Augusta) while William McIntosh and a band of his Cowetas were on the move. This letter is also the earliest known mention referring to the place as Standing Peachtree.

[375] Morris, Michael P. (2015) George Galphin and the Transformation of the Georgia-South Carolina Backcountry, Lexington Books
[376] Georgia in the American Revolution, An Exhibition from the Library and Museum Collections of the Society of the Cincinnati; Anderson House, Washington DC, (October 2003 – May 2004)
[377] Franklin M. Garrett; (1969) Atlanta and Environs: A Chronicle of Its People and Events, Volume 1; University of Georgia Press

1782 Letter Regarding Standing Peachtree

May 27, 1782

Dear Genl:

I have just had the pleasure of seeing our good firm and fast friend the Tallasee King, who has come down with a Talk to me and has brought about forty of his head Men and Warriors with him.

He informs me, that Mr. McIntosh with a strong party of the Cowetas, etc. were to rendezvous at the Standing Peach Tree the 26th of this month and they were afterwards to meet at the Big Shoal where they were to meet a number of Cherokees after which they were to fall on the Okonnys on our Frontiers, therefore we have every reason to expect that they will be in upon our back Settlements in about 8 or 10 days at the farthest. I doubt not my der Genl., you will take proper measures and endeavor to give us every and the most early assistance in your power – for God's sake exert yourself and come in to our timely aid, as delays are dangerous. I have wrote to Col. Clarke on this matter who I dare say will be happy to see you – In the meantime I am

Dr. Genl. Your Most Obt. Sert.
JNO Martin

Copy
The Honble. Genl. Pickins
So. Carolina[378]

---

[378] Franklin M. Garrett; (1969) Atlanta and Environs: A Chronicle of Its People and Events, Volume 1; University of Georgia Press

A grassy area in the Johnson field near the Lyon family home near Decatur was also called "Fortification Hill" because there was said to have been an Indian battle there during the Revolutionary War. The purpose and significance of this battle has unfortunately been lost to history.[379]

Nancy Hart and the Six Tories

There are many more stories of conflict in the backcountry farther from Decatur around Augusta. In one of these, a band of six Tories (British loyalists) stopped at the home of Nancy Hart who lived around 45 miles East of where Athens now lies. Hart was a fiery and ruthless patriot who confronted any British sympathizers she could find. Her husband was a lieutenant serving under Elijah Clarke. Nancy was left alone to defend her home and her children at most times during the war. When the group of Tories stopped at her home, they got far more than they had bargained for.

The men were in search of one of the Whig leaders who had just been by her cabin. When asked if she had seen the man, she denied it. The Tories didn't believe her and shot her turkey. The men then went into her cabin and started demanding she cook the turkey and bring them drinks. She started opening wine for them and told her daughter to go get some water from a nearby spring. In secret, she also told her daughter to blow on a conch shell that was kept

In 1912, they unearthed a grave where six skeletons had been neatly laid to rest under about three feet of earth that were estimated to be at least 100 years old.

on a stump near the spring as a secret signal to the neighborhood that there were Tories in the area and she needed help. As the men in her cabin continued drinking, she began to move their guns outside from where they had been stacked by the door. One of the men noticed and jumped to his feet, but Nancy coolly pointed the rifle at the man's chest and told him not to move. He moved toward her and she shot him dead. Nancy picked up another rifle as another of the men started to step forward and she shot him as well. The other four were held at gunpoint until help arrived. The remaining four men were then hanged from a tree near the cabin.[380]

There are several other stories about Nancy Hart from the Revolutionary days in Georgia, but it's hard to know which of them or how much is true. The reason I wanted to tell this one is that later evidence was found making it seem

---

[379] Price, Vivian (1997) History of DeKalb County, Georgia, 1822-1900; Wolfe Pub. Co.
[380] Ouzts, Clay (2005) Nancy Hart, The New Georgia Encyclopedia

completely true. In 1912, workmen were grading for a railroad that would pass near the old Hart cabin. During their work, they unearthed a grave where six skeletons had been neatly laid to rest under about three feet of earth that were estimated to be at least 100 years old.[381]

Georgia's Awkward Start in the Revolution

Prior to these clandestine meetings in Standing Peachtree that we know of, Georgia had an awkward start in the revolution. As revolution began to take shape farther north, there was enormous disagreement in Georgia about whether to commit support to it. Georgia was still a very young colony. In 1774, when the First Continental Congress began, Georgia was still just 42 years old and far more dependent on Britain than the more northern colonies.

In addition, Georgia was in a very dangerous location. If a war were to begin, Georgia would be exposed most directly to the Creeks from the south and the west. Georgia would also be the only colony directly exposed to an area that remained under British control.

At the time of the revolution, there were 15 colonies not 13. Britain had gained Florida from the Spanish in 1763 after they supported the French in the French and Indian War. They then divided it into two colonies, East Florida and West Florida. St. Augustine was the capital of East Florida and Pensacola was the capital of West Florida.[382]

> At the time of the revolution, there were actually 15 colonies not 13.

Each had a Royal Governor, and that was the extent of its formal government. There was no governmental infrastructure established there yet to debate, choose parish representatives and decide to join a coalition of other colonies. Both colonies remained British. However, there was a military presence in Florida.

The trend of sentiment among the Georgians was slowly moving toward separation. A charismatic Scotsman named Lachlan McIntosh of Darien emerged as a powerful leader encouraging separation. With revolutionary sentiment still low, Georgia still sent no delegates to the First Continental Congress in Philadelphia in 1774.[383]

There were three types of congresses that were important in moving the country and the state. There were Continental Congresses involving

---

[381] Ouzts, Clay (2005) Nancy Hart, The New Georgia Encyclopedia
[382] Florida of the British; British Colonialism in Florida 1763-1783, The Florida History Internet Center
[383] Golden, Randy (2017) Georgia Joins the Continental Congress, Our Georgia History

representatives from each of the colonies. Most of these were in Philadelphia. Then, in Georgia, Provincial Congresses were held involving representatives from the Georgia parishes. There were also eventually Constitutional Congresses in which the new US constitution was discussed and drafted.

In Georgia's absence from the First Continental Congress, the colony of South Carolina agreed to hold Georgia responsible for resolutions decided at the congress. Georgia had something akin to a big brother / little brother relationship with the much older and more established colony of South Carolina. Leaders from the older colonies seemed to take South Carolina more seriously and turn to this colony to represent the South overall. The colonial leaders of Georgia were considered by many to be rough and less sophisticated by comparison.

> Georgia sent no delegates to the First Continental Congress in Philadelphia in 1774.

The most important of these decisions was a resolution that the colonies would join in a coalition to ban all future trade with Britain.[384] A provincial congress was called in Savannah in January of that year to decide whether Georgia would join the ban on British trade and to nominate delegates for the upcoming Second Continental Congress.

Each of the colonies was divided into parishes that acted as the representative authority for the people living there. The same system was used in England. Even though people in these parishes might be very close to each other geographically, they were often very divided politically. Although people from similar backgrounds in general would naturally locate themselves together and have similar views, it was surprising how drastically wide these differences were. St. John's Parish was in the Southern Georgia, close to the Florida border. It was so opposed to the viewpoints of other parishes in Georgia and so frustrated with Georgia's reluctance to join the coalition of other colonies that the parish and its leader Lyman Hall, tried to break away from Georgia and become part of the colony of South Carolina. By the beginning of 1775, about a third of Georgians were Whigs (supporting the Revolution); another third were Tories (loyal to Royal Britain) and the rest remained undeclared.

The First Provincial Congress in Georgia still reflected the wide disparity of opinions of Georgia's parishes. Only five of the 12 parishes of the Georgia

---

[384] Jackson, Edwin L. and Stakes, Mary E. (2004) The Georgia Studies Book: Our State and the Nation; University of Georgia, Carl Vinson Institute of Government, Chapter 8

colony sent a representative. Those in attendance resolved to support the ban on British trade in gesture but not in spirit. They added several exceptions to the articles passed by the First Continental Congress to the point the ban would be all but ineffectual in Georgia. They also elected three representatives to attend the Second Continental Congress, Noble Jones, Archibald Bulloch and John Houstoun.[385]

The primary exception Georgia made in the ban on British trade was that it wanted to preserve its right to trade for British goods that could be traded with the local Indians. British relationships with the Creeks continued to be strong and Georgia feared cutting off trade would further strengthen this advantage and leave the colony more vulnerable.[386]

> As the Second Continental Congress got under way on May 10, 1775, in Philadelphia, Georgia still had not sent delegates.

As word reached Georgia that the first shots of the war had been fired in the Battle of Lexington and Concord in April 1775, revolutionary fervor began to take flame in the backcountry in many Georgia parishes, especially in Darien where many Scotsman who opposed the crown resided. [387] Powder and weapons from several town magazines were raided and their contents stockpiled in preparation for the war.

However, as the Second Continental Congress got under way on May 10, 1775 in Philadelphia, Georgia continued to be reluctant to fully commit to the war and still had not sent delegates. Responding to Georgia's lackluster support and its half-acceptance of the ban on British trade, the other colonies agreed to cut off trade with Georgia.

Royal Governor of Georgia, James Wright, responded to the increasing tensions by sending a letter to request greater military support from England in June 1775. His letter was intercepted, and a forged one was sent in its place saying everything in the colony was fine.[388]

Finally, a Second Provincial Congress met in Savannah on July 4, 1775. Unlike the previous Provincial Congress, this one was well attended with 102 delegates representing all but two of the Georgia parishes. St. Patrick and St. James

---

[385] Jackson, Edwin L. and Stakes, Mary E. (2004) The Georgia Studies Book: Our State and the Nation; University of Georgia, Carl Vinson Institute of Government, Chapter 8
[386] Golden, Randy (2017) Georgia Joins the Continental Congress, Our Georgia History
[387] Cobb, James C., University of Georgia, Inscoe, John C., University of Georgia, (2009); New Georgia Encyclopedia; Button Gwinnett
[388] Golden, Randy (2017) Georgia Joins the Continental Congress, Our Georgia History

Mark Pifer

parishes did not attend. On the second day, they accepted the provisions of the Continental Association and agreed to enforce the ban on British trade as it had been written in the First Continental Congress. Archibald Bulloch (the great grandfather of President Theodore Roosevelt) emerged as a clear choice among the other representatives to lead Georgia in becoming part of the new country. They elected him their President of the Council of Safety, the temporary government put in place prior to the establishment of Georgia's new state government and constitution and one of the delegates to the Second Continental Congress.[389]

Apart from Bulloch, the representatives also elected John Zubly, John Houstoun, Noble W. Jones and Lyman Hall to represent the colony. At the time he was elected as a representative, Lyman Hall was already at the Second Continental Congress and not in Georgia. He and his parish, St. John's, had already decided to go and show their support for the revolution regardless of what the other parishes decided. The other representatives arrived on July 20, 1775, a little over two months after the first meeting of the Congress had already convened.

Bulloch immediately impressed the other members of the Continental Congress when he arrived wearing homespun (normally he would have been wearing clothing imported from England) to show his support for a ban on British trade. They elected him to the Secret Committee, the group that would be responsible for making arms deals to supply the war effort.[390]

The most outspoken of the Georgia representatives at the Second Continental Congress was John Zubly. He quickly made himself unpopular by continuing to adamantly oppose any thought of the colonies breaking away from England.[391]

As word went out in Georgia that the colony had agreed to ban trade with Britain, enforcement of the ban was placed in the hands of local committees. There were still many Georgians who didn't support the ban at all and openly refused to abide by it. This resulted in Georgia's first violence as part of the war. When Thomas Brown, a British loyalist, openly defied the ban and called on others to resist, he was beaten, maimed and dragged through the streets of Augusta on August 2, 1775.[392]

The Battle of the Rice Boats

British warships made their first appearance in Georgia in January 1776. Col. Lachlan McIntosh was put in charge of the defenses of the city. Thinking the

[389] Schmidt, Jim (2002) Archibald Bulloch, New Georgia Encyclopedia
[390] Schmidt, Jim (2002) Archibald Bulloch, New Georgia Encyclopedia
[391] Schmidt, Jim (2002) Archibald Bulloch, New Georgia Encyclopedia
[392] Jackson, Edwin L. and Stakes, Mary E. (2004) The Georgia Studies Book: Our State and the Nation; University of Georgia, Carl Vinson Institute of Government, Chapter 8

warships were there to retrieve Royal Governor James Wright and bring him back to England, the Council of Safety put the governor under arrest and held him in a cell.

The ships were not there to retrieve the governor though, nor were they there to attack the city. They had come to capture ships full of grain in the harbor to bolster dwindling food supplies for their armies in the North. They succeeded in capturing several ships in what became known as the Battle of the Rice Boats. Governor Wright still somehow escaped and made his way to one of the warships and sailed away with them.[393]

As locations for gatherings in the Second Continental Congress changed, new representatives were elected to represent Georgia at the Second Continental Congress in Philadelphia. In addition to Lyman Hall, Button Gwinnett, George Walton, Archibald Bulloch and John Houstoun each accepted their nominations. Archibald Bulloch, as leader of the Council of Safety in Savannah, felt his presence was needed at home and John Houstoun needed to attend to family business. Therefore, neither of them was present to sign the Declaration of Independence on July 4, 1776.[394]

Both of these men played critical roles in Georgia's history and it is unfortunate that they did not receive the honor of signing the Declaration of Independence. In particular, Bulloch was a truly noble and admirable person whose important role in the history of Georgia and the United States was cut far too short (as you will read further on).[395]

The First Georgia Invasion of British Florida
One of the first tasks on the agenda for the Continental Congress and for Georgia was to disrupt the British in East Florida. Coastal Georgia settlers were frequently losing cattle and crops to the Florida Rangers raiding across the border. Many of these Florida Rangers were former Georgians who were loyal to British rule and had migrated south when the colony swung toward separation. St. Augustine was the primary base of operations for the British traders who held strong relationships with the Indians at the interior.[396]

The first offensive engagement was to be led by the popular Lachlan McIntosh. At that time, McIntosh was a Captain in the Georgia Militia. In the Summer of 1776, he raided several English plantations along the St. Mary's River and evicted the occupants. These raids were executed honorably and showed tangible results. Even so, the Continental Congress wanted larger

[393] Cashin, Edward (2005) Revolutionary War in Georgia, New Georgia Encyclopedia
[394] Cobb, James C., Inscoe, John C., (2009); New Georgia Encyclopedia; Georgia History: Overview
[395] Cashin, Edward (2005) Revolutionary War in Georgia, New Georgia Encyclopedia
[396] Golden, Randy (2017) Georgia Joins the Continental Congress, Our Georgia History

invasions of Florida led by the Continental Army instead of the Georgia Militia and tasked Maj. Gen. Charles Lee with the job.

As the First Invasion of Florida got under way later in 1776, the combined Continental Army and Georgia Militia first ran into transportation issues when there were not enough boats to carry the troops south as had been planned.

They were forced to split the troops. Some would go by sea and others by land. As the armies drew closer to Florida, the weather grew very hot. Disease broke out. Supplies ran low. Word then reached them that the Cherokees were attacking in the backcountry and the Creeks were on the move to support the British held garrison at St. Augustine. Members of the invasion force began to desert. Finally, there were betrayals within the troops by secret Tories who found ways to pass information about the Americans and their plans to the British in Florida. Though some of the troops did eventually reach Florida, none of them ever met with the British and all of them were back in their home bases by December. The First Invasion of Florida had ended with a quiet fizzle.[397]

The Demise of Archibald Bulloch and the Feud Between Lachlan McIntosh and Button Gwinnett

In 1777, the rivalry that had been simmering between two of Georgia's prominent revolutionary leaders, Lachlan McIntosh and Button Gwinnett, came to a boil. Lachlan McIntosh was the most influential leader of the conservatives, also called the City Party or the Merchant Party. Button Gwinnett led the Radical Party, also called the County Party. Caught between the two of them, moderating their bitter arguments, was Archibald Bulloch, the leader of the Council of Safety, the temporary executive branch before a true state government was established. As long as Archibald Bulloch was there to hold their rivalry in check, the two men and their followers continued to function with some effectiveness. As fate would have it though, Bulloch's ascension in leadership was short lived.[398]

In addition to disrupting the British in Florida, one of the first points of order for the fledgling state was to create a congress for the establishment of state laws and a state constitution to provide the process and guidelines by which this would occur. On February 5, 1777, at the urging of Archibald Bulloch, a state constitution was put in place of the "Rules and Regulations" that had governed the state during the previous nine months. They now needed to elect an executive leader (a governor of sorts). Bulloch was the clear choice to be this first executive leader of the state of Georgia and almost certainly its eventual first governor.[399]

[397] Golden, Randy (2017) Georgia Joins the Continental Congress, Our Georgia History
[398] Schmidt, Jim (2002) Archibald Bulloch, New Georgia Encyclopedia

However, the renewed action with British Florida and the renewed attacks made by Indians in the backcountry had rattled the confidence of the members of the Council of Safety. Instead of holding elections, they decided to give Bulloch full executive control of the state including all military action. The state wanted to be ready to respond to any future incidents at a moment's notice without having to call together the Council of Safety. Essentially, Bulloch would have full dictatorial powers over the state and it was obvious that he would soon be elected into office as Georgia's first executive leader. [400]

Just an hour after he was given full executive control on February 22, 1777, Archibald Bulloch turned up dead. He was just 47 when he died and had seemed in very good health. Many suspected he had been poisoned, but no clear evidence was ever brought forth.[401]

> **Just an hour after he was given full executive control of the state of Georgia, the popular Archibald Bulloch turned up dead.**

After Bulloch's death, Button Gwinnett was selected as Bulloch's replacement in the role of executive leader. At almost the same time, Lachlan McIntosh became a Brig. Gen. in the Continental Army and was given command of the southern forces as Charles Lee's replacement, the Maj. Gen. who had led the disastrously failed First Invasion of British Florida.

There was a natural tension between the Continental government and the Georgia government. Each struggled for control of the action in Georgia. In particular, there was disagreement over the proper execution of military operations and whether they should be led by the Continental Army or the Georgia Militia. Thus, McIntosh and Gwinnett, two very stubborn, strong willed rivals who already opposed one another, were now put in natural positions of conflict and had lost the strongest voice of reason between them. This would not end well.[402]

Gwinnett was the next to raise the stakes in the intensifying game he was playing out with his rival McIntosh. Based on very flimsy evidence, Gwinnett charged Lachlan's brother George McIntosh, another member of the Council of Safety, with treason. A letter from the Governor of East Florida had been intercepted in which, he speculated George might be somewhat supportive of the Tories. Gwinnett had George arrested and jailed. The rest of the Council of

[399] Schmidt, Jim (2002) Archibald Bulloch, New Georgia Encyclopedia
[400] Schmidt, Jim (2002) Archibald Bulloch, New Georgia Encyclopedia
[401] Golden, Randy (2017) Georgia Joins the Continental Congress, Our Georgia History
[402] Golden, Randy (2017) Georgia Joins the Continental Congress, Our Georgia History

Safety later agreed to release George during a session when Gwinnett was not present.[403]

The Second Invasion of Florida and the Duel Between Lachlan McIntosh and Button Gwinnett

As Button Gwinnett assumed power, he immediately began to make plans for a new invasion of East Florida to rout the British out of Georgia once and for all. As before, the invasion ran into difficulty before it began. First, Gen. Robert Howe the Commander of the Southern Department of the Continental Army and Brig. Gen. McIntosh's commanding officer, came to Savannah to meet with Gwinnett and discuss military plans. The two men failed to come to any kind of agreement or form any kind of working relationship. Gwinnett had his own ideas for how he wanted to operate military operations in Georgia and had no interest in Gen. Howe's thoughts on the subject. In response, Howe left Savannah in a huff and pledged no support from the Continental Army in Gwinnett's plans.[404]

After Gen. Howe had refused to provide support from the Continental Army, Gwinnett launched a recruiting campaign for the Georgia Militia. This proved to be another of Gwinnett's setbacks. Very few Georgians volunteered to join the militia. Despite their differences, Gwinnett swallowed his pride and went to Lachlan McIntosh to ask his assistance for the Second Florida Expedition. Though he despised Gwinnett, McIntosh's loyalty was to Georgia. Rather than let the expedition fail, he agreed to bring the Southern Continental Forces to support it.[405]

McIntosh was named leader of the expedition, but this in no way stopped Gwinnett from trying to assume command and make battle plans. The two men fought frequently and publicly to the point they were both eventually relieved of leading the expedition and ordered to return to Savannah. Command of the forces was given to Col. Samuel Elbert of the Continental Army.

Gwinnett had to return home to political defeat as well as his military failure. Just after the expedition headed south, an election was held on May 8, 1777 for Georgia's first governor after the delay in February that had just preceded the death of Archibald Bulloch. Though he had served as the state's executive leader up until then, Gwinnett was not elected. Georgia's first governor was John Adam Treutlen.

[403] Golden, Randy (2017) Georgia Joins the Continental Congress, Our Georgia History
[404] Golden, Randy (2017) Georgia Joins the Continental Congress, Our Georgia History
[405] Golden, Randy (2017) Georgia Joins the Continental Congress, Our Georgia History

Upon returning to Savannah, the animosity and fights between McIntosh and Gwinnett continued to escalate. They openly blamed each other for the problems of the Second Florida Expedition. On May 1, 1777, Brig. Gen. McIntosh stood in the General Assembly and called Button Gwinnett a "scoundrel" and a liar." An insult like this, said in public, was not something that could be overlooked without a public demand for satisfaction according to the rules of gentlemanly conduct. McIntosh knew this and was goading Gwinnett into a confrontation.

Gwinnett challenged McIntosh to a duel on May 16, 1777 outside Savannah. The odds of the duel were heavily in McIntosh's favor. Gwinnett was facing an experienced war veteran in a duel with firearms. A detailed account of the duel given by George Wells reveals some of the interesting procedures by which these events were conducted.[406]

> Lachlan McIntosh stood in the General Assembly and called Button Gwinnett a "scoundrel and a liar". An insult like this, said in public, was not something that could be overlooked.

"That late on the Evening of Thursday, the 15th of May instant [1777], a written challenge was brought to Genl. McIntosh signed Button Gwinnett, wherein the said Mr. Gwinnett charg'd the General with calling him a Scoundrel in public Conversation, and desir'd he would give satisfaction for it as a Gentleman before Sunrise next morning in Sir James Wright's pasture, behind Colo. Martin's house; to which the General humorously sent in answer to Mr. Gwinnett, that the hour was rather earlier than his usual but would assuredly meet him at the place and time appointed with a pair of pistols only, as agreed upon with Mr. Gwinnett's second, who brought the challenge.

Early the next morning, Mr. Gwinnett and his second found the General and his Second waiting on the Ground and after politely saluting each other the General drew his pistols to show he was loaded only with single Balls, but avoided entering into any other conversation but the business on hand. It was then propos'd and agreed to, that they shou'd go a little lower down the hill, as a number of spectators appear'd and when the Ground was chose the seconds ask'd the distance. Mr. Gwinnett reply'd 'whatever distance the General pleases.' the General said he believ'd Eight or 10 feet would be sufficient, and they were immediately measur'd to which the General's second desir'd another step might be added. It was then proposed to turn back to back. The General

[406] Lynch, Wayne (2014), Button Gwinnett and Lachlan McIntosh Duel, Journal of the American Revolution

answer'd 'By no means let us see what we are about' – & immediately each took his stand, and agreed to fire as they cou'd. Both pistols went off nearly at the same time, when Mr. Gwinnett fell being shot above the knee, and said his thigh was broke. The General, who was also shot thro' the thick of the Thigh, stood still in his place & not thinking his antagonist was worse wounded than himself – as he immediately afterward declar'd – ask'd if he had enough or was for another shot, to which all objected, and the seconds declar'd they both behav'd like Gentlemen and men of honor, led the General up to Mr. Gwinnett and they both shook hands."[407]

McIntosh survived the incident with little trouble. Gwinnett died three days later, perhaps due to an infection or damage to a major artery in the leg.[408] After their duel, friends of Gwinnett accused McIntosh of murder. A petition was put forth to charge McIntosh with the murder of Button Gwinnett. The

> **"Both pistols went off nearly at the same time, when Mr. Gwinnett fell being shot above the knee, and said his thigh was broke."**
>
> **~ George Wells (1777)**

General was ordered to appear before Gen. George Washington for a vote in the General Assembly but no formal action was ever taken against him.[409]

Meanwhile, the invasion of Florida now led by Col. Elbert after McIntosh and Gwinnett had been sent back to Savannah was going no better than the first attempted invasion. Elbert split his forces in two, taking half with him into seven ships while the rest proceeded to Florida on horseback under Col. John Baker.

Baker's group was the first to see the enemy face to face. The British were leading a combined force of 400 Florida Rangers and Creeks. In May 1777, the British sent a small band of Indians into the Georgia camp who successfully ran off their horses. The horses were later recovered by Baker's men, but the boldness of the Creeks convinced the Georgians that they were probably dealing with a significant British force. They decided to retreat. Anticipating this, the British were waiting in ambush along the road back north and surprised the Georgians. Thanks to some impressive horsemanship, most of the Georgians managed to escape the scene, but 40 were captured. Twenty-

[407] George Wells Affidavit, June 1777, Edward G. Williams, An Orderly Book of McIntosh's Expedition of 1778, (Western Pennsylvania History Magazine, March 1960), 3-4.
[408] Lynch, Wayne (2014), Button Gwinnett and Lachlan McIntosh Duel, Journal of the American Revolution
[409] Cashin, Edward (2005) Revolutionary War in Georgia, New Georgia Encyclopedia

four of these prisoners were then killed, reportedly by the Creeks, according to British officers who were there.

Elbert's part of the expedition fared no better. They had been stricken by illness while aboard ship and the small fleet proceeded very slowly. After the two halves of the Georgian force rejoined on Amelia Island in late May 1777, they withdrew back to Savannah. The second expedition into Florida had been another complete failure.

The Third Invasion of Florida

After the failure of the second Florida invasion, the Florida rangers out of St. Augustine resumed their harassment of the South with increasing temerity. Reports said they had come within five miles of Savannah and even entered the city of Augusta.[410]

On March 12, 1778, the Florida Rangers scored a significant victory in Georgia by capturing Fort Howe (built in the 1730s near Darien and later renamed from Fort Barrington) and thereby establishing a firm link to the British loyalists in South Carolina.[411]

Brig. Gen. McIntosh was away at the time responding to accusations of murdering Button Gwinnett. As a result, he was not part of the planning or the execution of the third attempt to invade Florida.[412]

> General Howe reviewed the battle plans and suggested that it might not be best to use the Georgia Militia in the invasion since many of them would be needed back on their farms.

As planning began for this third attempt, the leaders of the expedition still couldn't get out of their own way. Gen. George Howe, the commander of the Southern Department of the Continentals, was called by the Georgia Legislature to speak with them about the plans. Howe reviewed the plans and suggested that it might not be best to use the Georgia Militia in the invasion since many of them would be needed back on their farms. This suggestion indicated the Georgians were more farmers than fighting men. The Georgia Legislature considered this a great insult. They requested that Gen. Howe be censured for insubordination.

---

[410] Cashin, Edward (2005) Revolutionary War in Georgia, New Georgia Encyclopedia
[411] Cashin, Edward (2005) Revolutionary War in Georgia, New Georgia Encyclopedia
[412] Cashin, Edward (2005) Revolutionary War in Georgia, New Georgia Encyclopedia

Apparently, Georgia and the planners of Georgia's early revolutionary expeditions were incapable of learning from past mistakes. Even though conflicts of leadership led to many of the problems experienced by each previous invasion, the third expedition to Florida was given four different leaders with no clear structure or reporting relationships between them. Gen. Howe was in charge of the Continentals. Commodore Oliver Bowen was in charge of a small fleet of ships that worked their way down the coast. The new Governor John Houstoun, just elected in January, was in charge of the Georgia Militia. Col. Pinkney was in charge of the South Carolina Militia.[413]

On the other side of the conflict, the British were also bickering over who would control the Rangers and their other forces including the Creeks in Florida.[414]

The British were once again aware of the Americans' plans to invade. During their march south, the Georgia land forces accidentally came upon a force of Florida Rangers and Creeks and overtook them with little incident. After questioning a prisoner, they found out that the force they were looking to attack was well supplied and much larger than the attacking revolutionaries.

The revolutionary forces met with the British in minor skirmishes on June 29 and June 30, 1778 with no clear victor. The British then scored a surprise victory over a portion of the rear guard of the Americans on July 1. Then began a slow period of little action in which the supplies of the Georgia and Continental Forces ran low. They eventually all returned to Savannah in yet their third embarrassing failure in the South.[415]

Decatur resident James McNeil was probably present at this time as a member of the Georgia Militia.

Georgia is Returned to British Control

The British launched a full campaign to take Georgia back into British rule in late December 1778. Col. Archibald Campbell landed with 3,000 troops and easily took back the city of Savannah that was unprepared for the attack. Only a month after that, he took half his troops and marched them to Georgia's interior and took Augusta. Decatur resident James McNeil was likely there at this time as a member of the Georgia Militia in Augusta.

[413] Cashin, Edward (2005) Revolutionary War in Georgia, New Georgia Encyclopedia
[414] Cashin, Edward (2005) Revolutionary War in Georgia, New Georgia Encyclopedia
[415] Deaton, Stan, Georgia Historical Society, (2004); New Georgia Encyclopedia; Battle of Kettle Creek

The Battle of Kettle Creek

Before returning to Savannah, Campbell was awaiting reinforcements on their way from North Carolina to reinforce Augusta. These troops never arrived because they were defeated at the Battle of Kettle Creek.

Kettle Creek flows into the Little River in Wilkes County, Georgia. Indian fish traps are often called "kittle" and probably gave the creek its name.

The battle occurred on February 14, 1779. That morning, 600 British loyalists were camped on a hill overlooking a bend in the river on their way to Augusta to rendezvous with Col. Campbell's troops.

Their leader was named James Boyd of Raeburn South Carolina. Boyd had a commission from the British government to recruit Georgia soldiers. He had set out for Augusta on February 5, 1779 with 350 recruits and was joined at Kettle Creek by 250 North Carolinian recruits under the command of John Moore.

The British recruits had captured Fort Independence in South Carolina and an outpost at Broad Mouth Creek. They were then attacked by a garrison of Georgians from Cherokee Ford, but staved them off. They were still being pursued by a small group of militia, but the militia's pursuit was so far proving ineffectual.[416]

Three hundred forty militia from South Carolina and Georgia had assembled and were preparing to attack Boyd while they were camped at Kettle Creek. The American militia was under the command of Col. Andrew Pickens of South Carolina, Col. John Dooly and Lt. Col. Elijah Clarke of Georgia.[417]

Taken by surprise, Boyd and his men were driven across the creek. Nineteen of Boyd's men and Boyd himself were shot and killed.

Pickens had prepared a direct assault on Boyd with his 200 South Carolinians. Dooly and Clarke would attack from across the creek. The battle started earlier than Pickens had planned when one of his men fired a rifle prematurely and roused the loyalists. Boyd then attacked Pickens while Dooly and Clarke struggled through swampy areas in the flood plain to join the battle.[418]

A group of Clarke's Georgia Militia, struggling through the marsh suddenly found themselves walking into the middle of Boyd's camp. Taken by surprise,

---

[416] Cashin, Edward (2005) Revolutionary War in Georgia, New Georgia Encyclopedia
[417] Cashin, Edward (2005) Revolutionary War in Georgia, New Georgia Encyclopedia
[418] Cashin, Edward (2005) Revolutionary War in Georgia, New Georgia Encyclopedia

Boyd and his men were driven across the creek. Nineteen of Boyd's men and Boyd himself were shot and killed. Twenty-two more were taken prisoner.

Many more of the British loyalists surrendered after returning to their homes in the Carolinas. Seven of these were eventually hanged. Of the Americans, only seven of the Georgia Militia were killed and 15 wounded.[419]

Unable to connect with more Continental Troops from North Carolina, Campbell withdrew from Augusta. Campbell's troops, now under Col. James Mark Prevost, were pursued by a force of Georgia Continentals and South Carolina Militia. Prevost surprised the revolutionaries by turning on them. The British routed the Americans in the Battle of Briar Creek on March 3, 1779. The British had given up Augusta but were still firmly in control of the capitol city of Savannah.

The American victory at Kettle Creek was crucial to the northern part of Georgia remaining under American control while the city of Savannah still belonged to the British. This meant the Americans still controlled the Georgia backcountry which included Decatur.

The Siege of Savannah
After Campbell had taken back Savannah, Governor James Wright returned on July 14, 1779 and announced that the colony had been officially returned to English rule. This made Georgia the only colony where the British regained control during the war.

Just two months after this declaration by Wright, a French fleet arrived to take the city back from the British. The French had recognized the United States as a new nation and begun to support them in the revolution in 1778. A French squadron of ships under the command of Count Charles d'Estaing had made the crossing and taken part in a series of successful battles in Rhode Island and the West Indies.[420]

Charles-Francois Sevigny, the Marquis of Bretigny, was serving in the Continental Army in South Carolina and encouraged d'Estaing to lay siege to Savannah saying he believed the city could be taken "without firing a shot." D'Estaing agreed. On September 3, 1779, 38 French warships appeared off the coast of Tybee Island carrying around 4,000 troops.[421]

The French began to land troops around 14 miles south of Savannah on September 11, 1779. Landing operations went poorly. The French landing boats were getting lost and grounded in heavy rains among the shifting tidal creeks off the Georgia coast.

[419] Cashin, Edward (2005) Revolutionary War in Georgia, New Georgia Encyclopedia
[420] Smith, Gordon Burns (2013); The Siege of Savannah, New Georgia Encyclopedia
[421] Smith, Gordon Burns (2013); The Siege of Savannah, New Georgia Encyclopedia

Meanwhile, the Americans had assembled a force of around 600 Continental Troops under Gen. Lincoln, 200 legionnaires commanded by Count Casimir Pulaski and 750 militia who were struggling south to rendezvous with the French.

On September 16, 1779, D'Estaing demanded a surrender from Gen. Prevost in Savannah. Before making any reply, Prevost received reinforcements of 800 Scottish troops from South Carolina. This brought the number of British occupying the town to 3,500. The British demolished several buildings in Savannah and used the materials to further fortify the city.

Prevost rejected the offer of terms from the French, and the siege began. The French positioned their artillery in heavy rain and began bombarding the city. The savage bombing between October 3 to October 7, 1779, caused severe damage to the city's buildings but low casualties.

The ground assault on the city then began on October 8 at 5:00 a.m. The French and Continental Forces first made two diversionary assaults on the town near White Bluff Road to try and fool the British into thinking this would be the main assault. These diversions failed though, and the British were fully prepared for the main attack. British musket fire and

> The French and Continentals fought bravely and continued the attack but were decimated by the British.

grapeshot ripped through the attackers as they approached the British barricades.

The French and Continentals fought bravely and continued the attack but were decimated by the British. The American and allied forces lost around 1,094 people including around 650 French. Many more were wounded. The British lost around 40 soldiers and 63 wounded.

Among those killed were Casimir Pulaski, the Polish aristocrat who led a brave cavalry charge into the city but was cut down. His name now graces a fort in Savannah.[422]

Aftermath of the Siege of Savannah
Flush with victory from their defense of Savannah, the British then laid siege to Charles Town using Tybee island as their base. The city fell to the British on May 12, 1780. More British units were then sent out and took control of the backcountry towns Augusta, Cambden and Ninety-Six.

---

[422] Jackson, Edwin L. and Stakes, Mary E. (2004) The Georgia Studies Book: Our State and the Nation; University of Georgia, Carl Vinson Institute of Government, Chapter 7

Col. Elijah Clarke brought his Georgia troops to try once again to retake Savannah in September of 1780. They engaged the British in a brutal battle over four days but were again repulsed when the British troops were reinforced by soldiers from Ninety-Six. Col. Clarke was pursued in his retreat to North Carolina by troops under Col. Patrick Ferguson, but the British were swarmed upon and defeated at King's Mountain.

Col. Clarke then returned to lay siege to Augusta and was joined by South Carolina Militia under Gen. Andrew Pickens and a legion commanded by Gen. Henry "Light Horse Harry" Lee (the father of Robert E. Lee). Augusta returned to American control on June 5, 1781. It was ultimately a very crucial victory in the overall war because the coast of Georgia was still under British control.

John Adams, Thomas Jefferson, Benjamin Franklin and the other negotiators of the treaty that ended the war might not have had enough grounds to demand that Georgia be surrendered to the new United States had the victory not returned the backcountry to American control.

The British began to withdraw from America in 1782. They withdrew from Savannah on January 2 of that year. The Treaty of Paris officially ended the war in 1783.

During the revolution, Spain had supported the Americans. As a

> **Among those who ratified the new US Constitution was a Decatur resident, James McNeil.**

result, they were once again given Florida. The two countries disagreed on the placement of Florida's northern boundary. During the next 12 years, the Georgia border was under constant dispute.[423]

Georgia and the Early United States of America

Georgia sent four delegates to the Constitutional Convention in Philadelphia in 1787. These were William Pierce, William Houston, William Few and Abraham Baldwin. All four supported the new US Constitution, but only Baldwin and Few were still in town when the delegates signed it.[424]

Georgia was the fourth state in the United States to ratify the US Constitution on January 2, 1788.[425] Among those who ratified it was a later Decatur resident, James McNeil.

---

[423] Jackson, Edwin L. and Stakes, Mary E. (2004) The Georgia Studies Book: Our State and the Nation; University of Georgia, Carl Vinson Institute of Government, Chapter 8
[424] Cobb, James C. and Inscoe, John C. (2009), Georgia History: Overview, New Georgia Encyclopedia
[425] Cobb, James C. and Inscoe, John C. (2009), Georgia History: Overview, New Georgia Encyclopedia

The first State Constitution of Georgia established eight counties in place of the colonial parishes, each with their own officials, courthouse, schools and militia. The counties established were Liberty, Chatham, Effingham, Burke, Richmond, Wilkes, Franklin and Washington. [426]

Decatur Resident and Founding Father James McNeil

There are several veterans of the Revolutionary War who eventually came to settle in Decatur. Each of them has an interesting story. One of them also played a significant role in the history of our country, Col. James McNeil. Col. McNeil's family emigrated to America from England in 1757. James' father Godfrey McNeil was a Colonel in the British Army. His mother's name was Sarah.[427]

From the moment it began, James McNeil led an interesting life. He was born aboard ship while crossing from England to America. After making the crossing, the family first settled in Robeson, North Carolina. As the winds of the Revolutionary War began to blow through North Carolina, the McNeil family sided with the crown against the colonies. Young James, at only 17 or 18 years of age, chose otherwise and wanted to join the Revolution. He left Robeson behind him and joined the Colonial Militia in Augusta, Georgia.

James was now part of a small number of rebels called "Revolutionary Refugees" or "Refugee Patriots" – men and women who joined the revolution at the cost of losing their homes in America. In Augusta, James was soon promoted to Colonel and given command of the 1st Battalion of the Georgia Militia in Richmond County associated with the brigade of John Twiggs. It's not clear how much action McNeil saw during the Revolutionary War, but it's likely he participated in Elijah Clarke's siege of Augusta in September 1780 and the action that followed when Gen. Andrew Pickens and Light Horse Harry Lee joined Clarke to besiege Augusta again in May 1781.[428] . He further showed his character and commitment to the new United States of America after the Revolutionary War had concluded.

Having been a colonel in the militia, McNeil was popular in Richmond County and was elected as a representative to ratify the new US Constitution alongside William Few Jr. on January 2, 1788.

[426] Vyas, Amee, Association of County Commissioners (2002); New Georgia Encyclopedia; Georgia's County Governments
[427] Price, Vivian (1997) History of DeKalb County, Georgia, 1822-1900; Wolfe Pub. Co. p 77
[428] Cashin, Edward (2005) Revolutionary War in Georgia, New Georgia Encyclopedia

The Georgia Ratification of the US Constitution

"Wednesday, Jan. 2, 1788

We, the delegates of the people of the State of Georgia, in Convention met, having taken into our serious consideration the Federation Constitution agreed upon and proposed by the Deputies of the United States in General Convention, held in the City of Philadelphia, on the 17th day of September, in the year of our Lord 1787, have assented to, ratified, and adopted, and by these presents do, in virtue of the powers and authority to us given by the people of the said State for that purpose, for and in behalf of ourselves and our constituents, fully and entirely assented to, ratify, and adopt the said Constitution, which is hereunto annexed, under the great seal of the State.[429]

Done in Convention, at Augusta, in the said State, on the 2d day of January 1788, and of the Independence of the United States the 12th.

In witness whereof, we have hereunto subscribed our names.

-- John Wereat, President, and Delegate from the County of Richmond.
-- William Stephens and Joseph Habersham - Chatham County
-- Jenkin Davis and N. Brownson - Effingham County
-- Edward Telfair and H. Todd - Burke County
-- William Few and **James McNeil** - Richmond County
-- George Matthews, Florence Sullivan, and John King - Wilkes County
-- James Powell, John Elliot, and James Maxwell - Liberty County
-- George Handley, Christopher Hillary, and J. Milton - Glynn County
-- Henry Osborne, James Seagrove, and Jacob Weed - Camden County
-- Jared Irwin and John Rutherford - Washington County
-- Robert Christmas, Thomas Daniell, and R. Middleton - Greene County"

---

[429] Georgia Info, An Online Georgia Almanac

McNeil and the Yazoo Land Act[430]

McNeil was then elected as a member of the Lower House of the General Assembly in the Legislature of Georgia.[431] He truly showed his quality as a Senator when he refused the temptation to relinquish his ideals and opposed the infamous Yazoo Land Act of 1795, the biggest scandal in the history of the state.[432]

As a new state, Georgia had claim to vast land to the west, in what is now Mississippi and Alabama which was called the "Yazoo Land" for the river running there that joins the Mississippi. The territory was so large and wild that it created costly and insurmountable issues for the state to fortify its borders, organize settlement and effect the transfer of the land over from the Creeks to the state. During the 1780s, several proposals were made to the Georgia legislature for various parties to take over large portions of Georgia's western claims. In 1788, the state tried unsuccessfully to cede the land over to the Federal Government. It was still Georgia's problem.

In 1789, Georgia sold about 25 million acres of the Yazoo land to three land companies. That deal fell through when Georgia demanded payment in gold and silver instead of the currently weak American currency. The issue continued to rankle, and pressure continued to mount on the legislatures to find a solution.[433]

Finally, in 1795, James Gunn orchestrated a deal by which 35 million acres of the Yazoo land in current Mississippi and Alabama would be sold to a consortium of four land companies. When Governor George Matthews signed the Yazoo Land Act on January 7, 1795, there were immediate cries of fraud.[434]

> **When Governor George Matthews signed the Yazoo Land Act on January 7, 1795, there were immediate cries of fraud.**

The $500,000 the four companies had paid for the land was severely below its market value and the primary broker of the deal, James Gunn, had facilitated various bribes, including money and land for state legislators, state officials, newspaper editors and other people who could influence the approval of the deal.

---

[430] Lumplugh, George (2002) Yazoo Land Fraud, New Georgia Encyclopedia
[431] Franklin M. Garrett; (1969) Atlanta and Environs: A Chronicle of Its People and Events, Volume 1; University of Georgia Press
[432] Lumplugh, George (2002) Yazoo Land Fraud, New Georgia Encyclopedia
[433] Lumplugh, George (2002) Yazoo Land Fraud, New Georgia Encyclopedia
[434] Price, Vivian (1997) History of DeKalb County, Georgia, 1822-1900; Wolfe Pub. Co. p 77

The existence of these bribes was well known among the representatives. Only nine Georgia representatives voted to reject the Yazoo Land Act and refused to bend their principles. One of these was James McNeil.

One of McNeil's mentors, US Senator James Jackson returned from Washington. With the help of allies like his friend McNeil, he led an investigation into the Yazoo Land Act. It was declared a fraud and rescinded by an act passed in 1796. Jackson also made several changes to ensure an incident like the Yazoo Land Act could not be repeated, and the embarrassing ordeal for the state would be put to rest. He destroyed all the records associated with it to squelch further investigations, but he also worked hard to ensure all legislators associated with it were denied reelection, and he orchestrated a revision of the state constitution including articles of the rescinding act in 1798.[435]

Then, to further ensure another fiasco like the Yazoo Land Act was not instituted, Jackson orchestrated the passage of the Compact of 1802. This act would have enormous, far-reaching effects for every person in Georgia, both Americans and Indians. Under the terms of the compact, Georgia transferred the Yazoo land to the Federal Government for $1.25 million, and the Federal Government agreed to work toward extinguishing all Indian claims to this land and transferring it back to Georgia "as early as the same can be peaceably effected". This transfer of land and the promise that Indian claims to it would be extinguished, which the Federal Government was slow to accomplish, became one of the many turning points in the increasingly frosty relationship between the state of Georgia and the US government where the Creeks were caught in the middle.

The Yazoo land companies pleaded with the Federal Government for payment of the $1.25 million that they expected to profit from the deal, but the state of Georgia declared the contract null and rescinded. They continued to seek restitution and were denied until 1810 in the case of Fletcher v. Penn. The case went to the Supreme Court, and it was ruled that rescinding of the Yazoo Land Act was unconstitutional. It took another four years for Congress to issue $5 million from the proceeds of sales of the Yazoo Land to the land companies.[436]

> **McNeil's public career had ended before he married his cousin McNeil, in 1809. He was 52. She was 19.**

[435] Lamplugh, George (2002) Yazoo Land Fraud, New Georgia Encyclopedia
[436] Lamplugh, George (2002) Yazoo Land Fraud, New Georgia Encyclopedia

McNeil's Later Life in Decatur

McNeil's public career had ended before he married his cousin Sara in 1809. He was 52. She was 19.[437] They moved to Decatur in 1830 for its educational opportunities for their seven children. The McNeils lived on the Shallowford Trail (Clairemont Ave.) where he owned a saddle manufacturing business, which he operated with his son, Daniel.[438] Col. McNeil died in 1853 at the age of 96 and was buried in Decatur Cemetery.[439]

[437] Price, Vivian (1997) History of DeKalb County, Georgia, 1822-1900; Wolfe Pub. Co. p 77
[438] Price, Vivian (1997) History of DeKalb County, Georgia, 1822-1900; Wolfe Pub. Co. p 77
[439] Price, Vivian (1997) History of DeKalb County, Georgia, 1822-1900; Wolfe Pub. Co. p 77

The Final Resting Place of James McNeil in Decatur Cemetery[440]

CHAPTER 11:
THE CREEK WARS WITH AMERICA

The Change to Wanting Creek Land More than their Deerskins and Slaves

The final and most tragic chapter in the story of the Creeks and other Indian groups in the Southeast took place in the late 18th century and the early part of the 19th century. Several things happened in this timeframe that changed the relationship between the Europeans or Americans and the Indians, and ultimately, it led to forced removal of the Creeks from Georgia and the Cherokee Trail of Tears.

In the late 1700s, as in the past, the primary reasons for growing tension and eventual conflict were commercial ones. Indian culture had been forever changed when slave trading for profit was introduced into their society around 1600. It then changed again when the slave trade shifted from Indians to Africans around 1700, and the primary economic driver of activity at the interior of Georgia became trade in deerskins.

> The Indians around Decatur and the rest of the interior of Georgia had fewer customers around 1800 but enjoyed a brief period of relative peace.

After the Spanish and the French were driven out of the Southeast at the end of the French and Indian War in 1763, the closest colony on the coast was now Charles Town. The Indians around Decatur and the rest of the interior of Georgia had fewer customers but enjoyed a brief period of relative peace.[441] With the territory now under British control, English settlers quickly began flooding into Georgia and migrating west.

The Indians lost another significant source of their power when the United States became the only stable power on the East Coast. In the past, the Indians were important allies (or at least kept as satisfied neutral parties) for the British to enforce their claimed borders with the Spanish and the French and later the Americans. After the war, this became much less important.[442]

---

[441] Price, Vivian (1997) History of DeKalb County, Georgia, 1822-1900; Wolfe Pub. Co. , 1986
[442] Etheridge, Robbie; (2003) Creek Country, University of North Carolina Press

The population of white-tailed deer was decimated, and the wealth emanating from the Southeast began to decline. The basis for much of the power the Indians had in their dealings with the British declined with it.

Along with the decline in white-tailed deer, many of the most successful traders in the Southeast were ceasing operation. Trade with Britain was outlawed in most colonies before the war even began. All the British trading houses in places like Charles Town and Savannah were now out of business. The only British trading house that remained open in the Southeast was at the Port of Pensacola in the British colony of West Florida. This was Panton, Leslie and Company (later John Forbes and Company). It remained the primary trading house in the South until as late as 1830.[443]

> Land replaced deerskins as the most profitable and desirable thing the Americans could gain from the Indians.

The traders who operated in the Southeast nearly all operated in conjunction with British trading houses and were mostly British themselves. During the war, they nearly all took the loyalist side and paid the price. After the war ended, many were expelled or fled back to England. Many others had their property confiscated. Some were hanged.[444]

The last and hardest blow to Indian power was the increased profitability of raising cotton in the wake of the invention of the cotton gin in 1793. By 1766, there were already 18,000 settlers in Georgia. Ten thousand were white British and 8,000 were black slaves mainly working crops.[445] Land replaced deerskins as the most profitable and desirable thing the Americans could gain from the Indians. The role of the Indians in the American business model changed from being a necessary partner to an obstacle in possession of the land the Americans wanted, especially the land in the South. The results of that change were predictable. Anyone planning to settle in the American South wanted the Indians gone.[446]

By the end of the 18th century, the Lower Creeks were occupying most of the interior, southern half of Georgia.[447] The Upper Creeks lived on the Tallapoosa, Coosa and Alabama Rivers in Alabama This territory was at first

---

[443] Etheridge, Robbie; (2003) Creek Country, University of North Carolina Press
[444] Etheridge, Robbie; (2003) Creek Country, University of North Carolina Press
[445] Jackson, Edwin L. and Stakes, Mary E. (2004) The Georgia Studies Book: Our State and the Nation; University of Georgia, Carl Vinson Institute of Government, Chapter 6
[446] Etheridge, Robbie; (2003) Creek Country, University of North Carolina Press
[447] Etheridge, Robbie; (2003) Creek Country, University of North Carolina Press

part of the Yazoo land that Georgia ceded to the Federal Government and eventually became the state of Alabama in 1819. The Cherokees controlled North Georgia and into North Carolina and South Carolina. The Seminoles controlled the interior of Florida.

Alexander McGillivray, the First Leader of the Creeks as a "Nation"

Alexander McGillivray was the first among several fascinating and controversial leaders who rose to power from among the Creeks and took on the mantle of national leadership in dealing with the new United States and Georgia.

He was born around 1750 in the town of Little Tallassee near what is now Montgomery, Alabama.[448] His mother was named Sehoy, a Creek of the Wind Clan, a group with significant prominence among the Creeks and his father was Lachlan McGillivray, a Scot who had been a successful trader among the Creeks. The Wind Clan of the Creeks was a matrilineal society. Alexander was given full membership and rights in her clan.[449]

Alexander's life, like many of the Creek leaders, was an interesting dichotomy between British and Creek ways of life. As a half-European, he ran a plantation, owned African slaves and bred cattle. As a Creek, he obeyed Creek law, lived with them and followed Creek religious customs and rituals.[450]

While he was comfortable living among the Creeks, Alexander was also comfortable among the British colonists. His father, Lachlan McGillivray, moved the family to Augusta in 1774, before the Revolutionary War.[451] Young Alexander spent most of his childhood there. He was then educated in Charles Town, South Carolina and then worked as an apprentice in Savannah, Georgia.[452]

> As a half-European, McGillvray ran a plantation, owned African slaves, and bred cattle. As a Creek, he obeyed Creek law, lived with them, and followed Creek religious customs and rituals.

---

[448] Frank, Andrew K., (2002); Alexander McGillivray (ca. 1750-1793), New Georgia Encyclopedia
[449] Frank, Andrew K., (2002); Alexander McGillivray (ca. 1750-1793), New Georgia Encyclopedia
[450] Etheridge, Robbie; (2003) Creek Country, University of North Carolina Press
[451] Frank, Andrew K., (2002); Alexander McGillivray (ca. 1750-1793), New Georgia Encyclopedia
[452] Frank, Andrew K., (2002); Alexander McGillivray (ca. 1750-1793), New Georgia Encyclopedia

At the start of the war, in 1775, revolutionaries confiscated Alexander's father Lachlan's property in South Carolina. At the age of 27, Alexander then returned to Little Tallassee to live with his mother, and Lachlan returned to Scotland.[453]

During the war, Alexander became instrumental in creating and preserving alliances between the Creeks and the British. At one time, he even held a commission as a Colonel in the British Army and worked for the British superintendent of Indian Affairs.[454]

After the War, McGillivray fought passionately to retain the rights of the Creeks to their land from the new state of Georgia. He negotiated the Treaty of Pensacola with the Spanish in 1784, which protected Creek claims to land in Florida and guaranteed access to Panton, Leslie and Company.[455]

A large part of McGillivray's power among the Creeks derived from this relationship with the traders from Panton, Leslie and Co. McGillivray was instrumental to both sides in keeping the flow of deerskins running back to Britain. This made him a very powerful figure. Through his business relationships, he could influence preferential treatment for some Creeks in their trade relationship while doing the opposite for others.[456]

> Had the Creek Confederacy been able to survive as a separate nation from the United States Alexander McGillivray would have gone down in history as the father or their nation.

Within Creek society, McGillivray was the first to successfully organize the Creeks into a national entity with the power to negotiate as one nation with the Americans on somewhat equal footing. There had been previous treaties between the Creeks and the English and other nations. Those treaties did not truly represent the entire Creek Confederacy. In the past, each group within the Creeks had the power to negotiate their own agreements with outside parties. This was a tradition that dated back long before they had formed the Creek Confederacy. McGillivray successfully established a new law within the Confederacy that removed the right of individual groups to make their own agreements. Though it succeeded, the new law was passionately opposed by

---

[453] Frank, Andrew K., (2002); Alexander McGillivray (ca. 1750-1793), New Georgia Encyclopedia
[454] Frank, Andrew K., (2002); Alexander McGillivray (ca. 1750-1793), New Georgia Encyclopedia
[455] Frank, Andrew K., (2002); Alexander McGillivray (ca. 1750-1793), New Georgia Encyclopedia
[456] Etheridge, Robbie; (2003) Creek Country, University of North Carolina Press

some Creek chiefs and added to the tension growing between factions in the confederacy.[457]

President George Washington invited the Indian chiefs to come to New York in 1790 to form a treaty. McGillivray answered the call and brought a large number of other chiefs and braves to come with him. His trek north became a major event and passed right through the Decatur area, probably on the Shallow Ford Trail.

The entourage passed through Stone Mountain as was documented by the President's special envoy, Marinus Willett, who was sent to escort McGillivray to New York.

"June 9, at 9 o'clock a.m., arrived at the Stony Mountain about 8 miles from where we encamped. Here we found the Cowetas and the Curates to the number of eleven waiting for us; lay by until 3 o'clock p.m. and then proceeded 8 miles and encamped by a large Creek of the waters of the Ocmulgee. Course in general nearly east, north east. Pleasant day, shower of rain after we encamped. While I was at Stony Mountain I ascended the summit. It is one solid rock of circular form, about one mile across. Many strange tales are told by the Indians of this Mountain. I have now passed all Indian settlements and shall only observe that the inhabitants of these countries appear very happy."[458]

McGillivray signed the first Treaty with the United States on behalf of the Creek Confederacy representing them as a nation. This was the Treaty of New York signed in 1790 in which the United States agreed to defend Creek territorial rights.[459] This treaty also relinquished any Creek claims to the land between the Ogeechee and Oconee Rivers in Georgia, the first cession of Creek land to the United States

Creek rights laid out in their treaties were routinely ignored by settlers arriving in the territories, particularly in Georgia and by the new Georgia state government.

and by proxy, to the state of Georgia. There would be many more.[460]

McGillivray's successful consolidation of the Creeks into one nation was an amazing accomplishment. It's astonishing he was able get all the Creeks to act

[457] Etheridge, Robbie; (2003) Creek Country, University of North Carolina Press
[458] Price, Vivian (1997) History of DeKalb County, Georgia, 1822-1900; Wolfe Pub. Co.
[459] Frank, Andrew K., (2002); Alexander McGillivray (ca. 1750-1793), New Georgia Encyclopedia
[460] Etheridge, Robbie; (2003) Creek Country, University of North Carolina Press

in a different way from the past across around 47 disparate groups across all of Georgia and Alabama and down into Florida and somehow do this entirely through speech. There were no telephones, and the Creeks had no written language. Had the Creek Confederacy survived alongside the United States Alexander McGillivray would have gone down in history as the father of their nation.

On the other side of the table, the Americans after the Revolutionary War were debating between two opposing philosophies on how best to deal with the Indians. Despite just signing a treaty acknowledging Creek rights to their land, all Americans supported the westward expansion of the United States, but they disagreed on the best approach for accomplishing this. The enlightenment followers like Thomas Jefferson and his close friend Benjamin Hawkins, favored assimilation of the Indians into American society.

Benjamin Hawkins was another important player in this story. He was the first Creek agent for the Americans, responsible for managing the relationship between the Creeks and the Federal Government. In many ways, he can be thought of as the ambassador to the Creeks as a nation. He located the Creek agency along the Ocmulgee River in today's Crawford County, Georgia. The primary activity at the Creek agency was to listen to Creeks in their complaints about dealings with intruders. Hawkins would then do his best to settle each matter brought to him.

The central purpose to Hawkins' position was to manage the transfer of Creek land over to the United States. However, in his strong view toward assimilation of the Creeks, he worked very hard to convince them to adopt European practices and become farmers and prepare to become contributing members of the new United States. He also worked very closely with the Creeks to learn from them and understand the inner workings of their culture. Hawkins consistently dealt with the Creeks fairly and treated them as intelligent people, not interlopers or savages as many viewed them. He learned to speak Creek fluently. In the following years of conflict between the Creeks and the United States, Hawkins consistently fought for fair negotiations with the Creeks and tried his best to protect Creek land rights from intruding settlers. However, these efforts were often fruitless. Creek rights laid out in their treaties were routinely ignored by settlers arriving in the territories, particularly in Georgia and by the new Georgia state government.

It's debatable whether the view of assimilation was really in the best interest of the Creeks and the Indians in general over the long term. It still represents the destruction of their culture and in the modern view, the idea of a new culture absorbing a previous one entirely by converting all its members into the new way of life is more often considered not to be the wisest approach. In 1800, it was certainly preferable to the alternative view. Hawkins and Thomas Jefferson absolutely did what they thought best on behalf of the Creeks. I think the most revealing evidence of all the things Hawkins held most dear in his life and his clear affection for both the new United States and for the Indians in the Southeast is in the names of his children. He and his wife Lavinia had six daughters and one son. They named their son Madison and their daughters Georgia, Muscogee, Cherokee, Carolina, Virginia and Jeffersonia.

The opposing view to that of Hawkins and Jefferson in how to deal with the Indians was epitomized by Andrew Jackson, another central player in the drama that unfolded and eventually created Decatur. This view was much simpler and straight forward than assimilation. Jackson and most of the people in Georgia favored westward expansion through the expulsion of the Indians out of the Southeast United

> "Georgia political opinion is most rabidly anti-Federalist. Public professions of demagoguery and scorn for the President are often pushed to the point of insult and profanity."
> ~Duc de la Rochefoucald-Liancourt (1796)

States as soon possible. Failing that, extermination of the Indians would be necessary. Jackson was ready and willing to devote his efforts to either approach that became necessary in his view.[461]

After the debacle of the Yazoo Land Act, vast areas of land to the west of Georgia had been removed from the control of the state of Georgia and put under the management of the Federal Government. The Georgia government was furious about this and openly refused to cooperate in upholding the Creek land rights from the beginning. "Intruders" continued to settle on Creek land, and Georgia did nothing to discourage them.[462]

Francois Alexandre Frederic, Duc de La Rochefoucauld – Liancourt took note of this during his sojourn in Georgia in 1796.

"The newspapers are full of libelous articles, invective and challenges; simply reading them shows, with no other proof, the confusion and licentiousness in the State of Georgia. Georgia political opinion is most rabidly anti-Federalist.

[461] Etheridge, Robbie; (2003) Creek Country, University of North Carolina Press
[462] Etheridge, Robbie; (2003) Creek Country, University of North Carolina Press

Public professions of demagoguery and scorn for the President are often pushed to the point of insult and profanity."[463]

Despite his success in dealing with the United States, Alexander McGillivray hated the Americans and the people of Georgia. They had taken away all his father's property that he was meant to inherit. He was a British loyalist and enjoyed good relationships with the British that were undone by the Americans. Yet he was a pragmatist and did whatever was necessary to preserve a fragile peace between the Creeks and the United States.

Together, McGillivray and Hawkins kept a fragile peace within the Creek Nation and between the United States and the Creeks for roughly 20 years and usher in the new United States. Tensions within and between the two nations were ready to explode toward the end of the 16th century. McGillivray died in 1793, and with the loss of his leadership, the tensions quickly took flame.[464]

The Fight Over Georgia Land Explodes when Tecumseh Visits Georgia

After the death of Alexander McGillivray, there was a power struggle within the Creek Confederacy with no clear leader emerging to take McGillivray's place. The chiefs of Oakfuskee were some of the most prominent among the Upper Creeks and Menawa, their second chief was the popular chief among the young warriors. Menawa was destined to figure prominently in the history of Georgia and would become a legend.[465]

He was another of the new social class of Indians who lived a dual existence influenced by the European world as much as his Indian heritage. His father was a Scot trader, and his mother was a Creek woman from the town of Oakfuskee. During his youth, when Creek life in the backcountry was more isolated, Menawa was called Hothlepoya, "crazy war hunter" for the reputation he had already gained leading many raids in Alabama, Tennessee and Georgia and stole countless numbers of horses from settlers intruding on Creek land. Somewhere around 1811, he became the second chief of the Oakfuskee towns and was called Menawa, "The Great Warrior."[466]

Within the Creek Confederacy, there were two opposing views on how to deal with the Americans that reflected the mirror image of the opposing American views, assimilation or opposition. The supporters of each view had grown more divided to the point the two sections of the overall confederacy, the

[463] Lane, Mills (1973) The Rambler in Georgia, Beehive Press, pg 8
[464] Etheridge, Robbie; (2003) Creek Country, University of North Carolina Press
[465] Braund, Kathryn, Auburn University (2014); Menawa; New Georgia Encyclopedia
[466] McKenny, Thomas & Hall, James & Todd, Hatherly & Todd, Joseph. (1872) History of the Indian tribes of North America: with biographical sketches and anecdotes of the principal chiefs., Philadelphia: D. Rice & Co.

Upper Creeks and the Lower Creeks operated in many ways like two strong political parties. The lines of division had become distinct between the Upper Creeks from the towns along the Coosa and Tallapoosa Rivers and the Lower Creeks along the Chattahoochee and the Flint Rivers. In general, the Lower Creeks favored much more open relationships with the Americans.

As they felt their power waning and settlers continued to intrude illegally on Creek land in greater and greater numbers with no opposition from the state governments, the Upper Creeks and Menawa were becoming demoralized. The loss of all Creek land seemed increasingly unavoidable. They were becoming desperate for a new vision of hope and in 1811, Tecumseh, the famous Shawnee Warrior, brought it to them.[467]

> Menawa was called Hothlepoya, "crazy war hunter" for the reputation he had already gained leading raids into Tennessee and stealing countless numbers of horses from intruders.

After McGillivray's death in 1793, the Creeks had formed a National Council around 1800 that would make decisions and form written laws governing the confederacy. In 1811, Tecumseh came to visit the Council with a vision that had been articulated by his brother Tenskwatawa, a renowned Shawnee prophet. The Creeks had long held the Shawnee in high regard and were eager to listen. In very inspiring terms, Tecumseh communicated a vision that all Indians would join in a united force that would push the Americans back into the sea. They would then rid the land of all things American and return to a traditional Indian culture.[468]

Some of Tecumseh's eloquent and truly inspiring speech to the Cherokee's is preserved from reports. The speech to the Creeks would have been very similar with some poetic changes that I can imagine describing the Creek's deep, shaded forests more than the mountain glens of the Cherokees.

"Everywhere our people have passed away as the snow from the mountains melts in May. We no longer rule the forests. The game has gone like our hunting grounds. Even our lands are nearly all gone. Yes, my brothers, our campfires are few. Those that still burn we must draw together. Behold what

---

[467] McKenny, Thomas & Hall, James & Todd, Hatherly & Todd, Joseph. (1872) History of the Indian tribes of North America: with biographical sketches and anecdotes of the principal chiefs., Philadelphia: D. Rice & Co.,
[468] Etheridge, Robbie; (2003) Creek Country, University of North Carolina Press

the white man has done to our people! Gone are the Pequot, the Narraganset, the Powhatan, the Tuscarora and the Coree. We can no longer trust the white man. We gave him our tobacco and our maize. What happened? Now there is hardly enough land to grow these holy plants. White men have built their castles where the Indians hunting grounds once were, and now they are coming into your mountain glens. Soon there will be no place for the Cherokee to hunt the deer and the bear. The tomahawk of the Shawnee is ready. Will the Cherokee raise the tomahawk? Will the Cherokee join their brother, the Shawnee?"[469]

After the Shawnee's visit, several of the Creek leaders, including Menawa, traveled to the Great Lakes to meet with other followers of Tenskwatawa. They returned with more inspiring rhetoric and promises. Tenskwatawa's followers had taught them sacred rituals and dances to their deity Hisagati Misi, "The Master of Breath", that they believed would shield them from American bullets and cannon fire. In addition, they promised that Tecumseh's warriors and their old allies the British were gathering and would soon come to support them.[470]

> "The tomahawk of the Shawnee is ready. Will the Creek raise the tomahawk? Will the Creek join their brother, the Shawnee?"
> ~Tecumseh (1811)

In this way, Tecumseh masterfully intertwined his brother's vision and the frustration of all Indians with the brewing War of 1812 between the British and the Americans into his own vision for a united Indian nation.[471]

Tecumseh's warriors were known for carrying red war clubs. So, the followers of this movement became known as the Red Sticks (I would have thought this was also the origin for the name of the city of Baton Rouge which means Red Stick in French. The name of that city apparently refers to a tree that was stripped of bark and marked a boundary into Indian land).[472]

The wrath of the Red Sticks was as much focused on other Creeks as it was the Americans. They believed that the Creeks who had favored compromise and negotiation with the Americans had sold away their culture and their power in the New World. In general, the Upper Creeks tended to support the Red Stick

---

[469] WC Allen, the Annals of Haywood North Carolina (Waynesville NC, 1935) p. 44-46 (from NPS – Battle of Horseshoe Bend).
[470] Etheridge, Robbie; (2003) Creek Country, University of North Carolina Press
[471] Etheridge, Robbie; (2003) Creek Country, University of North Carolina Press
[472] Louisiana.gov

movement while the Lower Creeks supported continued relationships with the Americans, but this was not at all absolute. Many Creek towns were divided against each other and many people from each region left to join the other side. In addition, many Indians who were not Creek chose to join the Red Sticks.

The Red Sticks first efforts were to purge themselves of anything they viewed as an American influence. They destroyed Creek farms. They threw plows and looms into the river. They slaughtered any farm animals they found among the Creeks.

> **The wrath of the Red Sticks was as much focused on other Creeks as it was the Americans.**

The Battle and Massacre at Fort Mims

In the Spring of 1813, a group of the Red Sticks traveled to Pensacola to gather supplies from the British trading house there. They were probably being inspired by British soldiers who supplied them with weapons to further destabilize the Americans in the Southeast. On their way back, they were attacked by a group of Mississippi Militia led by Lower Creek headmen from the Tensaw and Bigbe settlements just north of Pensacola. In retaliation, on August 29, 1813, the Red Sticks attacked and defeated the garrison at Fort Mims near present-day Mobile, Alabama. They killed nearly every settler and Lower Creek Indian who had been living there.

The Red Stick War had begun.

In the following days and months, several quickly assembled armies from Mississippi, Georgia and Tennessee took to the field in the Red Stick War. The Americans were successful in putting the Creeks on the run and winning a series of battles through the rest of 1813. American soldiers marveled at the Red Sticks doing their dances to the Master of Breath in front of the cannons expecting that they couldn't be harmed. None of these battles were definitive enough to crush the Red Stick forces. Most of the Creeks were able to escape each confrontation and reassemble in another location.[473]

After the attack on Fort Mims, the Red Sticks attacked Fort Sinquefield. The first American victory occurred on November 3 when Gen. John Coffee used his 1,300 cavalry soldiers to attack the town of Tallushatchee. Around 200 Red Stick warriors were killed along with several women and children.[474]

A few days after Tallushatchee, the Red Sticks began a siege of the town of Talladega but were routed out by the combined force of Tennessee Militia,

---

[473] Braund, Kathryn, (2008) Creek War of 1813-14, Encyclopedia of Alabama
[474] Braund, Kathryn, (2008) Creek War of 1813-14, Encyclopedia of Alabama

cavalry and Cherokees commanded by Andrew Jackson. The Red Sticks lost about third of their 1,000 warriors in their escape.[475]

In October 1813, Creek residents of the town of Hilibi sent word to Gen. Jackson that they planned to take no part in the war and did not plan to support the Red Sticks. Nevertheless, they were attacked by Gen. Cocke's Tennessee forces. Seventy Creeks were killed and around 300 taken prisoner.[476]

Next, Gen. Floyd took his 1,000 Georgia Militia to the town of Autossee along with around 400 Creeks warriors from the Lower Towns commanded by William McIntosh. The Georgia and Lower Creek forces won the battle once again, but most Red Sticks escaped. Around 200 Red Sticks were killed. Gen. Floyd was wounded and retreated to Fort Mitchell on the Chattahoochee. It is not known for certain, but the battle at Autossee was probably the first meeting of William McIntosh and Menawa, whose rivalry determined much of Creek and Georgia history.[477]

In January of 1814, Floyd left Fort Mitchell and built Fort Hull around 40 miles to the west as a link in supply chain of forts. He then proceeded to Calabee Creek to establish the next link in the chain and was caught in a surprise attack and nearly routed by a group of Red Sticks. In the end, the Georgians turned the tide and fought off the Red Sticks. Floyd's army suffered 150 wounded but only 22 dead compared to 50 dead among the Red Sticks.[478]

The Critical Battle in the Creek Conflict with America, The Battle of Horseshoe Bend

By the Spring of 1814, Jackson's Army was the only one still active in the field, and the bulk of the remaining Red Stick forces had assembled near the town of Tohopeka. As the Americans approached Tohopeka and the Red Sticks made their preparations to meet them, each knew this would be the battle to decide the Red Stick War. The Red Sticks believed they had gathered a much larger force than the Americans and were determined to execute this battle differently from the sprawling town defenses they had made in the past.

The face-off between the Americans and the Red Sticks was not the only major confrontation taking place at Horseshoe Bend. The Upper Creeks and their greatest leaders were going to meet the leader of the Lower Creeks face-to-face and the civil war within the Creek Confederacy would also be decided.

On one side, leading the Red Sticks, was Menawa, the legendary chief and warrior from the powerful Creek town of Oakfuskee. It is not certain in which

[475] Braund, Kathryn, (2008) Creek War of 1813-14, Encyclopedia of Alabama
[476] Braund, Kathryn, (2008) Creek War of 1813-14, Encyclopedia of Alabama
[477] Braund, Kathryn, (2008) Creek War of 1813-14, Encyclopedia of Alabama
[478] Braund, Kathryn, (2008) Creek War of 1813-14, Encyclopedia of Alabama

battles Menawa participated before the Battle of Horseshoe Bend. There were probably several. He almost certainly fought with his kindred the Oakfuskee at Autossee, the Creek encampment of Emuckfau and the previous battle with Jackson's forces at Enitichopco Creek.[479]

On the opposite side of the conflict was William McIntosh, the leader of the Lower Creeks. Like Menawa, McIntosh was born to a Scotsman trader father, Captain William McIntosh and a Creek mother, Senoya of the influential Wind Clan. McIntosh's views on how to deal with the Americans were the mirror image of Menawa's. He favored assimilation and close ties in the American world. In fact, McIntosh was connected by family bonds to many Americans in government including his cousin George Troup. the Governor of Georgia at that time and Lachlan McIntosh, the General who commanded the Continental Troops in Georgia during much of the Revolutionary War.[480]

McIntosh was a Coweta, the clan that controlled the land around the Chattahoochee including the land where Decatur is now located. He led around 200 Lower Creeks into the Battle of Horseshoe Bend.

Menawa and McIntosh knew each other and their rivalry for leadership within the Creek Nation had already been growing for many years. Years before the Battle of Horseshoe Bend, one of the Upper Creek villages had been burned in retribution for the murder of an American settler. Some said the murder had been committed by Menawa's band. Menawa vehemently denied the rumors. He believed those false reports had been delivered by McIntosh whom he thought to be the real culprit of the murder in a scheme to play the Americans against him and further solidify McIntosh's own position as the primary Creek leader.[481]

The Red Sticks chose a spot where there is a sharp 180-degree bend in the Tallapoosa River near Tohopeka to make their stand. They had gathered around 1,000 Red Stick warriors and converted the bend of the river into a fortress. The river would serve as a natural moat at the back and on the sides. Then in front, where an army could approach on land, the Red Sticks dug out trenches and built up a barricade of logs with openings from which they could fire their weapons. Menawa oversaw much of the preparations. Menawa and his Red Sticks had done a masterful job of choosing a location and fortifying it which Jackson praised many times in descriptions of the battle.

"It is impossible to conceive of a situation more eligible for defence (sic) than the one they had chosen and the skill they manifested in their breastwork was

[479] Braund, Kathryn, Auburn University (2014); Menawa; New Georgia Encyclopedia
[480] Stock, Melissa, University of West Georgia (2007), William McIntosh, New Georgia Encyclopedia
[481] McKenny, Thomas & Hall, James & Todd, Hatherly & Todd, Joseph. (1872) History of the Indian tribes of North America: with biographical sketches and anecdotes of the principal chiefs., Philadelphia: D. Rice & Co.

really astonishing. It was from five to eight feet high and extended across the point in such a direction as that a force approaching would be exposed to a double fire, while they lay entirely safe behind it. It would have been impossible to have raked it with cannon to any advantage even if we had had possession of one extremity."[482]

Despite the Red Sticks excellent preparations at the front of the attack, they had left themselves vulnerable at the back where there was a small village containing women and children. During their preparations making Horseshoe Bend into a barricade, the first chief of the Oakfuskee whom Menawa followed, declared that he had learned through supernatural means that the attack would come from the thin opening of land in the horseshoe, not from across the river at the rear. His followers believed him and put all their efforts into fortifying this side of the Bend.[483]

On the morning of March 27, 1814, a day before the battle, Jackson made probably his most important maneuver by splitting his force in two. He sent Gen. Coffee ahead at 6:30 in the morning with the mounted Americans and most of the Indians; a force of 700 cavalry and mounted horsemen and about 600 Indian allies. The Indian forces consisted of around 400 Cherokees and William McIntosh with his 200 or so Lower Creeks.[484] Some of the Cherokees in the battle were from Standing Peachtree as was confirmed by James Montgomery who lived there and later in Dekalb County. It is almost certain that there were also Creeks from Sandtown battling with McIntosh.

> "It is impossible to conceive of a situation more eligible for defence (sic) than the one they had chosen and the skill they manifested in their breastwork was really astonishing."
> ~Andrew Jackson (1814)

Jackson did not plan to just win this battle. His objective was to "exterminate" the whole of the Indian force. Therefore, he wanted Coffee and his Cherokee and Lower Creek forces to "surround the bend in such a manner, as that none of them should escape by attempting to cross the river"[485] Sometime during the morning of March 28, Gen. Coffee sent McIntosh and most of the other

---

[482] National Park Service, Description of Horseshoe Bend National Historic Site
[483] McKenny, Thomas & Hall, James & Todd, Hatherly & Todd, Joseph. (1872) History of the Indian tribes of North America: with biographical sketches and anecdotes of the principal chiefs., Philadelphia: D. Rice & Co.
[484] Letter from Coffee to Jackson, April 1, 1814
[485] Letter from Jackson to Blount, March 31, 1814

Indians ahead of the American troops with orders to position themselves at the rear of the battleground across the river and behind the Red Stick's barricade.[486]

Around the time Coffee was approaching the battleground with his horses, about 10:00 in the morning, Jackson was approaching the barricade from the front with his force of around 2,000 regular soldiers and militia and two cannons. Upon sighting them, "a savage yell was raised" by the Indians in the barricade that must have bristled the hair on backs of the necks of the American forces.[487]

Jackson placed his two cannons (a six pounder and a three pounder) on a small hill around 150 to 200 yards from the front of the barricade. The battle began quickly and in earnest with the firing of the cannons into the front of the Red Stick's fortifications. The American forces supported the cannon fire with their rifles in both the front and the rear.[488]

Inside the fort, pandemonium ensued. As the battle opened, the Indians in the village began running for cover in a panic but were prevented from approaching the river by Coffee, McIntosh, and the Indians on the opposite bank firing across at them.[489] The cannon balls failed to completely break the front of the barricade as Jackson had intended. Many of them passed through and ripped apart any Red Stick warriors unlucky enough to be in their path.[490]

The next hours were the bloodiest and most brutal of all the engagements between the Creeks and the Americans. The Red Sticks knew this would be the day that decided whether they would continue as a people in the Southeast and believed they were being supported by their gods and rituals. They fought with the desperation that comes when there is no option for retreat.

> Upon sighting them, "a savage yell was raised" by the Indians in the barricade that must have bristled the hair on backs of the necks of the Americans.

Jackson described the action saying that each side "...maintained for a few minutes a very obstinate contest, muzzle to muzzle, through the port-holes, in which many of the enemy's balls were welded to the bayonets of our musquets." (meaning they would stick their bayonets down the muzzle of the rifles protruding from the barricade thereby plugging them as the Indians fired).[491]

---

[486] Letter from Coffee to Jackson, April 1, 1814
[487] Letter from Coffee to Jackson, April 1, 1814
[488] Letter from Jackson Mrs. Jackson, April 1, 1814
[489] Letter from Coffee to Jackson, April 1, 1814
[490] Letter from Jackson Mrs. Jackson, April 1, 1814
[491] Letter from Jackson to Blount, April 1, 1814

The American forces kept up this assault on both sides for the next two hours or so with a few brief interruptions. Around mid-day, several of the Indians at the rear under Coffee's command broke away from the line at the river bank and dove into the river to cross over into the village. Some of them grabbed canoes that were resting on the bank behind the village and began to ferry their comrades across.[492] Others proceeded into the village setting it on fire and advancing to the back of the barricade.[493]

> **Menawa took a small group of warriors and ran through the battle to find the first chief of the Oakfuskee and slew him on the spot.**

Sensing that this was the moment the Red Sticks would fall, Jackson ordered a charge from the front while the barricade was being attacked from behind. Jackson later described his troops at this moment.

"Never were men better disposed for such an undertaking than those by whom it was to be effected. They had entreated to be lead (sic) to the charge with the most pressing importunity and received the order which was now given with the strongest demonstration of joy."[494]

Menawa then realized the Red Sticks were being viciously attacked from the rear and the village had been set afire despite their false faith in the first chief's prophesy that the attack would come from the direction of the barricade. Amidst the chaos, he took a small group of warriors and ran through the battle to find the first chief of the Oakfuskee and slew him on the spot. Then, he gathered his closest Red Stick warriors about him and went to meet the Americans who were now storming over the barricade at the front and waded into their midst battling hand-to-hand.

Among those who stormed over the barricade in Jackson's infantry was another well-known figure to later history. A young third lieutenant named Sam Houston was wounded twice during the Battle of Horseshoe Bend.[495]

The entire battle lasted about five hours, but the killing continued until night time. In the morning, the river bank was strewn everywhere with the dead.[496] The Americans counted 557 Red Sticks lying dead on the ground. They estimated that another few hundred were killed and had been swept under by the Tallapoosa. Two-hundred fifty Indians were taken prisoner. All were women and children except for three.

---

[492] Letter from Coffee to Jackson, April 1, 1814
[493] Letter from Jackson to Mrs. Jackson, April 1, 1814
[494] Letter from Jackson to Blount, April 1, 1814
[495] Sam Houston Memorial Museum
[496] Letter from Jackson to Pinkney, March 28th, 1814

Many of the dead were killed by Gen. Coffee and his men as they tried to escape out the rear of the barricade. Jackson estimated that no more than 20 Red Stick warriors escaped alive.[497] Sixteen more Red Sticks were killed the next day when they were found hiding in the water under the river bank. The Army's final death count was 850 Red Sticks.[498] Among Jackson's force, there were 25 killed and 106 wounded.[499]

> Menawa was wounded by seven balls before he finally fell to the ground.

According to the Red Sticks in later accounts, the number who escaped was closer to 70 warriors of the total of 1,000 who had been in the battle.[500]

Three of the Red Sticks principal leaders were killed in the battle including the first chief of the Oakfuskee slain by Menawa and another chief named Monashee who had spoken strongly and convincingly against the Americans. Jackson took pleasure in noting in one of his letters that Monashee had received a grapeshot to the mouth thereby closing it for good. Grapeshot are iron balls that are fired from a cannon in a bunch.[501]

McIntosh showed himself well enough in the battle to get a mention in one of Jackson's accounts; "Major McIntosh, (the Cowetau) who joined my army with a part of his tribe, greatly distinguished himself." [502]

---

[497] Letter from Jackson to Pinkney, March 28th, 1814
[498] Letter from Jackson to Pinkney, March 28th, 1814
[499] Letter from Jackson to Pinkney, March 28th, 1814
[500] McKenny, Thomas & Hall, James & Todd, Hatherly & Todd, Joseph. (1872) History of the Indian tribes of North America: with biographical sketches and anecdotes of the principal chiefs., Philadelphia: D. Rice & Co.
[501] Letter from Jackson to Blount, April 1, 1814
[502] Letter from Jackson to Pinkney, March 28th, 1814

A Charge is Called in the Battle of Horseshoe Bend[503]

[503] Illustrations by Chulsan Um

Amazingly, Menawa, though he fought viciously in the thick of the battle, survived the ordeal. Meeting the Americans face-to-face as they stormed over the barricade, Menawa was wounded by seven balls before he finally fell to the ground. He awoke several hours later bleeding profusely on the ground yet still clutching his gun to his chest.

The bulk of the action had ceased, and the light of day was fading. He still heard intermittent shots being fired. He slowly rose to a sitting position and was confronted by a soldier who was inspecting the dead. Each man raised his rifle, and the two fired almost simultaneously. Menawa killed the soldier but received another wound as the bullet passed through his cheek near the ear and out the other side of his face taking out several of his teeth. He fell back once again unconscious but remained alive. He could feel the Americans walking over his body as they continued to search among the dead and night fell.[504]

Later that night, he awoke after full darkness feeling somewhat revived. He crawled over the bodies to the river bank and found a canoe there that he quietly entered. By rolling side to side while lying on the bottom, he slowly dislodged it from the bank and floated downriver. The canoe eventually reached the swamp at Elkahatchee where several women and children had been waiting since before the battle. Seeing the canoe approach, they pulled it to the shore and found their mangled chief lying unconscious in the bottom barely alive.

> **Menawa never returned to Horseshoe Bend on the Tallapoosa. It was said that he believed it to be haunted.**

Menawa was brought to a rendezvous point in the swamp where the survivors of the battle had chosen to meet should things go awry. For the next three days, the surviving Red Sticks held a secret council where they considered what to do next. During this time, they neither ate nor drank nor dressed their wounds. After three days, it was decided that each of them would return home and admit defeat. All of them surrendered to the Americans except Menawa who was still too badly wounded to travel.

When Menawa was finally able to travel, he returned home to a cold greeting in Oakfuskee. His village had been burned to the ground. Everything he owned had been taken away.

---

[504] McKenny, Thomas & Hall, James & Todd, Hatherly & Todd, Joseph. (1872) History of the Indian tribes of North America: with biographical sketches and anecdotes of the principal chiefs., Philadelphia: D. Rice & Co.

Menawa never returned to Horseshoe Bend on the Tallapoosa. It was said that he believed it to be haunted. Undoubtedly, he was indeed haunted by his memories of the place.[505]

The Creeks were then forced to sign Treaty of Fort Jackson in 1814 ending the Red Stick War. Benjamin Hawkins was there representing the Federal Government during the negotiations, but Andrew Jackson took over completely. Though he was supported by McIntosh and his Creeks in the war, Jackson was determined to remove any of the remaining power base of the entire Creek Confederacy. Upper Creeks and Lower Creeks together were forced to give up two-thirds of their remaining territory. Twenty-two million acres of Creek Land was ceded to the United States including a huge tract of Southern Georgia that was Lower Creek territory. The Creeks still had possession of most of the land west of the Ocmulgee River and north of what had been lost by the Treaty of Fort Jackson.[506]

Benjamin Hawkins protested before the signing of the Treaty that the border and the terms were too harsh and punished both factions of the Creeks even though many had supported the Americans against the Red Sticks. He was literally pushed aside from the table by Andrew Jackson.[507] Not long after the signing of the Treaty of Fort Jackson, Benjamin Hawkins resigned his post as Creek agent on February 15, 1815.[508]

Jackson closes a letter to Major Gen. Pinkney in 1814 saying "The Power of the Creeks is I think forever broken."[509] And in this, he was largely correct. The Upper Creek towns were now all destroyed. Their followers were scattered. Over the next several years, thousands of Red Stick followers fled to join the Seminoles to the south and continue resistance to the Americans. Others fled to Lower Creek towns like Coweta, Cusseta and Tuckabatchee where they admitted defeat and joined the Lower Creeks. Many others drifted back into the Decatur area and settled in Buzzard's Roost or Sandtown.[510]

---

[505] McKenny, Thomas & Hall, James & Todd, Hatherly & Todd, Joseph. (1872) History of the Indian tribes of North America: with biographical sketches and anecdotes of the principal chiefs., Philadelphia: D. Rice & Co.
[506] Stock, Melissa, University of West Georgia (2007), William McIntosh, New Georgia Encyclopedia
[507] Etheridge, Robbie; (2003) Creek Country, University of North Carolina Press
[508] Stock, Melissa, University of West Georgia (2007), William McIntosh, New Georgia Encyclopedia
[509] Letter from Jackson to Pinkney, March 28th, 1814
[510] Etheridge, Robbie; (2003) Creek Country, University of North Carolina Press

CHAPTER 12:
THE KILLING OF WILLIAM McINTOSH

The First Treaty of Indian Springs Gave Decatur from the Creeks to Georgia

The Red Stick War not only took away the Creeks' land and power but also swayed much of the American public sentiment against them. The Federal policy of assimilation over expulsion continued to weaken in the view of the public while the state's case for expulsion had strengthened.

In the compact of 1802 that followed the Yazoo Land Fraud, it was stipulated "that the United States shall, at their own expenses, extinguish, for the use of Georgia, as early as the same can be peaceably effected, on reasonable terms, the Indian title to the lands within the forks of the Oconee and Oakmulgee rivers, &c. &c.; and that the United States shall, in the same manner, also, extinguish the Indian title to all the other lands within the state of Georgia."

Despite more recent progress through the Treaty of Fort Jackson, Georgia was increasingly and openly critical of the Federal Government's progress in fulfilling this promise. The United States responded and redoubled efforts toward delivering the rest of what is now Georgia and Alabama. The Federal Government's primary partner in pushing forward a new round of agreements was William McIntosh.

> The 1821 Treaty of Indian Springs gave half of the land remaining to the Lower Creeks over to the Americans including Decatur.

Negotiating primarily with McIntosh and Tustunnugee Hopoie, another chief of the Lower Creeks, the Federal agents first tried to get the Creeks to cede land to the north of the Chattahoochee. They wanted to create a buffer of US land between the Cherokees and the Creeks to discourage an alliance between the Indian groups.

Cessions of Indian Land in Georgia[511]

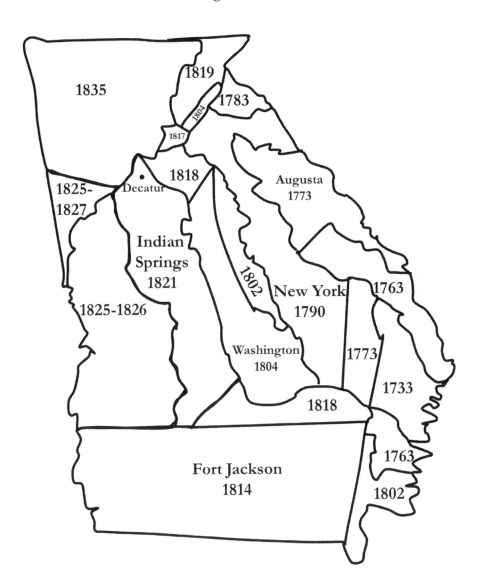

---

[511] Sketch by the author based on several sources

They also sought restitution for complaints settlers had lodged for stolen property (including runaway slaves) and destruction and asked that Creeks who had lived on land that was already ceded to the United States be relocated west of the Mississippi. The Creeks agreed to none of these terms but still agreed to sell another enormous tract of Georgia land to the United States.[512]

The land on which Decatur is located was officially given over to the United States by the Creeks in Indian Springs, Georgia, the plantation owned by William McIntosh about 50 miles south of Decatur, on January 8, 1821.[513] The 1821 Treaty of Indian Springs sold half of the land remaining to the Lower Creeks over to the Americans, approximately 6,700 square miles including Decatur. It included all the land between the Ocmulgee River and the Flint River and south of roughly where Alpharetta, Georgia is now.[514]

Under the terms of the agreement, the United States would pay the Creeks $10,000 at signing and $40,000 more when the treaty was ratified. The US government would also pay a total of $200,000 in various annual payments over the next 14 years. The parties also agreed that $250,000 would be paid to Georgia claimants as restitution for stolen and damaged property. McIntosh was personally paid $40,000 for arranging the treaty.[515]

The treaty also included a stipulation that if the boundary should "strike the Chattahoochee below the Creek village of Buzzard's Roost, there shall be a set aside made to leave the village 1 mile within the Creek Nation. There were more carve-outs of land for the Creeks of 1,000 acres around Indian Springs, a tract around the Creek agency that would be given to the United States when the agency was removed and 640 acres on the west bank of the Ocmulgee that belonged to Chief William McIntosh. This land is now a state park called McIntosh Reserve about 50 miles west of Decatur where the chief is now buried.[516]

Some years earlier, after the death of Andrew McGillivray, the Creeks had set down a law in the town of Broken Arrow that no more land could be sold to the United States on behalf of the Creeks without the full consent of the National Council. However, since the land that was given to the United States in the treaty of 1821 all belonged to the Lower Creeks and the two Creek leaders who had negotiated the treaty were the leaders of the Lower Creeks (McIntosh and Tustunnugee Hopoie), the National Council agreed to give its consent and the treaty was ratified. Now that nearly all the Creek land in

[512] Garrett; Franklin M. (1969) Atlanta and Environs: A Chronicle of Its People and Events, Volume 1; University of Georgia Press
[513] Maloney, Christopher (2011) Treaty of Indian Springs (1821), Encyclopedia of Alabama
[514] Maloney, Christopher (2011) Treaty of Indian Springs (1821), Encyclopedia of Alabama
[515] Maloney, Christopher (2011) Treaty of Indian Springs (1821), Encyclopedia of Alabama
[516] Maloney, Christopher (2011) Treaty of Indian Springs (1821), Encyclopedia of Alabama

Georgia belonged to the United States, the Creek National council was adamant that no more land should be handed over.[517]

The Second Treaty of Indian Springs Sealed the Fate of William McIntosh

In 1825, two agents of the Federal Government, Duncan G. Campbell and James Meriwether, were sent to the South to settle the Creek issue once and for all by procuring a final treaty that would give the remainder of Creek land to the United States in exchange for land west of the Mississippi River. The two agents first visited the National Council in 1825 to plead their case.[518]

Menawa, after being nearly killed in the Battle of Horseshoe Bend, had reemerged as an influential force on the Creek National Council. After recovering from his injuries in the secret hiding place in the Elkahatchee swamp along the Tallapoosa and returning home to find his village burned, Menawa had reassembled those who were left of the Oakfuskee and taken his place on the council as their chief.

He continued to oppose any attempts by the Americans to gain control of Creek lands. When the two agents came seeking a new treaty, Menawa was among those who vehemently opposed it, and the agents were sent away with no agreement.[519]

From there, the two agents went to visit William McIntosh and tried their best to achieve the same success the United States had just had with him in the Treaty of 1821. Another meeting was set at McIntosh's plantation in Indian Springs. Very few of the Creeks from the Upper Towns were present at the meeting which should have stopped the negotiations.[520]

McIntosh knew adequate participation from Upper Creek leaders would be necessary to any hope of having the treaty ratified by the Creek National Council but agreed to meet with the agents anyway.

Among the few Upper Creeks who attended was the chief of the Tuckabatchee (either the Chief Big Warrior or Opthle Yoholo),[521] one of the more powerful towns. Instead of agreeing once the proposal was laid out, this chief stood and said,

---

[517] McKenny, Thomas & Hall, James & Todd, Hatherly & Todd, Joseph. (1872) History of the Indian tribes of North America: with biographical sketches and anecdotes of the principal chiefs., Philadelphia: D. Rice & Co.
[518] Christina Snyder, University of Pennsylvania (2008); Encyclopedia of Alabama; Treaty of Indian Springs (1825)
[519] Christina Snyder, University of Pennsylvania (2008); Encyclopedia of Alabama; Treaty of Indian Springs (1825)
[520] McKenny, Thomas & Hall, James & Todd, Hatherly & Todd, Joseph. (1872) History of the Indian tribes of North America: with biographical sketches and anecdotes of the principal chiefs., Philadelphia: D. Rice & Co.
[521] Haveman, Christopher (2008) Opthle Yoholo, Encyclopedia of Alabama

Portrait of William McIntosh[522]

Mark Pifer

"You asked us to sell you more lands at Broken Arrow; we told you we had none to spare. I told McIntosh then, that he knew no land could be sold except in full council and by consent of the nation. We have met here at a very short notice. Only a few chiefs are present from the upper towns and many are absent from the lower towns. That is all the talk I have to make, and I shall go home."

With that, he departed.[523]

McIntosh's confidence wavered and was on the verge of calling off the meetings. The federal agents spoke with him in private and upon their assurances that he would have the full protection of the United States, the meeting resumed. The 1825 Treaty of Indian Springs was signed by all those still present. The treaty gave all remaining Creek land in Georgia to the United States. McIntosh and his follow ers each received $200,000 right away with further payments to occur once removal of the Creeks had begun. They each also received land in present-day Oklahoma, the location of the Creek Reservation. McIntosh was given permanent rights to Indian Springs, his plantation along the Chattahoochee River South of Decatur.[524]

Among those who signed the treaty were three chiefs from Sandtown, the Creek town just outside Decatur on the Chattahoochee. These were Konope Emautla, Chawacala Mico and Foctalustee Emaulta.[525] One of these chiefs appears to have also signed the 1821 Treaty of Indian Springs, Chawacala Mico, whose name is spelled Chaughle Micco on that treaty. Creek names, as they had no written language, had various spellings.[526]

The Trial and Conviction of William McIntosh

News of the signing of this treaty went off like a bombshell to the Creek Council. Menawa was once again at the forefront in condemning the actions of his old enemy McIntosh. The punishment for signing a treaty on behalf of the Creeks without the consent of the National Council carried the death penalty. The council met and

The council met and quickly tried and convicted McIntosh of breaking this law and issued a death sentence.

[523] McKenny, Thomas & Hall, James & Todd, Hatherly & Todd, Joseph. (1872) History of the Indian tribes of North America: with biographical sketches and anecdotes of the principal chiefs., Philadelphia: D. Rice & Co.
[524] Kane, Robert (2016), Second Creek War; Encyclopedia of Alabama
[525] (1825) Treaty with the Creeks, Indian Affairs: Laws and Treaties, Volume II, Treaties
[526] Indian Affairs: Laws and Treaties, Volume II, Treaties. Treaty with the Creeks, 1825

quickly tried and convicted McIntosh of breaking this law and issued his death sentence.[527]

The council then chose Menawa to issue the sentence. Somewhat surprisingly, Menawa at first refused and asked the council to choose someone who had less personal involvement in the matter. The council prevailed upon him, and Menawa agreed. He was soon leading a band of 100 of his Oakfuskee braves on the warpath to Indian Springs. They were also instructed to kill any of the other Creek chiefs found there who had participated in the fraudulent treaty. They arrived in Indian Springs just before dawn on April 30, 1825, only a little over two months after the signing of the infamous treaty.[528]

Surrounding McIntosh's house, Menawa called to those inside, "Let the white people who are in this house come out! And so, will the women and children! We come not to injure them! McIntosh has broken the law made by himself, and we have come to kill him for it!"[529]

The Americans who were inside then came out and were allowed to leave. Among them, McIntosh's son Chilly McIntosh slipped by unnoticed. His name was also on the death warrant issued by the Creek National Council as one of those who had signed the Treaty but being small and of mixed ancestry, he was able to pass himself off as a white child. Only two people remained in the house--William McIntosh and Eotmie Tustennuggee, the two Lower Creeks most responsible for the treaty.[530]

> **McIntosh and Tustennuggee were smoked out and upon appearing at the front door were torn down in a hail of bullets.**

Menawa and his warriors then set the house on fire. McIntosh and Tustennuggee were smoked out. Upon appearing at the front door, both were torn down in a hail of bullets. They both died there in the doorway.

Both of William McIntosh's sons-in-law, Samuel Hawkins and Benjamin Hawkins Jr., were also on the death warrant for their participation in the treaty.

[527] McKenny, Thomas & Hall, James & Todd, Hatherly & Todd, Joseph. (1872) History of the Indian tribes of North America: with biographical sketches and anecdotes of the principal chiefs., Philadelphia: D. Rice & Co.
[528] McKenny, Thomas & Hall, James & Todd, Hatherly & Todd, Joseph. (1872) History of the Indian tribes of North America: with biographical sketches and anecdotes of the principal chiefs., Philadelphia: D. Rice & Co.
[529] McKenny, Thomas & Hall, James & Todd, Hatherly & Todd, Joseph. (1872) History of the Indian tribes of North America: with biographical sketches and anecdotes of the principal chiefs., Philadelphia: D. Rice & Co.
[530] McKenny, Thomas & Hall, James & Todd, Hatherly & Todd, Joseph. (1872) History of the Indian tribes of North America: with biographical sketches and anecdotes of the principal chiefs., Philadelphia: D. Rice & Co.

Samuel was found later that day and hanged. Benjamin Jr. was fired upon and wounded but escaped.[531]

It appeared that Menawa had the final revenge upon McIntosh. The history that soon followed would show this to be a very hollow and short-lived victory indeed.

Four days after the McIntosh home was burned, his daughter, Jane Hawkins, and widow of Samuel Hawkins wrote a letter to the two agents of the Second Treaty of Indian Springs, Duncan Campbell and James Meriwether describing what had happened and begging for their assistance.

---

[531] McKenny, Thomas & Hall, James & Todd, Hatherly & Todd, Joseph. (1872) History of the Indian tribes of North America: with biographical sketches and anecdotes of the principal chiefs., Philadelphia: D. Rice & Co.

The Death of William McIntosh[532]

[532] Illustrations by Chulsan Um

Jane Hawkin's Letter Describing the Death of William McIntosh

May 4, 1825

"Col. Campbell and Major Meriwether,

My dear friends, I send you this paper, which will not tell you a lie, but if it had 10 tongues, it could not tell all the truth. On the morning of the 30th of April at break of day, my Father's house was surrounded by a party of hostile Indians to the number of several hundred who instantly fired his dwelling and murdered him and Thomas Tustunnuggee by shooting more the family no clothes (some not one rag) nor provision. Brother Chilly was at Father's and made his escape through a window under cover of a traveling white man who obtained leave for them to come out that way. It being not yet light, he was not discovered. While those hostiles were murdering my beloved father, they were tying my husband Col. Sam Hawkins with cords, to wait the arrival of Stockchunga Thloccocosconicco and Munnauca who were the commanders at Tatler to give orders for the other execution also which took place about three o'clock the same day, and these barbarous men not content with spilling the blood of both my husband and father to atone for their constant friendship to both your nation and our own, refused my hand the painful privilege of covering his body up in the very ground which he lately defended against those hostile murderers and drove me from my home, stript of my two best friends in one day, stript of all my property, my provisions and my clothing with a more painful reflection than these that the body of my poor murdered husband should remain unburied to be devoured by the birds and the beasts, was ever poor woman worse off than I?

I have this moment arrived among our white friends, who altho they are very kind, have but little to bestow on me and my poor helpless infant, who must suffer before any aid can reach us from you but I can live a great while ono very little, besides the confidence I have on you and your government. For I know by your promise, you will aid and defend us as soon as you hear from our situation. These murderers are the very same hostile who treated the with 10 years ago as they have now treated my husband and father, who say they are determined to kill all who had any hand in selling the land and when they have completed the work of murdering, burning, plundering and destruction, they will send the president word that they have saved their land and taken it back and he and the white people never shall have it again which is the order of the heads of the nation, by the advice of the agent.

We expect that many of our best friends are already killed but have not heard by reason of the water (Chattahoochee River) being too high for word to go quick, which is the only reason Co. Miller and other on his of the river were not killed.

We are in a dreadful condition, and I don't think there will be one ear of corn made in this part of the nation, for the whole of the friendly party have fled to DeKalb and Fayette County, two (sic) much alarmed to return to their homes to get a little grain of what corn they left for themselves and their families to subsist on, much more to stay at home to make more and we fear every day that what little provision we left will be destroyed. I am agreed you will think I make it worse of itself than any pen can write, my condition admits of no equal and mock me when I try to speak of it, after I was stript of my last frock but one humanity and duty called on me to pull it and spread it over the body of my dead husband (which was allowed no other covering) which I did as a farewell witness of my affection. I was 25 miles from any friend (but sister Catherine who was with me) and had to say all night in the woods surrounded by a thousand hostile Indians who were constantly insulting and affrighting us. And now I am here with only one old coat to my back and not a morsel of bread to save us from perishing, or a rag of a blanket to cover my poor little boy from the sun at noon or the dew at night, and I am a poor distracted orphan and widow.

Jane Hawking

PS: If you think proper, I wish this to be published. [533]

JH"

[533] Garrett; Franklin M. (1969) Atlanta and Environs: A Chronicle of Its People and Events, Volume 1; University of Georgia Press p. 49

The Creek Civil War Erupted into Violence in Five Points in 1825

Following the executions at Indian Springs, the state of Georgia was thrown once again into alarm that the Creeks were rising (hence the saying, "God willing and the Creek don't rise."). A violent confrontation erupted between the Lower Creeks and some of the Upper Creeks who had migrated to the Decatur area after the Red Stick War and taken up residence around Sandtown and Standing Peachtree. The battle occurred at Walton Springs, near the intersection of Indian trails that became Five Points in downtown Atlanta. A description of it appeared in the Atlanta Constitution in 1869.

"Two factions occupied enemy camps, one at Walton Springs, near what is now Spring Street and Carnegie Way, the other where the Union Station would be built. In the summer of 1825, fueled by liquor they purchased with animal skins in Decatur, the two groups began trading insults and blows. The fighting progressed to knives, tomahawks and guns. For more than two hours, the virgin forest rang with the clangor of arms and demoniac yells of drunken and infuriated savages.

The fight culminated in a battle in a grove of oak trees on Alabama, between Whitehall and Pryor (the Sandtown trail and the current location between Peachtree Fountains Plaza and Underground Atlanta). The carnival of death went on until every actor in the tragic scene was disemboweled, or rendered utterly helpless, while in the adjacent thicket were scattered the dead and the dying who were engaged in the fight. The whole numbering not less than fifty, which was probably the entire combative strength of the two factions."[534]

The Treaty of Washington Replaced the Second Treaty of Indian Springs

In the wake of the disastrous Second Treaty of Indian Springs, the Creek chiefs, led by Opthle Yoholo and including Menawa, went in another delegation to Washington to declare this treaty was unlawful. They were successful, at least at first. The US government nullified the treaty on January 24, 1826 because it did not have the support of the National Council of Creeks.

In its place, the Treaty of Washington was negotiated. Menawa was a primary negotiator in the terms along with other of the principal chiefs of the Creeks. Realizing the inevitability of removal, the Creeks agreed to cede all Creek land in Georgia to the United States with the exception of 3 million acres in Alabama. The Creeks would retain all their land until January 1, 1827.[535]

---

[534] Price 89Author Unknown, June 7, 1931, Indian War Near Five Points, Atlanta Journal Magazine, pg 27, reprinted from the Atlanta Daily New Era, August 1, 1869)

[535] McKenny, Thomas & Hall, James & Todd, Hatherly & Todd, Joseph. (1872) History of the Indian tribes of North America: with biographical sketches and anecdotes of the principal chiefs., Philadelphia: D. Rice & Co.

Unfortunately, the Creek land rights set down in the Treaty of Washington were ultimately ineffectual.[536] Settlers continued to ignore Creek land rights in Georgia and Alabama and in many cases, defrauded Creeks out of their land. With the Treaty of Washington, most of the Creek chiefs, including Menawa had agreed to a final peace and never again opposed the United States. There was not a final peace with the Creeks.[537]

Georgia and Governor Troup, William McIntosh's cousin, refused to recognize the Treaty of Washington and announced that he planned to proceed with the Land Lottery that would distribute the land gained in the Second Treaty of Indian Springs to Georgia settlers. President John Quincy Adams attempted to enforce the authority of the Federal Government and even threatened to intervene by bringing US troops down to Georgia. Governor Troup called his bluff and began to raise the Georgia Militia. Adams backed down and the lottery proceeded.[538]

Has History Treated William McIntosh Fairly?

It's painful to see the division among the Creeks that resulted in Menawa and McIntosh facing off on opposite sides of the Red Stick War and the eventual death of McIntosh. Each of them supported opposing viewpoints in how to deal with the Americans that were ultimately each irrelevant. The results, either way, were unavoidable. The Americans and to be sure the Georgians, were going to take the land from the Creeks and impose their own culture and government under either plan-- assimilation or removal.

The mere notion of creating treaties with the United States and buying their land from them represents assimilation and the Creeks were falling victim to one of the same conflicts that led to the American Civil War. The Federal Government's opinion about how to deal with the Indians was very different from that of the states. Each felt they had the more legitimate right to decide

> Overall, I believe the driving force in William McIntosh's mind was probably family honor.

how to deal with the conflict. In various treaties, the US government tried to at least recognize that the Creeks had certain rights, and the states should abide by these rights as set down in federal treaties. However, the states and their citizens did not feel these rights were valid and acted as they saw fit. Settlers in

---

[536] Kane, Robert (2016) Second Creek War; Encyclopedia of Alabama
[537] McKenny, Thomas & Hall, James & Todd, Hatherly & Todd, Joseph. (1872) History of the Indian tribes of North America: with biographical sketches and anecdotes of the principal chiefs., Philadelphia: D. Rice & Co.
[538] (1970) Early DeKalb County History, prepared by and Furnished as a service of the DeKalb Chamber of Commerce

Georgia were unapologetic for taking land that had been set aside as belonging to the Indians.

Under these circumstances, there wasn't any hope that the approach supported by Menawa to hold the line and never give more land to the Americans was ever going to work. This became especially true after Andrew Jackson became President in 1829. With his election, the attitude of the Federal Government drastically swung from assimilation to expulsion.

For many people familiar with the story, the name William McIntosh is now infamous in Native American history and Georgia history for being the man who allowed himself to be bribed into giving away the last of the Creek land in Georgia and the chief who took up arms against his brethren, the Creeks. I can see this point of view but in all, I don't think it's a fair one.

First, the Creek confederacy was an agreement between many different groups of Indians to act on each other's behalf. Many of these groups never saw eye-to-eye for a long, long time before they came into contact with Europeans. The notion that he betrayed his own blood is not completely accurate or if it is, then betrayal of blood was a common practice among the Creeks.

Second, McIntosh passionately supported assimilation his entire life, and he had defended that commitment with his life. He loses a lot of credibility when it is pointed out that the Governor of Georgia was McIntosh's cousin, that he was given personal payments for brokering Creek treaties and that he owned large pieces of land and slaves, but Creek family ties among the Americans were common during this period because of interrelationships fostered mainly by traders and these other practices were common among other Creek leaders, especially among those tied by kinship to white America including Menawa.

Lastly, it's fair to point out that McIntosh's view may have been correct. I don't think assimilation ever had any chance of working and allowing the Creeks to remain among the Americans as US citizens, but it was certainly more possible to have succeeded than opposition of a much more organized nation with superior weapons and resources that was clearly growing well beyond the population of the Creeks. McIntosh was also descended from Scotsman. It's not difficult to envision how he would have likened the Creek situation in America with the history of the Scots in their relationship with England.

Who was William McIntosh? He was an Indian with strong roots in a powerful Creek clan. He was an American with strong roots going back before the revolution. To many Creeks, he was a traitor. To many other Creeks, he was visionary leader. And to many Americans, he was a patriot. He was a contrarian. He was also a collaborator.

Overall, I believe the driving force in William McIntosh's mind was probably family honor. He came from a long line of luminaries in US and Georgia history. Other relatives had reached higher stations in life during their lifetime. He saw the situation with the Creeks as the moment for which he was born and would create his legacy in history. He would be the man who consolidated Georgia into one union, an American union in which he hoped he could live and the Creek people could live as well, as Americans.

Ultimately, this dream of McIntosh's was not to be and there was little hope for it under any circumstances. Menawa and the Red Sticks removed any possibility that the Creeks would join with the Americans to be one country and gave Andrew Jackson the political support he needed to exile all Creeks from the South including both the Upper Creeks led in part by Menawa and the Lower Creeks led by McIntosh.

McIntosh accepted exorbitant personal payments and parcels of land in exchange for selling off Creek land to America. Some of this land, he had no right to sell. He also constructed a vision for the survival of his people that was similar to that of Benjamin Hawkins and Thomas Jefferson. He bravely fought for that vision at great personal risk, including taking up arms to achieve it, and he ultimately paid with his life. I can't say whether William McIntosh was a visionary, a scoundrel or both.

> I can't say whether William McIntosh was a visionary, a scoundrel or both.

William McIntosh is now buried at McIntosh Reserve in Carroll County, on the land that had been set aside for him in the Second Treaty of Indian Springs. A large, granite boulder under a tree marks the grave and a granite gravestone was added later. A nearby bronze plate was erected by the William McIntosh Chapter of the Daughters of the American Revolution in 1921.

"To the Memory and Honor of Gen. William McIntosh, 1778 – 1825. In 1905, the distinguished and patriotic son of Georgia whose devotion was heroic, whose friendship was unselfish and whose service was valiant, who negotiated the Treaty between the Creek Indians and the State for all lands lying west of the Flint River, who sacrificed his life for his patriotism."[539]

---

[539] Garrett; Franklin M. (1969) Atlanta and Environs: A Chronicle of Its People and Events, Volume 1; University of Georgia Press pg 50

The Final Resting Place of William McIntosh[540]

CHAPTER 13:
SANDTOWN AND STANDING PEACHTREE

I had a short list of questions I wanted to try to answer when I started thinking about writing this book. At the top of that list, there was a challenge: To confirm that Indians were living in Decatur and the nearby areas around Decatur continuously all the way up to removal and the Trail of Tears in the later 1830s --longer than most people generally think.

When I started doing some initial research and asking about the history of the Indians living in the area before the city was founded, I was told that Decatur was in a "buffer zone" between the Cherokees and the Creeks and that it was "only used as hunting grounds." This was disappointing, but I now know enough to say that both of those statements are false.

These two phrases were a direct quote from Vivian Price's excellent book about the History of DeKalb County. They were not meant to imply that the area was desolate of Indians. In fact, as was discussed earlier in this book, the Decatur area was well populated by early people. Known and confirmed Indian history in Decatur goes back at least four thousand years and there were very probably people living in the area much earlier than that.

The comment about a "buffer zone"[541] refers to a later period after the Yamasee War in 1715 when many of the Creeks were migrating to the west from the Ocmulgee toward the Flint and the Chattahoochee. There were Creeks living in the area and along the Chattahoochee and near Utoy Creek and Peachtree Creek this whole time.

If Standing Peachtree is the Indian settlement that eventually became Atlanta, then I think it's fair to say Sandtown is the Indian settlement that spawned Decatur.

The divisions of the Upper and Lower Creeks became much more apparent after the Yamasee war – the Upper Creeks who lived along the Tallapoosa in Alabama and the Lower Creeks who mostly lived on the Chattahoochee. However, there are no Creek towns identified on the maps from that time in

---

[541] Price, Vivian (1997) History of DeKalb County, Georgia, 1822-1900; Wolfe Pub. Co. Pg. 31

the Decatur area. The nearest Lower Creek town on the Chattahoochee is the town called "Chattahoochee" about 65 miles to the south.

An Aerial View North Over Buzzard's Roost Toward Utoy Creek[542]

The two large Creek towns in the area were Sandtown and Standing Peachtree. There has been a lot more attention paid to the history of Standing Peachtree than Sandtown, probably because it has so much to do with the founding of Atlanta and the naming of several parts of the city. Peachtree Road is literally the Peachtree Trail, so named because it ran to the town of Standing Peachtree. If Standing Peachtree is the Indian settlement that eventually became Atlanta then, I think it's fair to say that Sandtown is the Indian settlement that spawned Decatur.

Sandtown is in fact much older and richer in history than Standing Peachtree. The primary trail that runs through Decatur ran straight to this old Creek village and many of the people who passed through the area all the way through its founding were coming to trade with the Indians who lived in Sandtown.

---

[542] Photo by the author

Sandtown was Occupied at Least as Far Back as 1,800 Years Ago

During archaeological work performed in Sandtown in 1938, two human skeletons were found, one seated upright, legs crossed, leaning against a stone slab, arms crossed at the wrists. However, there is not a lot of additional information from this excavation.[543] At one time, a village that contained several mounds existed exactly where Six Flags Over Georgia is now located. Mounds are a feature of the Indians who lived in the Southeast around 2,000 years ago. Unfortunately, we will never know the age of this site because it was destroyed when Six Flags Over Georgia was constructed in 1967 without being studied.

In the furor of public outrage that followed the destruction of this site, a dig was funded at Sandtown on the east bank of the Chattahoochee River just north of Utoy Creek. However, the beginning of this dig led to the discovery of a more pristine and possibly much older site on the other side of Utoy Creek. This site, dubbed 9FU14, was found to date back to the early Woodland to Middle Woodland period.[544] It was a village of 25 structures that seem to be houses except for one much larger one that was probably a ceremonial house. Radiocarbon dating put the age of this village at 1,800 years. A similar site was excavated on the grounds of Pebblebrook High School a little farther north.[545]

The Name "Sandtown" Comes from the Hilibi Creeks

The next clue about when the Sandtown area was occupied has to do with the origin of its name and when that name is likely to have been established. Sandtown is a little unusual for having been one of the few places that was called by the same name among the Creeks and the Americans. The Creeks called the place Okthasasi and the translation for this word in Creek is "place where the sand is abundant." Ironically to its name, Sandtown is not at all sandy. It is made of the same Georgia red clay found across most of the area. The name was probably applied by Hilibi Indians who arrived from a town of that name in Alabama.[546]

The Hilibi group was one of the original 12 tribes that joined the Creek Confederacy. Before the arrival of the Europeans, these original 12 tribes were generally moving from west to east. Hilibi was a town of the Upper Creeks, but many of the towns of the Upper Creeks eventually moved as far

---

[543] Price, Vivian (1997) History of DeKalb County, Georgia, 1822-1900; Wolfe Pub. Co. pg 8
[544] Kelly, Arthur and Meier, Larry. (1969) A Pre-Agricultural Village Site in Fulton County, Georgia, Bulletin No. 11; Proceeding of the Southeastern Archaeological Conference
[545] Whites, Max E (2002) The Archaeology and History of the Native Georgia Tribes; University Press of Florida
[546] Price, Vivian (1997) History of DeKalb County, Georgia, 1822-1900; Wolfe Pub. Co.

Boat Rock Park was a Common Meeting Place Near Sandtown[547]

This boulder field in the Sandtown area of Atlanta is probably one of the main

reasons the Indians chose it as a place to settle as far back as 214AD.

---

[547] Photo by the author

east as the Ocmulgee. There is still a town in northwest Georgia called Hilibi Creek. The first mention of a town called Hilibi appears in the census lists of 1738 and 1750 (spelled Ylape). During other periods, it appeared in maps and historical descriptions along the Coosa River and near the Tallapoosa River.

Somewhere around this time, the name Buzzard's Roost became interchangeable with Sandtown. This name persists as the name of an island in the Chattahoochee at this location today as shown on the 1818 map on page 185.

It also appears that the name of Tuckabatchee was occasionally used in place of Standing Peachtree. Tuckabatchee is easily identified on the 1813 map on page 184. It then appears as Standing Peachtree on the 1818 map on page 185 and the 1839 map on page 186. As the tribe moved, it appeared that they may have also taken over the area of Sandtown sometime around the mid to late 1700s.

The town of Hilibi can be seen on the Tallapoosa River on the 1797 map on page 183 and on the Coosa River on the 1780 map on page 181. Buzzard's Roost appears on the Flint River on the 1795 map included on page 182. Then the name Buzzard's Roost moves to the location of Sandtown on the 1818 map on page 185 and as Sandtown on the 1839 map on page 186.

There Were Very Few Europeans Passing Through the Sandtown Area Before 1800

If the Hilibi were living in Sandtown in the 1700s, why does it not appear on any maps that were created by the English, Spanish or French as they were trying to establish closer relationships with the Creeks? I think it's possible it was overlooked. Little attention was initially paid to the Decatur area by the first Europeans to arrive in the New World. The earliest expeditions of the Spanish all traveled closer to the coast, up into the mountains and then west, bypassing the interior of Georgia along the upper Chattahoochee. No known Spanish expeditions ever travelled through the Decatur area.

The first Europeans in the Decatur area didn't arrive until around 1674 when Henry Woodward and other Carolina and Virginia traders began making contact with Indians living along the Chattahoochee and convinced them to begin trading and making slave raids, mainly against those Indians who were allied to the Spanish to the south.[548] There is really no reason to say the Sandtown area was not occupied during this time.

---

[548] Ethridge, Robbie (2002), English Trade in Deerskins and Indian Slaves, New Georgia Encyclopedia

By the end of the 17th century, the Spanish and the French had been driven out of what is now Georgia, and the closest English colony was Charles Town well to the north. The Indians were the only people in the area and kept no records of who was living where.[549]

Later, as trade was being established with the Spanish and the French, Sandtown was not on the principal trading route called the "Upper Path" that ran from Old Savannah Town near modern Augusta, to Coweta and Kashita towns near the head of the Ocmulgee River, then west across the upper reach of the Flint to Chattahoochee Town and then northwest to Oakfuskee on the upper part of the Tallapoosa.[550] This route is shown on the 1797 map shown on page 183. It is also shown on the map at the front of this book.

By the mid-1700s the Cherokees were arriving in the area that is now DeKalb County, pushed by the Iroquois to the north and other slave raiding tribes to the east around Savannah. There was a general migration of Indians in Georgia toward the south.[551] The Creeks all assembled in the later incarnation of Sandtown around 1800 as the Cherokees took over Standing Peachtree.

In 1793, there was one documented incident of violence between the Americans and Indians in the vicinity of Sandtown. Lt. John Axom O'Neal, Jr. who served the Wilkes County Militia and the Greene County Militia, was killed by two or three Coweta Indians seven miles north of Sandtown during the Oconee War while he was on an expedition to the Chattahoochee. The Oconee War was one of the early conflicts over land between the Americans and the Creeks. Lt. O'Neal is now buried in an unknown spot somewhere along the banks of the Chattahoochee River.[552]

Standing Peachtree Was the Other Indian Settlement Just Upriver from Sandtown

Just upriver from Sandtown was the connected village of Standing Peachtree at the confluence of Peachtree Creek and the Chattahoochee River. This town was first occupied between 1034 and 1154, almost 400 years before the first Europeans set foot on the America continent.[553]

---

[549] Price, Vivian (1997) History of DeKalb County, Georgia, 1822-1900; Wolfe Pub. Co.
[550] Southeast Archeological Center, The Creeks
[551] Ethridge, Robbie (2002), English Trade in Deerskins and Indian Slaves, New Georgia Encyclopedia
[552] (1793) Georgia Gazette, November 14th, 1793
[553] Price, Vivian (1997) History of DeKalb County, Georgia, 1822-1900; Wolfe Pub. Co.

The Spanish brought peaches to Georgia in the late 16th century. One of these peach trees evidently made its way to the Atlanta area at some point and became the basis for the naming standard of much of Atlanta.[554]

The first mention of Standing Peachtree was not until May 27, 1782, in a letter written by John Marten to Gen. Andrew Pickens that has been transcribed on page 105. It may also have been identified on a map in 1796 as the town labeled "Tuckabatchee" located on the "High T" trail (Hightower Trail) in the 1812 map shown on page 174.[555] It was first

> The Spanish brought peaches to Georgia around the late 16th century.

definitively identified as a Creek town by the Early map of 1818 shown on page 185.

There was also once a mound site at Standing Peachtree and a village. Each was mostly destroyed by the Atlanta Waterworks pumping station. Since it was a sprawling settlement with homes spread out over a wide area, it's very probable that there are still parts of it waiting to be studied in the vicinity of the Chattahoochee and Peachtree Creek. The village may have extended north of the pumping station as far as Nancy Creek. Eleven houses and more than 50 archaeological structures were identified in 1971 and 1973 that have been attributed to an early Cartersville occupation.[556][557]

As a result of both Treaties of Indian Springs and then the Treaty of Washington in 1826, the land on the south side of the Chattahoochee that belonged to the Creeks was ceded to the United States. The land on the north side remained under control of the Cherokees. This, of course, only lasted until Cherokee removal after the Treaty of New Echota in 1835. [558]

---

[554] Price, Vivian (1997) History of DeKalb County, Georgia, 1822-1900; Wolfe Pub. Co.
[555] Southeast Archeological Center, The Creeks
[556] Southeast Archeological Center
[557] Smith, Martin (1992) Historic Period Indian Archaeology of northern Georgia, University of Georgia Lab of Archaeology Series, Report Number 30
[558] Southeast Archeological Center, The Creeks e

Aerial View of the Location of Standing Peachtree[559]

James McConnell Montgomery, a Founding Settler of Atlanta and Decatur

One of the earliest settlers in the Decatur area was James McConnell Montgomery who also had much to do with the settlement of Standing Peachtree in the years before Decatur was founded. As early as 1814, Montgomery was living in the area and residing at Standing Peachtree.

In response to continued unrest among the Creek Indians during the early 19th century, the US government established a series of forts stringing together strategic locations in the frontier. These forts were intended to establish a supply line from Gen. Pinkney at Charles Town, South Carolina south to Brig. Gen. Floyd at Fort Mitchell at the Falls of the Chattahoochee and then Gen. Jackson at Columbus, Georgia. One of these stops in the supply line was intended to be Fort Peachtree at Standing Peachtree. Another was placed at Hog Mountain in Gwinnett County.[560]

A young James McConnell Montgomery was put under the command of George Rockingham Gilmer with 21 other soldiers, to establish the fort and put it in order as a boatyard and supply stop on the Chattahoochee River. He

---

[559] Photo by the author
[560] Price, Vivian (1997) History of DeKalb County, Georgia, 1822-1900; Wolfe Pub. Co. – pg. 42

had no idea at that time of the deep effects Standing Peachtree would have on the rest of his life.

Montgomery had served as a teamster with the Quartermaster Dept. under Gen. Floyd and was cited for his courage. He was commissioned a major of the 52nd Battalion on March 19, 1808.[561] He received the assignment to establish a boatyard at Standing Peachtree on February 18, 1814.[562]

As a detachment of soldiers, they were lightly equipped having only "a lot of flintlocks that nobody else wanted that had seen more service at the annual musters than at the firing line" and "some loose powder and a small quantity of unmolded lead for bullets."[563]

A compound consisting of a large log blockhouse, six dwellings and a storehouse was placed on the east side of the river opposite the creek. The fort was placed on the north side of Peachtree Creek and the boatyard on the south bank of the creek. They also built a bridge half a mile from the fort.

There were two minor incidents where the troops at Fort Peachtree were called into soldierly duty. In the first case, Cherokees came to the soldiers one night to inform them that a group of Creek warriors were on their way to attack the fort. Preparations were made and the soldiers lay in trenches ready for an attack that never came. The incident was probably fabricated by the Cherokees as an attempt to persuade the soldiers to abandon the area.

The second incident was a result of the American victory of Andrew Jackson over the Red Stick Creeks in the Battle of Horseshoe Bend. Captain Gilmer heard gunshots in the village of Standing Peachtree and called his soldiers to arms from their work cutting trees in the woods for lumber. As it turned out, the gunshots were a celebration by the Cherokees who had returned from the battle with 18 scalps that they were parading door-to-door on a pole.[564]

> As it turned out, the gunshots were a celebration by the Cherokees who had returned from the battle with 18 scalps that they were parading door-to-door on a pole.

---

[561] Price, Vivian (1997) History of DeKalb County, Georgia, 1822-1900; Wolfe Pub. Co.

[562] Price, Vivian (1997) History of DeKalb County, Georgia, 1822-1900; Wolfe Pub. Co. pg 43

[563] Price, Vivian (1997) History of DeKalb County, Georgia, 1822-1900; Wolfe Pub. Co. – pg. 42

[564] Franklin M. Garrett; (1969) Atlanta and Environs: A Chronicle of Its People and Events, Volume 1; University of Georgia Press

1812 Map of Georgia

The map below shows the town labeled "Tuckabatchee" on the Hightower Trail using the same labeling as the 1796 map. [565]

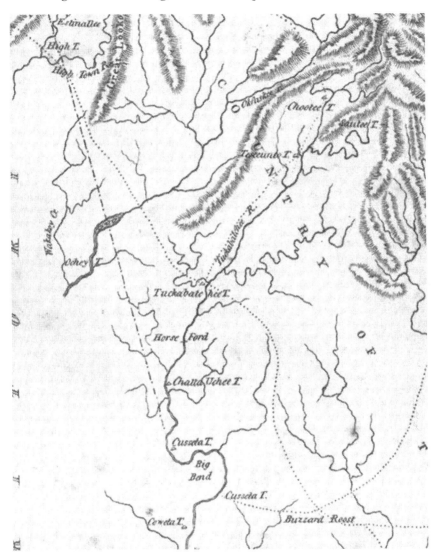

---

[565] Lewis, Samuel (1812), Thomas & Andrews

Overall, the establishment of the supply stop at Fort Peachtree was a failure. Only five of the intended 10 boats were built and these failed to stand up to the Chattahoochee's shoals and fell apart. The efforts at creating a boatyard were abandoned in May 1814 after just a few months of effort.

Montgomery left Fort Peachtree at that point, but he had fallen for the place and spent much of the rest of his life trying to find support to return there and establish it as a town. He wrote to Gen. Jackson on July 24, 1814 to request that he be able to stay on there to act as a supply agent and that the fort continue to be garrisoned.

A Replica of Fort Peachtree in Fort Peachtree Park[566]

"I would just state to you that this is a nice place in the Creek country and will no doubt be a convenient place for a public garrison. It is thought to be in the direction from Augusta and Milledgeville to Huntsville MS and Colo. Huger said would be kept up as a Sub. Agency or something of that kind. It is no doubt a very healthy place and has cost the Government not less than five thousand dollars and it appears like a pity to abandon it. However, as all trust rests with you, you can do which you think best. If a public stand was made there such as an Agency, or factory, I would be glad to have any appointment that you might think I merited at that place...."

ackson and Montgomery were acquainted with each other having both been born in Lancaster County, South Carolina, attended school together and served together in the Revolutionary War.

Montgomery wrote several letters to Jackson and most included requests for payment of his services. None of these were ever returned by Jackson. Montgomery wasn't paid until May 19, 1824 when the US Congress passed "An Act for the Relief of J.M.C. Montgomery."[567]

Montgomery Street: Named for James MC Montgomery[568]

Receiving no response or appointment at Standing Peachtree, Montgomery returned home to his farm in Jackson County and, always an ardent public servant, resumed his positions as sheriff, tax receiver, mail carrier and justice of the peace. His heart remained in Standing Peachtree, and he returned to it several times while it was still within Indian territory.

Once the land of Standing Peachtree became part of DeKalb County, Montgomery left the farm and returned to settle there around 1820 with his wife Nancy Farlow Montgomery and their 14 children. He became Postmaster of Standing Peachtree in 1825. He later ran a ferry on the Chattahoochee River, the namesake for Montgomery Ferry Drive in Atlanta. Montgomery's Ferry (later DeFoor's Ferry) was located at the present crossing of the Seaboard

[567] Price, Vivian (1997) History of DeKalb County, Georgia, 1822-1900; Wolfe Pub. Co. pg 74
[568] Photo by the author

Airline Railroad bridge.[569] He and Thomas Dobbs were county commissioners for Fayette County, and Montgomery also served as the first senator from DeKalb County.[570] He was also Clerk of the Court of the Ordinary in 1823 and helped with the census of 1830.

Montgomery died on October 6, 1842 and is buried with his wife in the Montgomery family cemetery near their Standing Peachtree homestead.[571] The Montgomery family cemetery is located on the west side of Marietta Blvd. a quarter of a mile South of Bolton Road.[572]

Sandtown Was Well Known to People in the Area When Decatur was Founded

By 1825, there was no question that Sandtown was a well-established Creek town that was big enough to have three of the Lower Creek leaders living there. Konope Emautla, Chawacala Mico and Foctalustee Emaulta each signed the Treaty of Indian Springs in 1825 as Sandtown headmen.[573]

Tunison Coryell and the Coryell Family

In a way, the counterpart to JMC Montgomery in Standing Peachtree was the Coryell family in Sandtown. The Coryell family is one with many members that resided in DeKalb County in the pioneer days and took a prominent role in establishing the settlement of Sandtown. Tunison Coryell was the first of the family to arrive from New Jersey to the DeKalb area sometime before 1828. He was named postmaster of Sandtown. He also shows up as being a resident of DeKalb County in the census of 1830. Tunison also drew in the land lottery of 1832 as a resident of Campbell County (which later became Fulton County). He was only a resident of the area for a short time though and died in 1842. His estate was left jointly to Joseph H. and John H.

> **Vestiges of Sandtown can still be found along Campbellton Road in Southwest Atlanta.**

Coryell and guardianship of his three daughters went to John H. Coryell in January 1842.[574] John H. Coryell took over Tunison's position as postmaster in Sandtown on March 23, 1835.[575] Joseph Coryell later took over the postmaster job in 1848.

---

[569] Georgia Historical Society, Georgiahistory.com
[570] Collections of the DeKalb Historical Society, Year Book, 1952
[571] Price, Vivian (1997) History of DeKalb County, Georgia, 1822-1900; Wolfe Pub. Co. pg. 79
[572] Georgia Historical Society, Georgiahistory.com
[573] Compiled by Kappler, Charles J. (1904); Indian Affairs: Laws and Treaties; Treaty with the Creeks, 1825, Government Printing Office
[574] Probate Records, 1854-1947, Indexes, 1854-1921; Author: Georgia. Court of Ordinary (Fulton County); Probate Place: Fulton, Georgia
[575] Record of Appointment of Postmasters, 1832-1971. NARA Microfilm Publication, M841, 145 rolls. Records of the Post

By 1855, Joseph owned around 1,500 acres of farmland in Campbell County. Many of the residents of Sandtown are buried in the Utoy Primitive Baptist Church Cemetery. This is also the location of Owl Rock shown on page 179.

Vestiges of the original Sandtown can still be found along Campbellton Road in Southwest Atlanta.[576] Even today, there is a community near the intersection of Campbellton Road and Camp Creek Parkway called Sandtown.[577]

There Were Indians Living in Decatur Continuously Into the 1830s

Here's my overall point. We know that there were people living in Decatur as far back as 4,000 years ago continuously through the time we know there were people living in the Sandtown area about 2,000 years ago and in Standing Peachtree around 1,000 years ago. They are confirmed to be living in the area again during the mid-1700s. The Indians living near Decatur were not just confined to Standing Peachtree and Sandtown. There were many of them in the area, concentrated mainly along the South River and Peachtree Creek.[578]

The only period there seems to be any question about who was occupying the area is during the early days of European arrival, and there were no Europeans or Americans visiting the area during this period. There's no reason to think Indians weren't actively occupying the area the entire time.

As you research history, especially reading things that were written in the past about the distant past, you tend to find a lot of interpretation that reflects the view of the writer. The history of the Indians in this area often describes them as "troublesome" and "warlike" as a way to imply that Americans had no choice but to remove them.

It has occurred to me that perhaps the notion that there were no Indians living in the Decatur area was created long ago from a view that was convenient to Georgia pioneers. As Caroline McKinney Clarke put it in her book, "The Story of Decatur", "The most compelling concern for most Georgians throughout this period – Indians – getting rid of them in Georgia and making their lands available for settlement."

Under those circumstances, I can easily envision a story that got repeated over time that there were no Indians regularly living in the Decatur area until after the Americans took control of it. In other words, "Well, we should be able to take this land anyway. It's not like they were using it."

Office Department, Record Group Number 28. Washington, D.C.: National Archives.
[576] Price, Vivian (1997) History of DeKalb County, Georgia, 1822-1900; Wolfe Pub. Co., pg. 34
[577] Price, Vivian (1997) History of DeKalb County, Georgia, 1822-1900; Wolfe Pub. Co. pg 8
[578] Price, Vivian (1997) History of DeKalb County, Georgia, 1822-1900; Wolfe Pub. Co.

Owl Rock Way Marker Near Sandtown[579]

Owl rock, so named because it was carved long ago by the Creeks to look like an owl, continues today as a well-known marker of the Sandtown area.

---

[579] Photo by the author

1752 Map of the Southeast[580]

This early map from the pre-revolutionary era shows the location of the Coweta (spelled Caoitas) along the Ocmulgee River. The northernmost Creek town on the Chattahoochee is shown as Catahooche. This town was about 65 miles South of Decatur near where Franklin, Georgia is today.

[580] Bowen, Emmanuel (1752) A new & accurate map of the provinces of North & South Carolina, Georgia &c., Library of Congress Geography and Map Division Washington

193

1780 Map of Georgia[581]

This French map shows the town of Hilibi on the Coosa River. Sandtown was occupied by a group from the Hilibi tribe who gave it that name.

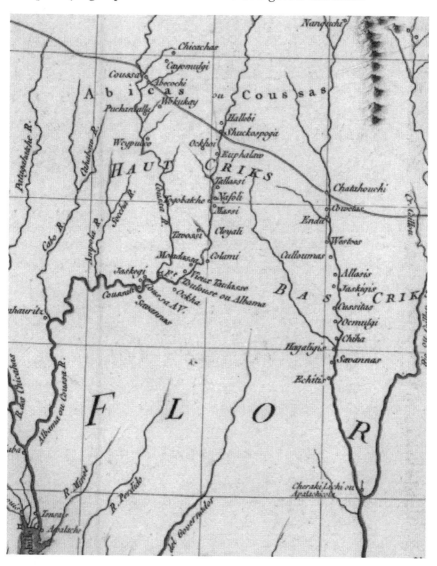

---

[581] Valet, PJ (1780) Tardieu's Florida and Georgia, State Library of Florida, Florida Map Collection

1795 Map of Georgia[582]

The map below shows the location of a town called "Buzzard's Roost", a name which became synonymous with Sandtown. However, the location of this Buzzard's Roost is on the Flint River, not the Chattahoochee River. It's possible that the those who started this town later moved to the Chattahoochee River area.

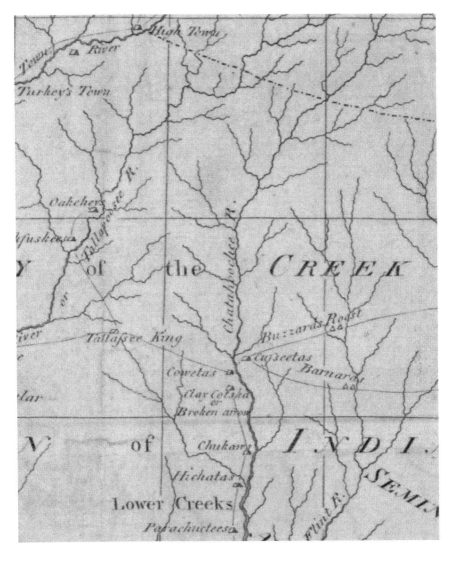

---

[582] Barker, William and Mathew, Carey (1795) Georgia, from the best authorities, Library of Congress Geography and Map Division

1797 Map of Georgia[583]

An early map showing the general direction of the Upper Creek Trading Path that bypasses Sandtown to the south.

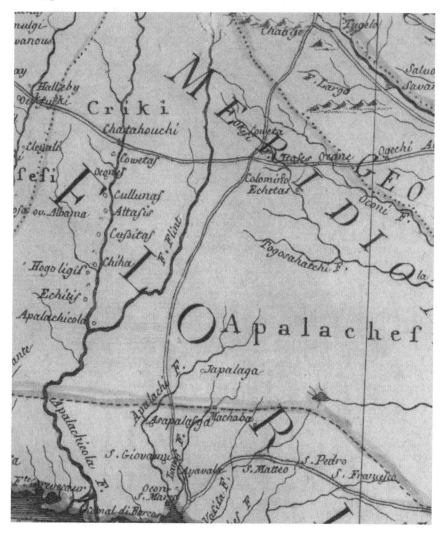

[583] (1797) Map of Southern Parts of the United States of America, Hagrett Library Rare Map Collectin, Univ. of Ga.

1813 Map of Georgia[584]

The map below shows the town of Tuckabatchee in the approximate location of Standing Peachtree. It also shows the shallow ford and the intersection of trails that correlates well with the location of the Shallow Ford trail, now Clairemont Avenue.

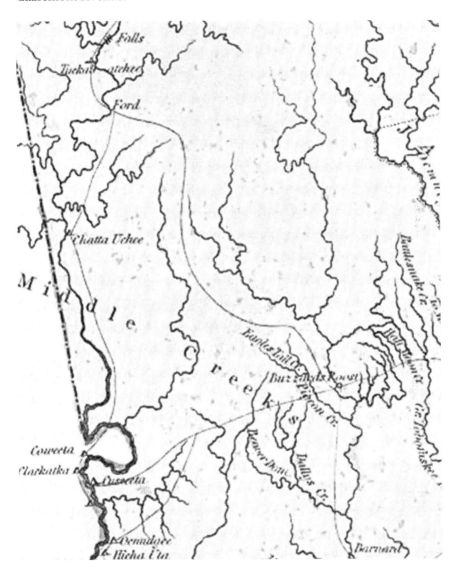

---

[584] Georgia / S. Lewis, del. ; H.S. Tanner, Sc. (1813) Hargrett Rare Book & Manuscript Library, Univ. of Georgia

1818 Map of Georgia[585]

This map shows the towns of Standing Peachtree and Sandtown (called Buzzard's Roost here) clearly on the Chattahoochee River. Also shown is the "Rock Mountain" which is, of course, Stone Mountain.

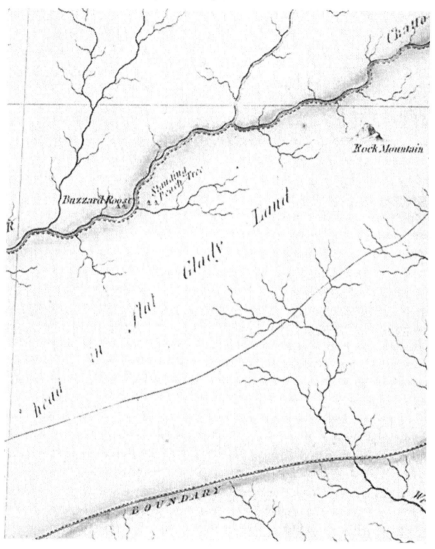

---

[585] Sturges, Daniel (1818) Map of the state of Georgia / prepared from actual surveys and other documents, Library of Congress Geography and Map Division

1839 Map of Georgia[586]

The map below specifically shows the locations of Sandtown and Standing Peachtree (as well as Flatrock, the Latimer Store and Stone Mountain) on trails out of Decatur.

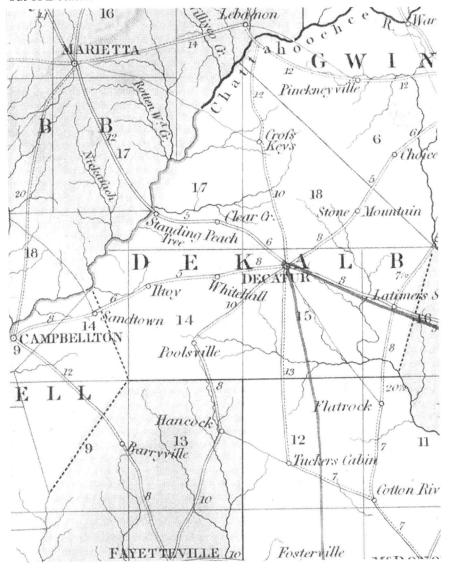

---

[586] David H. Burr (1839) Map of Georgia & Alabama exhibiting the post offices, post roads, canals, rail roads & c.; Library of Congress Geography and Map Division

CHAPTER 14:
THE DECATUR PIONEERS

Local Settlers Before the Land lottery of 1821

Even though the land still belonged to the Creeks until just before the Land Lottery of 1821, it's clear there were plenty of Americans living in the Decatur area before that. A letter written by R. Fullwood to Governor Mitchell in August 1813 suggested to the governor that Fullwood should "take command of a few persons…to keep a sharp lookout from Alcofa Mountain to Stone Mountain and from thence up to the frontier of Jackson County" to quiet the alarm among residents of that area that the Creeks would soon be arriving in their region on the warpath.[587]

This letter definitively reiterates three points important to this period of Decatur history. First, the Georgia settlers were present in large numbers and were routinely settling on land that belonged to the Creeks long before the treaties of 1821 and 1825 were even being negotiated. Second, the intrusion of settlers onto this land that belonged to the Creeks was not viewed as anything the settlers should be concerned about, at least insofar as a violation of the law. Third, at least implied in Fullwood's offer, the position of the Georgia government was not only that these settlers did not need to be evicted (at least until the land lottery when the land would go to other Americans) but even that settlers expected that the Georgia government should act on their behalf to defend their settlements.

> In 1821, Decatur was a trading post at the crossroad of several major trails containing only a few shanties and Indian lodges.

By 1820, still before the Treaty of 1821, Decatur had already become a small village. It was a very modest one that "could scarcely be dignified as a settlement," much smaller than the nearby town of Sandtown. It was a trading post at the crossroad of several major trails containing only a few shanties and Indian lodges, but it was a permanent area of residence for a few people all the same. The trails running to and from Decatur were still so narrow and closed in by trees that they could only be traveled by foot or perhaps horse. Even the

---

[587] Miller, Dorothy Burke (1952), Creek Indians of DeKalb County, Year Book of 1952, DeKalb Historical Society

width of a person on horseback caused some difficulty between the close trees and thick forest.[588] There was also a settlement in Stone Mountain before the city of Decatur began.[589]

These trails were now becoming filled with travelers. Some were refugees with no firm place to go. Many were wayward Indians headed west. Others were settlers in search of new spots for a homestead. An alarming number were criminals looking for easy prey to rob.

Adam Hodgson, a traveler from Scotland in 1820 gave a first-hand account of the state of the roads between the Ocmulgee River and the Chattahoochee.

"In the course of the day, we passed some Indians with their guns and blankets and several wagons of emigrants from Georgia and Carolina to Alabama. We also saw many gangs of slaves whom their masters were transporting to Alabama and Mississippi and met one party returning from New Orleans to Georgia…we did not pass a single house or settlement, but our pine avenue was literally without interruption for thirty miles."[590]

Hodgson may not have seen many homesteads on his journey, but there were many in the region. After an inspection of the land north of the Chattahoochee River in January of 1820, Andrew Jackson sent a report back to President John C. Calhoun saying, "I found a great many intruders and those on the north of the Chatahoochey (sic) not only numerous but insolent and threatening resistance."[591]

Later that same year, the Federal Government sent Jackson back across the Chattahoochee to further inspect the Cherokee land. After doing so, he posted this notice at the shallow ford on the Chattahoochee River near the current location of Roswell, just north of Decatur.

"Intruders on Cherokee lands, beware. I am required to remove all white men found trespassing on the Cherokee lands not having a written permit from the

Federal authorities ousted people who were living on Indian land illegally. Many Decatur settlers were evicted, including James Diamond, who later surveyed the land for Decatur.

[588] Author Unknown (1931), Indian War Near Five Points, Atlanta Journal Magazine, reproduced from the Atlanta Daily New Era, pg. 6
[589] (1970) Early DeKalb County History, prepared by and Furnished as a service of the DeKalb Chamber of Commerce
[590] Lane, Mills (1973) The Rambler in Georgia, Beehive Press, pg. 58
[591] Price, Vivian (1997) History of DeKalb County, Georgia, 1822-1900; Wolfe Pub. Co.

agent, Colo. R. J. Meigs. This duty I am about to perform. The Regulars and light horse will be employed in performing this service, and any opposition will be promptly punished. All white men with there (sic) livestock found trespassing on the Indian land will be arrested and handed over to the civil authorities of the United States to be dealt with as the law directs, there (sic) families removed to US land, there (sic) crops, houses and fences destroyed…"[592]

This warning was of course, not at all directed at protecting Indian land rights. It was directed at removing American intruders in preparation for the land to be distributed to new settlers as part of the expected land lotteries.

Federal authorities then ousted people who were illegally living on Indian land set aside for the Land Lottery of 1821. Many settlers, including James Diamond, who later surveyed the land for Decatur, had set up residence along the Chattahoochee, South River and major creeks in the area. They were evicted and many of their homesteads and crops were destroyed.[593]

The Georgia Land Lottery System and the Distribution of Georgia Land

With each treaty that sold another piece of land from the Indians to America, the land was then disbursed to American citizens. After the original plots were disbursed in the colony, Georgia used a land lottery system to distribute land to be developed and farmed.[594]

In each lottery, the names of those eligible to draw were written on a piece of paper and the numbers of each of the land lots to be distributed were written on another piece of paper. As each name was drawn, the drawer would come forward and draw out a number, usually from a barrel, indicating the plot of land they could buy and the draw was then recorded in a ledger.

A plot of land distributed by the lottery was normally hundreds of acres. The first lottery in 1805 divided the available land in Wayne County into 490 acre plots and land in Baldwin and Wilkinson Counties into 202.5 acre plots that were sold at a price of four cents per acre. Future lotteries valued the land at seven cents per acre, still much lower than their market value at that time. Those eligible to draw on the lottery were families (consisting of a husband, wife and at least one child), widows with children and white men who had been living in the state for at least one year.[595] The lottery system operated for 28 years during which time three-quarters of the land in Georgia was distributed to more than 100,000 lottery drawers.[596]

---

[592] Garrett; Franklin M. (1969) Atlanta and Environs: A Chronicle of Its People and Events, Volume 1; University of Georgia Press pg. 5

[593] Price, Vivian (1997) History of DeKalb County, Georgia, 1822-1900; Wolfe Pub. Co. p. 92

[594] Gigantino, Jim, University of Georgia, (2006) New Georgia Encyclopedia; Land Lottery System

[595] Gigantino, Jim, (2006) New Georgia Encyclopedia; Land Lottery System

[596] Gigantino, Jim, (2006) New Georgia Encyclopedia; Land Lottery System

Altogether, there were eight land lotteries that distributed Georgia land between 1805 and 1833. The 1805, 1807, 1820, 1821 and 1827 lotteries all involved land that had belonged to the Creeks. The 1832 and the 1833 lotteries disbursed the Georgia land that had belonged to the Cherokees.[597] These last lotteries in 1832 and 1833 distributed Georgia land even though it was not ceded until 1835. This cession followed a similar story to that of William McIntosh in that the primary negotiators, Major John Ridge and Elias Boudinot were not authorized to negotiate the treaty by the overall Cherokee nation and were killed for breaking Cherokee law.[598]

The Georgia system was unique from other southern states in that it was constructed to ensure the land would go to smaller farmers and not to large, wealthy landowners. In other states, the elite ended up owning most of the land for vast plantations. At least during the land lotteries, Georgia land was primarily under the control of less affluent land owners.[599]

The Land Lottery of 1821 that Gave Creek Land to the Decatur Pioneers

The drawings for the land lotteries of 1821 that distributed the land where Decatur is now located were held between November 7 and December 12, 1821. This was just four months after the First Treaty of Indian Springs. They divided the land lots between the new counties of Dooly, Fayette, Henry, Houston and Monroe.[600] The Decatur land was located inside the original borders of Henry County.[601]

> If you had been there to enter the lottery in 1821, you could have gotten an acre of land in downtown Decatur for nine cents.

The DeKalb Historical Society is in possession of one of the original deeds that was granted as a result of the Land Lottery of 1821.[602]

---

[597] Gigantino, Jim, (2006) New Georgia Encyclopedia; Land Lottery System
[598] (2017) American Indian Land Cessions in Georgia, About North Georgia
[599] Gigantino, Jim, (2006) New Georgia Encyclopedia; Land Lottery System
[600] 1821 Land Lottery in Georgia, Georgia Archives
[601] Garrett; Franklin M. (1969) Atlanta and Environs: A Chronicle of Its People and Events, Volume 1; University of Georgia Press pg. 5
[602] Records of the DeKalb Historical Society.

Georgia Land Lotteries[603]

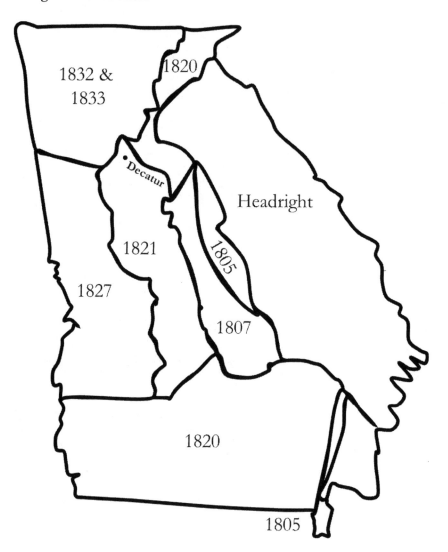

[603] Sketch by the author based on several sources including University of Georgia, Georgia Archives and map by Marion Hemperley

If you had been there to enter the lottery in 1821, you could have gotten an acre of land in downtown Decatur for nine cents. The lots were each 202.5 acres and sold for $19.00 each.[604]

Those eligible to draw in the lottery of 1821 were bachelors over 18 years old who had lived in Georgia for at least three years (1 draw); Georgia resident families with at least one child (1 draw); Georgia resident widows (1 draw); families of orphans under 21 years of age (1 draw if one or two family member; 2 draws for families of three or more); widows of a husband killed in the Revolutionary War, War of 1812 or one of the Indian Wars (2 draws); Orphans of a father killed in the Revolutionary War, War of 1812 or one of the Indian Wars (2 draws); or a child or family of a convict (terms the same as if an orphan).[605]

Anyone who had a successful draw in a previous lottery; refused to give military service when called; was a convict in the penitentiary; defaulted on taxes or absconded under a debt, was not eligible to draw in the lottery.[606]

Founder's Day and the Early Decatur Pioneers

The lucky drawers in the land lottery of 1821 then became Decatur's first (legal) settlers. The Decatur settlers mainly came from the Carolinas and Virginia. They were mostly of Scottish, Irish and English descent. A good number of the settlers also arrived from Gwinnett County as shown in the 1820 census. These included Meredith Collier, James Diamond, William Hairston and Dempsey Perkerson.[607]

> The Decatur settlers mainly came from the Carolinas and Virginia. They were mostly of Scottish, Irish and English descent.

"For the most part, the pioneers [of DeKalb County] were poor and meagerly educated but were generally industrious and temperate, qualities needed in the wilderness they sought to conquer. Their original homes were usually log cabins, owner built and occupied."[608]

---

[604] University of Georgia – Georgia Archives, 1821 Land Lottery
[605] University of Georgia – Georgia Archives, 1821 Land Lottery
[606] University of Georgia – Georgia Archives, 1821 Land Lottery
[607] Price, Vivian (1997) History of DeKalb County, Georgia, 1822-1900; Wolfe Pub. Co.
[608] Garrett; Franklin M. (1969) Atlanta and Environs: A Chronicle of Its People and Events, Volume 1; University of Georgia Press p. 31

The Founding of Decatur

After Gwinnett county was established in 1818, just before the land cessions of 1821, it already had a white population of 4,741 by 1820.[609] As more and more settlers flowed into the area, the distance for many of the pioneer homes in Henry County and Fayette County became too great over bad roads. It was decided that another county was needed. On December 9, 1822, an act of Georgia Assembly created DeKalb County from parts of Henry County, Fayette County and Gwinnett County.[610]

Two other jurisdictions in Georgia were already named for major heroes of the American Revolution-- Washington and Lafayette. Baron Johann DeKalb followed this tradition. Baron DeKalb was the only Revolutionary War general to die on the battlefield. Baron DeKalb received 11 wounds, fighting in hand-to-hand

> "The settlers of the Georgia backcountry are lazier and more given to drunkenness and lawlessness than any other state in the Union."
> ~Duc de la Rochefoucald-Liancourt (1796)

combat alongside his soldiers before he fell in the Battle of Camden. Legend has it that an English officer expressed his sympathy and attempted to help DeKalb toward a comfortable death. In thanks, Baron DeKalb shook the English officer's hand and said, "I thank you for your generous sympathy, but I die the death I always prayed for, the death of a soldier fighting for the rights of man."[611]

A bust of DeKalb graces the grounds of the Old Decatur Courthouse, a gift from the country of his birth, Germany.

When DeKalb County was established, its description included several landmarks that are still visible today. "Beginning at the high shoals of the Apalachee River (the easternmost corner of Monroe County) the line ran along the High Tower Path to the shallow ford on the Chattahoochee River (just downriver of Roswell Road); thence up the east bank of the Chattahoochee River (now Gwinnett County); thence along a direct line to the head of Apalachee, then down the river to the beginning point at high Shoals."[612]

[609] Price, Vivian (1997) History of DeKalb County, Georgia, 1822-1900; Wolfe Pub. Co. p. 59
[610] (1970) Early DeKalb County History, prepared by and Furnished as a service of the DeKalb Chamber of Commerce
[611] Trotti, Louis Haygood (1952), DeKalb County Georgia, The DeKalb Historical Society's Year Book - 1952
[612] Price, Vivian (1997) History of DeKalb County, Georgia, 1822-1900; Wolfe Pub. Co. pg 46

In an act of the Georgia General Assembly on December 23, 1822, it was decided that they would "fix on a public site for the courthouse and jail to be as near the center of DeKalb County as convenience will admit" The spot chosen was land lot 246 in the 15th district. Before the courthouse was constructed, they chose the house of William Jackson on South McDonough Street as the place for the first meeting of the county courts.[613]

The newly organized court issued an order on July 28, 1823 that the site on Land Lot 246 would be the permanent site of the court and the public site would be known by the name of Decatur. Decatur was incorporated as the county seat on December 10, 1823. Its location was a trading post at the intersection of the Shallowford Trail, the Stone Mountain Trail and near several other trails.[614] It was incorporated under an act of the General Assembly on December 19, 1823 as the first city in the County of DeKalb.[615]

When settlers arrived, their conditions were extremely rustic. They would most often camp out in the open until they could build a small cabin to live in. Campsites were normally placed next to a stream or river. Household water was normally dipped from a stream and carried back to the family site in buckets. Cooking was done over an open fire. Apart from a few dry goods like coffee, salt and sugar, everything they ate they either raised themselves or hunted or foraged from the surrounding areas. Livestock was often allowed to run free in the woods and was collected as the need arose. The livestock supplied much of their protein and fat as well as clothing, harnesses and soap. Many of the settlers grew cotton which they spun and dyed to make their own clothes.[616]

Southern frontier families were noted for their roughness and lack of respect for authority of any kind. One traveler noted, "the settlers of the Georgia backcountry are lazier and more given to drunkenness and lawlessness than any other state in the Union."[617]

Decatur "Blacksmith Nathan Wansley had part of his ear bitten off in a fight. The perpetrator, whose name is unknown, was found guilty of "mayhem".

A group of ruffians called the "Pony Boys" was notorious for pulling rough pranks late at night, mainly on travelers who had come to town

613 (1970) Early DeKalb County History, prepared by and Furnished as a service of the DeKalb Chamber of Commerce
614 Dekalb History.org
615 (1970) Early DeKalb County History, prepared by and Furnished as a service of the DeKalb Chamber of Commerce
616 Price, Vivian (1997) History of DeKalb County, Georgia, 1822-1900; Wolfe Pub. Co. pg 90
617 Creek Country, Etheridge – Lane, Mills (1973) The Rambler in Georgia, Beehive Press, p. 12.

and found themselves enjoying too much liquor on the square before heading home.[618]

"It was very common between 1824 and 1826 to get up of a morning and find a crate swinging up to a horse-rack with one or two men in it with their faces so black you could not tell who they were or if not swung under the horse rack, they were under a crate or cart body with perhaps half of a cord of wood or rock piled on it so they could not get out."

In 1825, they went into Mr. Reuben Cone's horse lot and cut off one ear each of 13 horses. Among them was Judge Shorter's and Solicitor General C.J. McDonald's (afterward Judge and Governor of Georgia) and put a wagon on top of the courthouse.

"On another occasion, the boys annoyed the people of the village by ringing the academy bell at midnight. Some of the sober old men went to them to reprimand them, but they were met with the reply: Pat Farrel has married the widow Scaife and we ae giving them a serenade…"[619]

"Blacksmith Nathan Wansley had part of his ear bitten off in a fight. The perpetrator, whose name is unknown, was found guilty of "mayhem" and sentenced to stand in the stocks. For some reason, to avoid embarrassing attention to the criminal and his punishment, Sherriff George A. Harris hung a blanket in front of the stocks.

Indians Still Living in and Around Decatur at Founding Day
The land just adjacent to DeKalb County still belonged to the Indians until 1835, and the Cherokees were not all officially sent on the Trail of Tears until 1838. For the first 12 years after the founding of Decatur, Indians were certainly a common sight in the area. After it was founded, Decatur was still mainly an Indian trading post. The Indians continued to make their way into town in groups of 30 or 40 to sell pelts, baskets, moccasins and other wares.[620]

After it was founded, Decatur was still mainly an Indian trading post.

The Indians in Sandtown and Standing Peachtree were sometimes harassed by the rougher Decatur residents who would rustle their cattle or pillage from the town.[621]

[618] Price, Vivian (1997) History of DeKalb County, Georgia, 1822-1900; Wolfe Pub. Co.
[619] Price, Vivian (1997) History of DeKalb County, Georgia, 1822-1900; Wolfe Pub. Co. – pg 130 – Willard Levi, 1920, The Early History of Decatur Written Many Years Ago: DeKalb New Ear – Note: Available on Microfilm at the University of Ga.,
[620] Hoyt, S. B. (1886) The Shumate Family; The Story of Some of the Pioneers of DeKalb County; The Atlanta Constitution

The Lyon family settled along the South River, and there are various tales of seeing Indians in the woods when they would drive the cows home from the fields. The Lyon children of this era also remembered seeing their parents give food to the local Indians. A group of Cherokees lived in the woods for a long time after Founder's Day along Lawrenceville Highway in a spot where two small creeks came together to form a small waterfall.[622]

Several Cherokees who lived near the Perkerson family and avoided the Trail to Tears are said to be buried in their family cemetery. The cemetery is located on River Road at Fork Creek. Land Lot 38, 15th District.[623]

[621] Price, Vivian (1997) History of DeKalb County, Georgia, 1822-1900; Wolfe Pub. Co.
[622] Price, Vivian (1997) History of DeKalb County, Georgia, 1822-1900; Wolfe Pub. Co. ; pg 37
[623] Price, Vivian (1997) History of DeKalb County, Georgia, 1822-1900; Wolfe Pub. Co.

Profiles of Some Decatur Pioneers
The names of the leading families of the new city of Decatur became evident from the day it was founded and appear in the ledgers again and again whenever there was a duty to perform or a post to fill on behalf of the town. Names such as Hairston, Akins, Shumate, Cone, Diamond, Latimer, Coryell, Kirkpatrick, Adair and Calhoun. I've profiled some of the interesting settlers already like James McNeil and James Mc. Montgomery and some others here.

Early Male Settlers of Decatur
During his Bicentennial address, Charles Murphy Candler mentioned a list of 191 of the prominent, early, male settlers of Decatur. Settlers discussed in this book who made the list are shown in bold text.

William Akers	William Gresham	Charles Murphey
Thomas Akins	Rev. Josiah Grisham	Moses Murphey
Thomas Austin	Rev. Bedford Gunn	Robert Murphey
Dr. James Avary	**William Hairston**	**John B. Nelson**
S. T. Bailey	Zachariah Hallaway	William New
William Baker	George K. Hamilton	Robert Ozmer
William Beauchamp	Naman Hardman	James Paden
Samuel Binion	Charles Harris	Isaiah Parker
James Blackstock	George Heard	Rev. William Parks
E.J. Bond	Charles C. Hicks	William Pendley
J. B. Bond	James Hicks	**Dempsey Perkerson**
Dr. W. P. Bond	William Hill	T. J. Perkerson
John W. Born	Robert Hollingsworth	L. Pitts
William L. Born	Hines Holt	Ebenezer Pitts
Jacob R. Brooks	John W. Hooper	Joseph Pitts
Fanning Brown	Asa W. Howerd	**Dr. Chapmon Powell**
John Brown	Dr. P. F. Hoyle	Samuel Prewitt
Robert M. Br Sr.	Eli J. Hulsey	Joel Pritchett
John Bryce	Hardy Ivy	John C. Ragsdale
G. B. Butler	William Jackson	Leonard Randall
Dr. E.N. Calhoun	John Jennings	Thomas Ray
James M. Calhoun	Archibald Johnson	J. M. Riddling
Larkin Carlton	Daniel Johnson	William Rogers
Benjamin Carr	Gabe Johnson	William Scaife
J. M. Carroll	Lochlin Johnson	Berryman D. Shumate
William Carson	William W. Johnson	**Mason D. Shumate**
Tully Choice	John Jones	Asa Simmons
Jacob Hupp	Robert Jones Sr.	Simeon Smith
Oliver Clark	Seaborn Jones	David R. Silliman

Rev. William H. Clark	David Kiddo	David M. Simpson
Jesse F. Cleveland	Alex Kirkpatrick	Leonard Simpson
James T. Cobb	**James H. Kirkpatrick**	G. K. Smith
Lemuel Cobb	James W. Kirkpatrick	Rev. John M. Smith
John Collier	Watson Kittredge	Robert H. Smith
Meredith Collier	**Charles Latimer**	William R. Smith
Merrill Collier	H. B. Latimer	Benjamin Sprayberry
Reuben Cone	Drury Lee	Harris Sprayberry
Alex Corry	James Lemon	Harris Sprayberry
James Crockett	Robert Lemon	Rev. Uriah C. Sprayberry
E. A. Davis	James Ligon	Joel Starnes
Moses W. Davis	John C. Maddox	Isaac Steele
Robert F. Davis	John E. Maguire	M. A. Steele
James Diamond	Rev. James Mangum	John Stephens
T. A. Dobbs	Ezekiel Mason	John Stephenson
Samuel Dodson	Samuel C. Masters	M. R. Stephenson
W. J. Donaldson	J. R. McAlister	**Thomas Stevens**
James R. Evans	John McCullough	Elijah Steward
William Ezzard	Rev. John McElroy	Joseph Stewart
John Y. Flowers	Samuel McElroy Sr.	Daniel Stone
Drury Fowler	William McElroy	John N. Swift
John W. Fowler	C. W. McGinnis	Asa Thompson
Minty Fowler	J. W. McLain	Dr. Joseph Thompson
Charles Gates	Malcolm McLeod	Ebenezer Tilley
Banks George	John W. McCurdy	Stephen Tilley
Rev. James R. George	P.B. McCurdy	Lewis Towers
J. W. George	**Daniel McNeil**	William Towers
Tunstall B. George	Robert McWilliams	Walter Wadsworth
Joseph W. Givens	John Meadow	Joseph Walker
Robert Givens	W. H. Minor	James White
John Glen	**J. Mc. Montgomery**	Levi Willard
A.J. Goldsmith	Joseph Morgan	Ammi Williams
James W. Goldsmith	L. S. Morgan	Jonathan B. Wilson
William Goldsmith	Joe Morris	James J. Winn
Alston H. Green	William Mosely	William Wright

1866 Map of Decatur Court Square[624]

This map of the Decatur square was created over 40 years after the founding of the town, but it still shows the locations of many homes and businesses of many of the first residents.

Marshall Street

Ponce de Leone Ave. (previously Greens Ferry Ave. and Broad St.)

Stable

Blacksmith

Atlanta Ave.

JB Wilson Residence

Masonic Lodge

Reynolds Hotel

Levi Willard store & residence

Tin Shop

Capt. Miltion A. Candler Residence

Hat Shop

Saloon and Store

JP Crocket Resident

West Court Square

Saloon -- Billy Hill

E Mason Residence

Court house

Clairmont Ave (previously Shallowford Rd)

Washington Hotel -- TB George

Post Office (property owned by Mrs. Bradshaw)

East Court Square

Judge William Ezzard Residence

Sycamore Street

Saloon

Col. RM Brown Residence

Dr. Calhoun

Ramspeck Store

Capt. Milton Candler Law Office

Augusta Eddleman Residence

Shoe Shop

Col. Thomas Akin Dry Goods and Grocery

JW Kirkpatrick Residence

Lawrenceville Road – Later Church Street

Blacksmith

Livery Stable

N →

Dr. Chapmon Powell and His Medicine House

Dr. Chapmon Powell is my favorite Decatur pioneer in a close race with James McNeil and Dempsey Perkerson. Powell was a very humble, very intelligent and very kind man who spent many many years helping whoever came to his door and left behind an interesting legacy of which, I think he would be very proud.

He was born in Wake County, North Carolina on August 10, 1798. He married Elizabeth (Betsy) Hardman on April 7, 1824. Chapmon followed some of his other family to Georgia, moved to DeKalb County and settled on land lot 61 in 1825. Dr. Powell then acquired all or part of land lots 52, 53, 58, 59 and 60 which are all along Clairemont Avenue near South Peachtree Creek.

> The Veteran's Administration Hospital, portions of Emory University Hospital, and parts of the CDC are all located on land once owned by the kind and caring Doctor Powell.

They built a small log cabin on land lot 51 but later moved it to Land Lot 61. The "Chapmon Powell Medicine House," as it came to be called, moved many times, but its primary location was at 1218 Clairemont Avenue, where the Public Storage is now located near the intersection of Clairemont and South Decatur Road.

Chapmon Powell's Medicine House welcomed all people and unlike most doctors, it was known to be a place Indians could visit to receive care.[625] The Medicine House was a said to be "a haven of rest and cheer; and many a travel-worn, footsore Cherokee found comfort in the medical skill and care of Dr. Powell who was famed and loved for his kindness of heart."

Dr. Powell's medical practice ran much more in the traditions or herbal medicine than those of other local Decatur doctors like Ezekiel Calhoun. When one visited him to receive treatment, it was well known that he expected his patients to also bring a gallon of whiskey in which the herbs and roots he used would be pulverized to make the treatment.

As a teenager, it was Powell's son John's job to ride across the Chattahoochee to trade gold for Indian herbal medicines. Powell's daughter Martha knitted socks for the Indians.[626]

[625] Price, Vivian (1997) History of DeKalb County, Georgia, 1822-1900; Wolfe Pub. Co. pg 143
[626] Price, Vivian (1997) History of DeKalb County, Georgia, 1822-1900; Wolfe Pub. Co. p.37

The Chapmon Powell Medicine House at Stone Mountain[627]

Mittie Bulloch, who was the granddaughter of a Revolutionary hero of Georgia, Archibald Bulloch and mother to President Teddy Roosevelt, was a close friend of Dr. Powell's daughter Amanda. Mittie often visited Amanda at the Powell Medicine House.

The original cabin in which Dr. Powell lived along Clairemont Avenue, and in which he was proud to say all his eight children were born, is now located in the Antebellum complex of Stone Mountain Park.

When his wife Betsy died in 1850, Dr. Powell moved to Atlanta and built the second house ever constructed on Peachtree Street.[628] He died in 1870 and is buried next to his wife in the Hardman Cemetery, now within the property of the University Apartments on a hill above South Peachtree Creek. To avoid vandalism, their obelisk monuments were later removed and replaced with flat markers. The two obelisks are now in Decatur Cemetery.

---

[627] Photo by the author
[628] Price, Vivian (1997) History of DeKalb County, Georgia, 1822-1900; Wolfe Pub. Co.

The Interior of the Powell Medicine House[629]

Dr. Powell's persisting legacy is that the Veteran's Administration Hospital, portions of Emory University Hospital and the Centers for Disease Control are all located on land once owned by the kind and caring Doctor.[630] I like to think that is not a coincidence and somehow the land is imbued with a natural tendency to care for those who are ailing.

[629] Photo by the Author
[630] Price, Vivian (1997) History of DeKalb County, Georgia, 1822-1900; Wolfe Pub. Co. pg. 159

The Thomas-Barber Cabin in Adair Park[631]

George and Martha Thomas and the Thomas-Barber Cabin

George and Martha Thomas came to DeKalb County in a covered wagon from South Carolina some time close to the founding of the city. They settled on the Decatur-McDonough Road about halfway between the two towns. There, George built them a twenty-foot by thirty-foot cabin with a large fieldstone fireplace. He fired his rifle through the front door to create a peep hole the family could use to see who was coming down the road without revealing themselves. Martha made the family beds by stuffing mattresses with wheat straw.[632]

Today, you can still visit the Thomas-Barber cabin and still see the peep hole George made with his rifle in the Adair Park Historical Complex on West Trinity Place.

---

[631] Photo by the Author
[632] Price, Vivian (1997) History of DeKalb County, Georgia, 1822-1900; Wolfe Pub. Co. pg 90

216

The Biffle Cabin in Adair Park[633]

John Biffle and the Biffle Cabin

John Biffle was a native of Germany born in 1744. He was a Private in North Carolina during the Revolutionary War. He came to DeKalb County with his son Leander and his wife Sally in 1822.

Biffle owned around 800 acres in the original DeKalb County and gradually sold it off to other settlers. The Biffles originally lived on a knoll overlooking Barbashela Creek close to where Biffle Road is now in the Hidden Hills Subdivision. The original one room cabin the Biffles lived in is preserved at the DeKalb Historical Society's Adair Historical Complex on West Trinity Place.

John and his wife Sally are both buried somewhere in an unmarked grave in the churchyard of the Macedonia Baptist Church.

[633] Photo by the Author

The Calhoun Brothers: Dr. E.N. Calhoun and James Calhoun

The Calhouns are perhaps most remembered for each of their roles in the Creek War of 1836. Dr. Calhoun was born on October 23, 1799 in Abbeville, South Carolina. His father, a state senator, was 50, and his mother Floride was 29 when Ezekiel was born. He had five brothers and four sisters. His father's cousin was John C. Calhoun who would go on to become US president.[634]

Ezekiel graduated in 1823 from the University of Pennsylvania School of Medicine. He opened his practice in Decatur in 1826 or 1827 with his partner Dr. Joseph Thompson. He and his wife Lucy B. Wellborn raised nine children in Decatur. He was a well-respected physician in Decatur at a time when they were sorely needed. The average life expectancy in the area at the time is given to have been only about 28 years. Residents were constantly threatened by malaria, bilious fever, pleurisy, pellagra, hookworm, yellow fever and smallpox.[635] After returning home from the Creek War of 1836, Dr. Calhoun died on March 13, 1875, having lived a long life of 75 years. He is buried in Atlanta.

Ezekiel's little brother, James Calhoun, would also became a well-known Decatur resident and a famous person in Atlanta. James was born in 1811 in the Abbeville District of South Carolina. When the brothers' parents died in 1821, John went to live with his brother Ezekiel in Decatur.[636] He attended Kiddoo's Decatur Academy and then began studying law in the offices of Hines Holt in 1831. He was admitted to the bar in 1832.[637]

Captain James Calhoun returned home from the Creek War of 1836 (discussed in the following chapter) as a Colonel. In 1837, he was elected to the State Legislature as a Whig. In 1851, he was elected to the State Senate and moved to Atlanta in 1852. After the resignation of Atlanta's mayor, Jared Whitaker in 1861, Alderman Thomas Lowe took the post but chose not to seek reelection, and James Calhoun was elected Mayor of Atlanta. He was reelected three times, and during that time, it became his duty to surrender the city to Gen. Sherman's Army.[638] James died on October 1, 1875 and is buried with his wife Emma Eliza Dabney in Oakland Cemetery. [639]

---

[634] Price, Vivian (1997) History of DeKalb County, Georgia, 1822-1900; Wolfe Pub. Co.
[635] Price, Vivian (1997) History of DeKalb County, Georgia, 1822-1900; Wolfe Pub. Co.
[636] Oakland Cemetery, Oakland Resident Spotlight: James Calhoun
[637] Oakland Cemetery, Oakland Resident Spotlight: James Calhoun
[638] Oakland Cemetery, Oakland Resident Spotlight: James Calhoun
[639] Oakland Cemetery, Oakland Resident Spotlight: James Calhoun

The Hairston, Towers and Mehaffey Families, First Settlers along Barbashela and Snapfinger Creeks

Another of the original settlers in the Decatur area were the Hairstons who settled along Snapfinger and Barbashela Creek in the Redan area, just to the west. Peter and Martha Baker Hairston moved from Abbeville, South Carolina to Barbashela Creek along with the Towers family and the family of Thomas MeHaffey sometime before DeKalb County was officially organized.

The Hairston home was located just north of where Covington Highway crosses over Snapfinger Creek.[640] Isaac Hairston and his brother William Hairston "cleared some of the land...and made a crop on it...It was the first timber cut anywhere on Snapfinger Creek. The virgin forest had been unbroken by the woodman's axe until then. Both creeks were fine ranges and were heavily timbered."[641]

In the Spring of 1827, Thomas Hairston "made a house raising and built a two-story dwelling out of large hewn log. William Hairston and his father-in-law Isaac Towers built the first sawmill in the area on Snapfinger Creek.[642] Once the house was built, the Hairstons' raised sheep. "There was a large unbroken range. Sheep went where they please coming home occasionally to be salted. At the time of the new moon in September, our fathers would go to the forest and drive the sheep home and shear them, and our mothers would wash the wool and card and spin it, as there were no factories there in the twenties."[643]

Thomas Mehaffey, who had traveled to the area along with the Hairstons, was a wheelwright by trade. He made all the spinning wheels that were used to make homespun cloth in the early days of the county. Mehaffey and his wife and several children are buried in a family cemetery in Land Lot 2 of the 16th District of DeKalb. There are not inscribed markers in the cemetery.

---

[640] Price, Vivian (1997) History of DeKalb County, Georgia, 1822-1900; Wolfe Pub. Co. pg. 90
[641] Price, Vivian (1997) History of DeKalb County, Georgia, 1822-1900; Wolfe Pub. Co. pg. 90
[642] Price, Vivian (1997) History of DeKalb County, Georgia, 1822-1900; Wolfe Pub. Co. pg. 90
[643] Price, Vivian (1997) History of DeKalb County, Georgia, 1822-1900; Wolfe Pub. Co. pg. 90

Reuben Cone, Owner of Decatur's First Hotel

Reuben Cone was an Inferior Court Judge and one of the first County Commissioners along with William Morris, James White, Thomas A. Dobbs and William Gresham.

He arrived in town in 1844 or 1845 and opened the town's first hotel on the Decatur City Square.[644] It's unclear where Reuben Cone came from, but it was one of the northern states.[645]

Though he owned a hotel, Mr. Cone's most prized possessions were his horses. He owned many and was proud of two in particular. The first, named Spot, had spent a lot of time on ships and would rock back and forth in his stall whenever there was a rainstorm as if he were still aboard ship in a rolling sea. The other, Cone claimed, was ridden by Gen. Packenham in the Battle of New Orleans.[646]

In 1825, Decatur's earliest band of ruffians, the "Pony Boys" went into Mr. Cone's horse lot and cut off one ear each of 13 horses. It's not clear if these 13 included his two most prized horses.

He married Lucinda Shumate, the daughter of Mason Shumate who rented space in his hotel and started Decatur's first tavern.[647]

Cone was instrumental in the growth of Atlanta as a city by dividing his vast land holdings into smaller lots which, he sold at reasonable prices. He owned around 300 or 400 acres of land that is now Atlanta including most of Marietta Street and Peachtree Street. He donated the land where the First Baptist and First Presbyterian Churches are located.[648] Cone's ownership of the land in downtown Atlanta is commemorated with the name of Cone Street between Marietta Street and Carnegie Way. You may notice that Marietta Street is lined by trees today. This was also Mr. Cone's doing. As far as I can tell, none of the trees currently lining the street are ones that he planted, but, it was Mr. Cone who first planted trees all along this street.[649]

Reuben Cone died in April 1852 in Atlanta.[650] He had 10 children -- four sons and six daughters.

Mason Shumate, Owner of Decatur's First Tavern

Mason Shumate was descended from French Huguenots like those who founded Port Royal and built the first fort in the United States north of

[644] Hoyt, S. B. (1886) The Shumate Family; The Story of Some of the Pioneers of DeKalb County; The Atlanta Constitution
[645] Hoyt, S. B. (1886) The Shumate Family; The Story of Some of the Pioneers of DeKalb County; The Atlanta Constitution
[646] Price, Vivian (1997) History of DeKalb County, Georgia, 1822-1900; Wolfe Pub. Co. pg 137
[647] Hoyt, S. B. (1886) The Shumate Family; The Story of Some of the Pioneers of DeKalb County; The Atlanta Constitution
[648] Hoyt, S. B. (1886) The Shumate Family; The Story of Some of the Pioneers of DeKalb County; The Atlanta Constitution
[649] Records of the DeKalb Historical Society
[650] Hoyt, S. B. (1886) The Shumate Family; The Story of Some of the Pioneers of DeKalb County; The Atlanta Constitution

Savannah in 1562. Mason was born in 1761 in Fauquier County, Virginia. He married Nancy Gatewood and the two of them moved to Spartanburg, South Carolina in 1804. They moved to Decatur in 1824 and opened the town's first tavern in a room they rented in Reuben Cone's hotel. Mason Shumate was also one of the founders of the Presbyterian Church in Decatur.[651]

At the time Mason Shumate arrived, there were only around 12 log buildings in Decatur. After living in town a few years, he moved to his plantation around a mile west of the courthouse, near the intersection of Upland Road and West Ponce de Leon Avenue. He owned much of the land that is now Edgewood which he used as a hog range.[652]

> At the time Mason Shumate arrived, there were only around 12 log buildings in Decatur.

He died in 1849 leaving nine children; Joseph D., Lucinda, Harriet, Berryman, Sarah, Cynthia, Elizabeth, Franklin and Eliza. He was accounted to be a very kind and generous man who highly valued learning and worked hard to ensure all his nine children had a good education.[653]

One of his sons, Joseph D. Shumate, married the Amelia Montgomery, the daughter of Major JMC Montgomery. Joseph and Amelia moved to Texas in 1865. Lucinda Shumate married Reuben Cone, the owner of the town's first hotel.[654]

---

[651] Hoyt, S. B. (1886) The Shumate Family; The Story of Some of the Pioneers of DeKalb County; The Atlanta Constitution
[652] Hoyt, S. B. (1886) The Shumate Family; The Story of Some of the Pioneers of DeKalb County; The Atlanta Constitution
[653] Hoyt, S. B. (1886) The Shumate Family; The Story of Some of the Pioneers of DeKalb County; The Atlanta Constitution
[654] Hoyt, S. B. (1886) The Shumate Family; The Story of Some of the Pioneers of DeKalb County; The Atlanta Constitution

Dempsey Perkerson, Early Settler in Panthersville

Dempsey Perkerson and his wife Nancy Ward Perkerson were some of the first to settle along the South River. The Perkersons owned six land lots in the area where Waldrop Road crosses the South River. [655]

Children of the Perkerson and Waldrop families used to play with Cherokee children whose parents were friends with their parents. The Indians lived in "wigwams" by the South River.[656]

Dempsey Perkerson died on July 28, 1875 at the ripe old age of 97. He is buried in the family cemetery on River Road. Several Cherokees who lived on the Perkerson's land with them are said to be buried in the Perkerson-Waldrop family cemetery.[657] The Dempsey Perkerson Family Cemetery is located on River Road at Fork Creek. Land Lot 38, 15th District.[658]

John Adair, Decatur's First Wagon Maker.

The first of the Adair family to arrive in the area was John Adair who was born in the Laurens District of South Carolina on December 3, 1785. He moved to Decatur from Morgan County in 1825 and settled along the South River.[659]

Adair Street: Named for Decatur's First Wagon Maker[660]

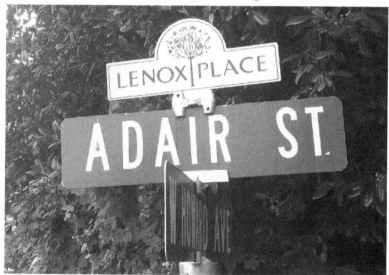

[655] Price, Vivian (1997) History of DeKalb County, Georgia, 1822-1900; Wolfe Pub. Co. pg 94
[656] Price, Vivian (1997) History of DeKalb County, Georgia, 1822-1900; Wolfe Pub. Co.
[657] Price, Vivian (1997) History of DeKalb County, Georgia, 1822-1900; Wolfe Pub. Co. p. 37
[658] Price, Vivian (1997) History of DeKalb County, Georgia, 1822-1900; Wolfe Pub. Co. pg. 37
[659] (1970) Early DeKalb County History, prepared by and Furnished as a service of the DeKalb Chamber of Commerce
[660] Photo by the Author

Charles Latimer, Owner of Decatur's First Store

Charles Latimer started the first store in Decatur located in a room he rented in Reuben Cone's hotel. The store was later moved outside town and is shown on the 1839 map on page 186. He also built the Panola Plantation.[661]

Another well-known resident of Decatur, Charles Latimer's daughter, **Rebecca Latimer Felton**, had the enormous and historic distinction of becoming the first woman to ever serve in the United States Senate, though it was only for a day.

She entered a political career later in her life and became well known in the fight for women's rights, including the right to vote. Unfortunately, she used racial arguments to support her arguments for women's rights. She was quoted as saying, "I do not want to see a negro man walk to the polls and vote on who should handle my tax money, while I, myself, cannot vote at all. Is that fair?"[662]

She was also the last slave owner to serve in the United States Senate but did go on record acknowledging the wrongness and evil of slavery. Her most clarifying statement on the subject of slavery was that, "All I owned was invested in slaves and my people were loyal and I stood by them to the end…Nevertheless, I am now too near the borderland of eternity to withhold my matured

> Decatur resident Rebecca Latimer Felton had the enormous and historic distinction of becoming the first woman to ever serve in the United States Senate.

conscientious and honest opinion. If there had been no slaves there would have been no war. To fight for the perpetuation of domestic slavery was a mistake. The time had come in the United States to wipe out this evil. The South had to suffer, and even when our preachers were leading in prayer for victory, during the war, and black-robed mothers and wives were weeping for their dead ones, who perished on the field of battle, I had questions in my own mind as to what would be the end of it."[663]

---

[661] Buchanan, Matthew (2016) The Daily Dose, October 3, 1922: Rebecca Felton becomes the First Woman United States Senator
[662] The Daily Dose, October 3, 1922: Rebecca Felton becomes the First Woman United States Senator
[663] The Daily Dose, October 3, 1922: Rebecca Felton becomes the First Woman United States Senator

Col. Thomas Akins – Patriarch of Decatur Merchants
Col. Thomas Akins was born around 1790.

Thomas J. Akins and William Gresham were two very early merchants in Decatur. Thomas Akins came to DeKalb County sometime before 1830 with his wife Elizabeth Ross. Thomas was a tall, large man. He served many public offices including as a State Senator in 1826.[664]

He took over space in the hotel owned by Reuben Cone from William Latimer and created a dry goods store. The store was later damaged by a fire in the hotel in 1846.

He seems to have been a very friendly man as you would expect of the man who operated the longest lasting business in town for that time, earning him the nickname "Patriarch of Merchants." His loud, hearty laugh was said to often echo in the Decatur square loud enough for anyone to hear. He also had many long-lasting partnerships in town including one with Jacob R Brooks, the proprietor of the first ferry in the County that crossed the Chattahoochee at the shallow ford. Akins also made a partnership with Leonard Randall in a mercantile firm they called Leonard and Akins.

When the call went out to supply soldiers for the Creek War of 1836, the DeKalb Independent Volunteer Rifle Company of DeKalb County was formed with 65 officers and men and Thomas Akins was elected captain.[665]

After the death of Elizabeth, his first wife, Thomas remarried Lucinda Hairston in 1849. Sadly, Lucinda died only two years later, and Thomas married again in 1852 to Sarah S. King.[666] Through his three marriages, Thomas had 16 children. The youngest, Daniel S. Akins, was born when Thomas was 55 years old. He died on March 10, 1873.[667]

The Akins family cemetery is one of the largest ones in DeKalb County. It is located on Shasta Way near the intersection of Briarcliff Road and Shallowford Road.

[664] Price, Vivian (1997) History of DeKalb County, Georgia, 1822-1900; Wolfe Pub. Co. pg 118
[665] Hudgins, Carl T. (1952) Collection of the DeKalb Historical Society, The Year Book – 1952
[666] Price, Vivian (1997) History of DeKalb County, Georgia, 1822-1900; Wolfe Pub. Co. pg 118
[667] Profile of Thomas J. Akins; Biographical file in the DeKalb Historical Society.

James Diamond, Surveyor of Decatur

James Diamond was a true pioneer of Georgia having been among the first to arrive in more than one region before it was made open to Americans. He and his future wife Nancy Cornwell both settled in Jackson County's around 1801, years prior to the land lottery that distributed Jackson County land.[668] Later, James did the same thing he had during his childhood when he settled in the Decatur area as one of the Georgia "intruders." He took up residence along Stone Mountain Creek on the Cherokee side and was later evicted and his crops destroyed. He then moved to DeKalb County in the Lithonia area.

Before moving to Decatur, James served in the Red Stick War in 1813 as part of captain Joshua Hagerty's company.[669] James Diamond is most connected to Decatur as the person who surveyed land lot 246 where downtown Decatur is now located. The district where James Diamond lived, north of Lithonia is now named for him. He was described as a very tall man, over six feet, blonde and "always ready for a fight."[670]

James died in 1849 after having been elected to several public offices including the State House of Representatives in 1835 and State Senate in 1840.

He is buried in the Diamond Family Cemetery.[671] The cemetery is located on the right side of Kimberland Road between two houses near Deshon Road.[672]

Joseph Emmanuel Lyon, Revolutionary Veteran and Settler Along the South River

Joseph Emmanuel Lyon was born February 13, 1754, in England. He was a jeweler and then came to the colonies as a British soldier. During fighting in Germantown, Pennsylvania on October 4, 1777, he was captured by the Americans. Obviously, a pragmatic soul, he took the oath of allegiance to the United States and joined the Colonial Army.

He was later wounded at the Battle of Cowpens, South Carolina on January 17, 1781. Lyon family history holds that Joseph had been left for dead and a "passer-by saw that he was alive and carried water to him in his hat. He then then carried him to his home and cared for him until he recovered. He was ever after crippled and was a teacher...." Lyon said that while he lay wounded on the battlefield, wild hogs came from the forest to eat of the decaying bodies on the battlefield. He feared they would eat him alive. He made a bargain in his mind that if the hogs didn't eat him alive he would never eat hog meat again.

---

[668] Records in the DeKalb Historical Society Biographical files
[669] Records of the Dekalb County Historical Society Biographical files
[670] Price, Vivian (1997) History of DeKalb County, Georgia, 1822-1900; Wolfe Pub. Co. pg. 95
[671] Price, Vivian (1997) History of DeKalb County, Georgia, 1822-1900; Wolfe Pub. Co. pg. 95
[672] Price, Vivian (1997) History of DeKalb County, Georgia, 1822-1900; Wolfe Pub. Co. pg. 95

He lost an arm as a result of his wounds. The hogs left him alone and for the rest of his life, Lyon never ate hog meat.

Joseph married Ann Marshbank around 1785 in South Carolina. He died about 1830. Their house, much modified since Joseph built it, is still home to members of the Lyon clan. Lyons Road, off Browns Mill, is named for this family.[673]

John B. Nelson, Nelson's Ferry Proprietor and Decatur's first Murder Victim

John B. Nelson, one of the first DeKalb Academy trustees and proprietor of Nelsons' Ferry on the Chattahoochee, became the county's first murder victim. He was killed in April of 1825 by John W. Davis. Governor George M. Troup offered a $250 reward for the apprehension of Davis who was caught and incarcerated in the dungeon of the DeKalb County Jail in downtown Decatur.

Col. Samuel T. Bailey served as lead defense attorney for Davis. His fee was $200 and a black boy named Jeff. Assisting Bailey were "a judge Strong and a man named Warner from Monticello".

Strong and Warner split the $200 and Bailey kept Jeff. There are no records of the outcome of the trial. Later, on August 4, 1849, the DeKalb Inferior Court declared the perpetrator, John W. Davis a "pauper lunatic" and committed him to the state Lunatic Asylum in Milledgeville.

John B Nelson is buried in his family cemetery close to the old ferry landing, now part of Fulton County.[674]

---

[673] Price 76, Hochim, Mrs. Eldred Martin, 1990, DAR Patriot Index, Centennial Edition Part I, National Society of the DAR, pg 431; Arnold Ross and Burnham, H. Clifton, Georgia Revolutionary War Soldier' Graves, pg 175; Johnson, Mr and Mrs J Wallace, n. d. Lyon Family History unpublished manuscript.
[674] Price, Vivian (1997) History of DeKalb County, Georgia, 1822-1900; Wolfe Pub. Co.

James H. Kirkpatrick, The Namesake for Kirkwood

James Hutchison Kirkpatrick has the distinction of being the first native-born Irishman to settle in Decatur. He came to Decatur from Morgan County, Georgia, in 1827. Between that time and his death in 1853, Mr. Kirkpatrick established the largest estate in the history of Decatur or DeKalb County which included thousands of acres west of Decatur. He was also probably the first tanner in Decatur.[675] Most of Kirkpatrick's land is now part of Kirkwood. He is buried in Decatur Cemetery.

Mural at the Intersection of DeKalb Ave. and Rocky Ford Rd.[676]

---

[675] Price, Vivian (1997) History of DeKalb County, Georgia, 1822-1900; Wolfe Pub. Co. pg. 139
[676] Photo by the Author

Decatur's Black Pioneers[677]

It's difficult to know the story for about half of Decatur's pioneers. Much of the very early history of African Americans living in the Decatur area is very difficult to document for obvious reasons and demands more research. One of the many tragedies of slavery is the loss of roots. It's possible to document how many African people and their early descendants were living in the area before the founding of Decatur but, documentation normally included only a name and age. Very few records were kept of people's relationships. As families were split up or moved to different areas, the connections were usually lost. In 1830, there were 8,388 white citizens living in DeKalb County and among them were 1,699 slaves and 17 freemen.[678]

Most Decatur residents kept few slaves in comparison to more rural communities. "Possession of a dozen or more was the exception rather than the rule and the majority of the early citizens, down to the time of the Emancipation Proclamation, owned none or at most, one or two house servants. Large plantations, such as were known in the older East and Middle Georgia counties, did not exist in early DeKalb."[679]

"In the early days of DeKalb County, indeed until slavery was abolished, there were no black churches. Slaves were often allowed to become members of white churches and in the larger town churches provision was always made for the separate seating of slaves, usually in galleries. It was a general custom of slave owners who were members of the church to give their slaves religious instruction. The field workers would meet in one of their cabins and the house servants around the family altars of their masters."[680] The oldest African-American congregation in Decatur, Antioch AME Church, was founded by freed slaves in 1868.[681]

Section Six of the Decatur cemetery was dedicated as an African American section soon after the Civil War and contains more than 900 graves. The oldest confirmed, known graves in section six are those of Dorcas Henderson, Simon Read and Israel Sanford who all passed away in 1887.[682]

Another large section of slave burials is located just north of the Lyon farm on a knoll above a small tributary of the South River. It was a spot too rocky to easily till and with a reputation as an Indian graveyard. It later became a place where slaves were buried that is now called Flat Rock Cemetery. Half of the

[677] Brown, John (1855) Slave Live in Georgia
[678] (1970) Early DeKalb County History, prepared by and Furnished as a service of the DeKalb Chamber of Commerce
[679] Garrett; Franklin M. (1969) Atlanta and Environs: A Chronicle of Its People and Events, Volume 1; University of Georgia Press p. 31
[680] Garrett; Franklin M. (1969) Atlanta and Environs: A Chronicle of Its People and Events, Volume 1; University of Georgia Press p. 39
[681] A Brief History of Decatur's African American Community, City of Decatur
[682] The Beacon Community, City of Decatur, Ga., Website

land is now owned by the Flat Rock Archives. Tours of the cemetery are available by appointment.[683]

There is also a section of slave burials in the cemetery of Utoy Primitive Baptist Church Cemetery near Sandtown.

Photo of "A Georgian Cotton Field" in 1907

The photo below depicts African Americans picking cotton in 1907. It was taken by a Decatur resident, Marcus L. Brown. Though it was taken well after slavery was abolished, it depicts a scene that would have looked very similar in the early days of DeKalb County and Decatur when John Brown was a slave of Thomas Stevens.

A Georgia Cotton Field.   Copyright 1907, by Marcus L. Brown, Decatur Ga.

---

[683] (2009) Georgia Archaeology Month, Society for Georgia Archaeology

Mason Shumate's Estate and Slaves

An appraisal of the estate of Mason Shumate gives us a window into how slaves in Decatur were managed and the values that were placed on human beings as possessions. The appraisal was made by Ezekiel Mason in 1849. Mr. Shumate made his living as a hotel owner. These slaves were most likely responsible for a lot of the maintenance and daily management of the hotel and were probably treated more humanely than other slaves who were forced to work in the fields.[684]

Cash on hand	$18.30
House and lot	$420.00
Frances Sophia, a mulatto girl	$420.00
Rosella, a negro woman, and her child, Savannah	$650.00
Mary, a mulatto woman	$620.00
Mary Emily, a black girl	$230.00
Caroline, a mulatto girl	$575.00
Elvira, a black girl	$470.00
Minerva, a mulatto	$430.00
Eli, a mulatto boy	$590.00
Frances Isabella, a girl	$371.00
Mary Loduska, a girl	$261.00
Adalaine and her child, John Albert	$775.00
Felix, a mulatto boy	$670.00
Emaline, a mulatto woman	$560.00
Huldah, a girl	$455.00
One yoke oxen	$25.00
One cow and calf	$10.00
One cow and calf	$10.00
One sorrel filly	$69.00
One lot stock hogs, 17 head	$40.00
One small wagon	$40.00
One lot kitchen furniture	$6.50
One lot farming tools	$7.00
One man's saddle	$3.00
One spinning wheel and reel	$3.00
3 featherbeds, One bedstead and furniture	$30.00
One pattent clock	$3.00
Other furniture	$13.00

---

[684] Garrett, Franklin (1969), Estate of Mason Shumate Reveals Slave Worth More than his House, DeKalb News

The Chronicle of John Brown, a Slave in Decatur

The richest source we have of what life was like for a slave who lived in the Decatur area around the time of its founding comes from the narrative of John Brown who was born into slavery but eventually escaped and made it to England.

John Brown (called "Fed" as a slave) was born around 1810 in Southampton County, Virginia. His parents were Nancy Moore[685] and Joe Benford.[686] Joe's grandfather had been kidnapped from the area that is now Nigeria where he was a member of the Eboe (sic) tribe. The Eboe (more commonly "Igbo") is an interesting tribe of practicing Jewish people in Nigeria who believe they are the descendants of the "Lost Tribes" that were exiled from Israel in Biblical times.[687]

> **John Brown was brought to Jones County Georgia, where he was sold to Thomas Stevens, one of Decatur's earliest residents.**

In 1820, at only about 10 years of age, John was pulled away from his mother and sold to a slave speculator who intended to bring him to Georgia where the market for slaves had risen in response to the rise in cotton prices. He was then brought to Jones County, Georgia where he was sold to Thomas Stevens, one of Decatur's earliest residents.

At that time, the Stevens growing farm where John was put to work was about eight miles from Milledgeville. Stevens then moved to DeKalb County where he owned 31 slaves including John Brown and making him the owner of the greatest number of slaves in DeKalb County per the 1830 census.[688] In 1825, he owned some land along the Chattahoochee River between the forks of Nancy Creek and Peachtree Creek and bought land lot 143 in Decatur for $400 in 1831 along a branch of South Peachtree Creek.[689] On December 22, 1832, Thomas Stevens became a commissioner of the Decatur Burial Ground (Decatur Cemetery).

John's typical duties were agricultural, working long hours in the fields planting, hoeing, ploughing, tending and harvesting crops for Thomas Stevens. A typical work day, even for a boy of 10, was 19 hours long.

---

[685] The slave owner of Nancy was Betty Moore – Nancy had no actual last name.
[686] The slave owner of Joe was a man named Benford. Joe had no actual last name.
[687] Nigeria's Igbo Jews: 'Lost tribe' of Israel?; CNN; Chika Ohuah; Feb 4th, 2013.
[688] 1830 Federal Census
[689] DeKalb County Land Records, Deed Book H p. 368, on file at Courthouse, Decatur, Georgia

John Brown describes interactions with several other residents of Decatur in his narrative. One of them was Jessie Cleveland who lived in the building where the Pythagoras Lodge is now located and owned the first piano to be seen in Decatur.[690]

Stevens had at first been a carpenter but found more success making alcohol. He then started planting crops including Indian corn and other ingredients needed for making beer and whiskey.

> On another occasion, John was lent out to a Doctor Hamilton by Stevens, so that the doctor could perform a series of barbaric medical experiments with a human subject.

In Brown's description, Stevens was a Welshman of about middle height with black hair and fair skin. He always seemed to have a smiling expression on his face and laughed out loud often, but his laughter was mocking, not jovial.[691] He was a very cruel man who frequently subjected his slaves to savage beatings. In one of these beatings, he delivered a kick to John Brown's face that broke his nose and "cut the leaders of his right eye" causing it to sag for the rest of Brown's life.

On another occasion, John was lent out to a Doctor Hamilton by Stevens, so the doctor could perform a series of barbaric medical experiments with a human subject. For one of these experiments, a pit was dug and heated with coals. Brown was placed sitting in the hole on a stool and the top of it was covered with blankets so that the doctor could administer different treatments for heat stroke to see which was most effective. The doctor also blistered up the skin on John Brown's arms and legs with heated iron so that he could see how deeply John's black skin went into his body.

Amid his own hardships, John Brown was inspired by the tragic story of another slave who was owned by Thomas Stevens, John Glasgow. Glasgow was a free, black, merchant marine from England who was seized, jailed and sold into slavery, apparently for no other reason than being black in America rather than England, while his ship was in port in Savannah, Georgia.

[690] McKinney Clarke, Caroline (1973) The Story of Decatur 1823-1899; Higgins-Macarthur/Longing & Porter
[691] Brown, John (1855) Slave Live in Georgia

Glasgow was to be held in jail until his ship was ready to depart, and his captain came to retrieve him. However, there was a "jailing fee" required to be paid by the captain for Glasgow's release. The captain chose not to pay. Perhaps he saw the double benefit of having already gotten Glasgow's labor on the journey to Savannah and having to pay neither Glasgow's wage as an able-bodied seaman nor the jailing fee. Glasgow was then sold into slavery by the city of Savannah and ended up in Decatur. Descriptions of England and how black citizens were treated much more as equals there inspired John Brown to commit himself to one day make his escape and reach London.

In 1839, Thomas Stevens suffered an apparent stroke that left him paralyzed on one side of his body and unable to speak (I find that interesting to note the coincidence of Stevens losing the use of one side of his face after what he had done to John Brown's face). Soon after the stroke, Thomas Stevens died and John Brown was left to Stevens' son, Decatur Stevens.

Decatur Stevens was no kinder to his slaves than his father had been. John made his escape from this new master around 1845. He was recaptured in New Orleans and sold to Theodoric J. James who owned a large plantation in Mississippi.

Brown made his final escape from James shortly after arriving at the James Plantation and made his way to the North with the help of many sympathetic Americans, both black and white. He then took the name of John Brown as his free man name (recall he had been called "Fed" up to this point). For a while, he lived in Michigan and then Canada. In 1850, he fulfilled his life's ambition and left America for England.

In England, he wrote a chronicle of his experiences and delivered many lectures about his experiences as a Georgia slave and the story of John Glasgow. He married an Englishwoman, became an herb doctor and died in London in 1876, a free man.

Mary Gay

Mary Gay was not one of the original Decatur pioneers but she deserves to be mentioned here as a sort of epilogue to the story of John Brown. Mary Gay was an accomplished author who lived in Decatur and published several books that recount what life was like in Antebellum Georgia and during the Civil War. Her most well-known book is "Life in Dixie During the War". It tells of how she was one of few who chose to stay in her home in Decatur during its occupation by Union Troops, even after they had set up camp on her front lawn. She tells several interesting stories with Southern pride and willingness to endure hardships for a principle as central themes. Some of her stories were the inspiration for elements of "Gone with the Wind" and were borrowed in Mark Twain's "Tom Sawyer." This inclusion in Mark Twain's writing was not a complimentary one though and Mary knew it. She included a scolding of Twain in the foreword to one of her own books.[692]

The Mary Gay House in Adair Park[693]

Mary Gay is also the granddaughter of Thomas Stevens, the previous owner of the slave John Brown. Her depictions of the relationships between slaves and their white owners differs dramatically from those of John Brown and his experiences with her grandfather. There was a vast difference in how slaves in the field like John Brown were treated and those who lived in the house with whom Mary Gay would have had a much closer relationship, but she was certainly familiar with what life was like for a slave owned by the Stevens family and that it was a very different story in each situation. Both stories involve one person being owned by another of course. I have little doubt that the publication of John Brown's narrative was a part of the inspiration for Mary Gay to tell her side of the story. The house in which Mary Gay lived in Decatur is now part of the DeKalb Historical Society's Adair Historical Complex on West Trinity Place.

---

[692] Clark, Kathleen Ann (2009) Georgia Women: Their Lives and Times, University of Georgia Press
[693] Photo by the author

A List of Firsts in Decatur [694]

- **First African-American Owned Business**: A blacksmith shop owned by Henry Oliver. Date unknown.[695]
- **First Bar**: Part of William Hill's grocery started on the square. Popular beverages were peach brandy, apple brandy and corn liquor.[696]
- **First Blacksmith**: Carlisle Johnson.[697]
- **First Burial in Decatur Cemetery**: A small child of unknown or who had no name. The next was Dr. Ormand L. Morgan, a promising young physician who arrived sometime after Dr. Hopkins had left in 1826 or 1827 but died suddenly and unexpectedly.[698]
- **First Clerk of Courts**: Thomas A. Dobbs. Thomas Dobbs built his own office in 1823 which extended 10 feet into the street!
- **First Courthouse**: A small log building on the north side of the square. It was equipped with stocks out front.
- **First Doctor**: Dr. Hopkins. He was in Decatur in 1826 but left soon thereafter. He was replaced by poor Dr. Morgan (see first burial) and later by Dr. E.N. Calhoun and Dr. Chapmon Powell among others.
- **First Ferry**: The first ferry in DeKalb County was started by Jacob R. Brooks at the shallow ford across the Chattahoochee in 1824.[699] The first permit for a ferry was given to William Blake in 1823. Blake soon sold the permit to a man named Nelson who started "Nelson's Ferry" over the Chattahoochee.[700]
- **First Furniture Factory**: Established by Joseph Morgan in 1832. Joseph first made chairs but was later joined by his brother LS Morgan. The factory expanded to include cabinet furniture. Joseph married the daughter of James H. Kirkpatrick, Jane M. Kirkpatrick.
- **First Grist Mill**: Dr. Peter F. Hoyle operated a water-powered grist mill in the very early days of Decatur somewhere on the south side. It was probably located within the city limits, but no sign of it can be found today.[701]
- **First Grocery**: Started on the square by William Hill.

694 (1970) Early DeKalb County History, prepared by and Furnished as a service of the DeKalb Chamber of Commerce
695 The Beacon Community, City of Decatur, Ga., Website
696 DeKalb County centennial celebration at Decatur, Georgia, November 9, 1922: Historical address
697 McKinney Clarke, Caroline (1973) The Story of Decatur 1823-1899; Higgins-Macarthur/Longing & Porter
698 Price, Vivian (1997) History of DeKalb County, Georgia, 1822-1900; Wolfe Pub. Co..
699 Price, Vivian (1997) History of DeKalb County, Georgia, 1822-1900; Wolfe Pub. Co. pg. 109
700 Price, Vivian (1997) History of DeKalb County, Georgia, 1822-1900; Wolfe Pub. Co.
701 Hudgins, Carl T. (1952) Collection of the DeKalb Historical Society, The Year Book – 1952

➤ **First Hanging**: A Mr. Crowder was hanged in the city square in 1829 for killing his wife and burning his house down with three children inside.[702]

➤ **First Hat Maker**: Jonathan B. Wilson[703]

➤ **First Hotel**: Built by Reuben Cone, a judge of the inferior court. The hotel burned down in 1846 due to a fire that began in Judge Cone's living quarters. It also burned Col. Thomas Akins's store, Thomas Dobb's office, another dwelling and the post office on the corner.

➤ **First Institution of Higher Education for Women**: Hannah Moore Female Collegiate Institute established by Act of the General Assembly on December 22nd, 1857. Its first President was Reverend John S. Wilson, the first pastor of the Decatur Presbyterian Church.

➤ **First Jail**: Small log building on McDonough Street. It included a dungeon which was entered through a trap door in the floor above.

➤ **First Jug Maker**: Jess Potter Jones[704]

➤ **First Murder in DeKalb County**: John B. Nelson, the proprietor of Nelson's Ferry was murdered by a man named John W. Davis. Davis was later committed to an insane asylum in Milledgeville.[705]

➤ **First Newspaper**: The DeKalb Gazette, established by Samuel Wright Miner in 1830.

➤ **First Church**: Macedonia Baptist Church was organized in 1823.[706]

➤ **First Postmaster in Decatur**: Leonard Randall. JMC Montgomery was the first Postmaster of Standing Peachtree. Tunison Coryell was the first Postmaster of Sandtown.

➤ **First Presiding Judge of the Court** Charles J. McDonald. The first court located in William Jackson's home in 1823.

➤ **First Railroad**: The Georgia Railroad. The first journey passing through DeKalb County passed from Augusta to Terminus (Atlanta) on September 15, 1845.

➤ **First Representative of DeKalb in the Legislature**: James Hicks

➤ **First Rifle Maker**: Joe Martin[707]

➤ **First Saddle Maker**: James McNeil (see the section on James McNeil) [708]

➤ **First School (in DeKalb County):** The DeKalb County Academy, established on November 10,1823 under a resolution of the General

---

[702] McKinney Clarke, Caroline (1973) The Story of Decatur 1823-1899; Higgins-Macarthur/Longing & Porter
[703] McKinney Clarke, Caroline (1973) The Story of Decatur 1823-1899; Higgins-Macarthur/Longing & Porter
[704] McKinney Clarke, Caroline (1973) The Story of Decatur 1823-1899; Higgins-Macarthur/Longing & Porter
[705] Price, Vivian (1997) History of DeKalb County, Georgia, 1822-1900; Wolfe Pub. Co.
[706] Price, Vivian (1997) History of DeKalb County, Georgia, 1822-1900; Wolfe Pub. Co.
[707] McKinney Clarke, Caroline (1973) The Story of Decatur 1823-1899; Higgins-Macarthur/Longing & Porter
[708] McKinney Clarke, Caroline (1973) The Story of Decatur 1823-1899; Higgins-Macarthur/Longing & Porter

Assembly. Lotteries were held to raised money for the school raising $1,267 in 1829. The School's first rector was Reverend Alex Kirkpatrick.

➤ **First School for African-Americans**: The first school for African-Americans in Decatur was a small parochial school started by a Presbyterian minister. In 1902, the first public school for African-Americans opened. That school relocated in 1913 and became known as Herring Street School.[709]

➤ **First Senator from DeKalb in the State Legislature**: James McConnell Montgomery (see profile section about James Montgomery).[710]

➤ **First Set of County Commissioners**: Reuben Cone, William Morris, William Gresham, James White and Thomas A. Dobbs[711]

➤ **First Set of Inferior Court Justices**: Charles Gates Sr., William Baker, Mason D. Shumate[712]

➤ **First Sherriff of Decatur**: George Harris. The sheriff in those days was required to take an oath that "he had not since the first day of January 1819, been engaged in a duel, either directly or indirectly, either as principal or second or in any character whatsoever, in this state."[713]

➤ **First Store**: Started by Charles Latimer in a rented room of Cone's hotel. He later bought a lot and built a store on the southwest corner of the square as well as one further outside the city. Col. Thomas Akins later took over the room for a store. William Gresham also began a store around this time (see profile section about Charles Latimer and Thomas Akins).[714]

➤ **First Tanner**: James Hutchison Kirkpatrick (see profile section about James Kirkpatrick).

➤ **First Tavern**: Opened by Mason D. Shumate in a rented part of Reuben Cone's hotel (see profile section about Reuben Cone).

➤ **First Tin Smith**: Walter Wadsworth. His shop was located on the northeast corner of what is now Church Street and East Ponce de Leon Ave. [715] Walter Wadsworth came to Decatur in 1827 and was employed by Eskow & Reece and a journeyman tinner. When Sherman's army arrived in Decatur, Mr. Wadsworth's shop was looted.[716]

➤ **First Wagon Maker**: John Adair. [717]

---

[709] The Beacon Community, City of Decatur, Ga., Website
[710] Records of the DeKalb Historical Society
[711] DeKalb County centennial celebration at Decatur, Georgia, November 9, 1922: Historical address
[712] DeKalb County centennial celebration at Decatur, Georgia, November 9, 1922: Historical address
[713] DeKalb County centennial celebration at Decatur, Georgia, November 9, 1922: Historical address
[714] DeKalb County centennial celebration at Decatur, Georgia, November 9, 1922: Historical address
[715] McKinney Clarke, Caroline (1973) The Story of Decatur 1823-1899; Higgins-Macarthur/Longing & Porter
[716] (1970) Early DeKalb County History, prepared by and Furnished as a service of the DeKalb Chamber of Commerce
[717] McKinney Clarke, Caroline (1973) The Story of Decatur 1823-1899; Higgins-Macarthur/Longing & Porter

Origins of Some Important Names Used in the Decatur Area

"Creek" Indians: The word Creek is a shortening of the phrase "Ocheese Creek". "Ocheese" is an old name for the Ocmulgee River where many of the Lower Creeks were living when the English came into contact with them. The English coined the term calling these Indians the Creeks.[718]

Adair Road: I'm not sure exactly which Adair the road was named for, but the Adair family is one of the original large families who settled the area. John Adair was Decatur's first wagon maker among many other posts important to the town.[719]

Chamblee: Was incorporated August 17, 1908 and was named for a Mr. Chamblee who had petitioned for a Post Office to be put in this location.[720]

Chattahoochee: There was a creek town along the river in what is now Heard County called Chattahoochee. The town was probably named for the river and not the other way around. The word "Chattahoochee" comes from a combination of two Creek words, "Chatto" meaning "stones" and "Hoochee" meaning "flowered." It was said that there were stones in the river with markings that resembled flowers on them.[721]

Clairemont Avenue vs. Clairmont Road: The "e" in Clairemont and the name of the street are both in honor of Claire Ridley, the eldest daughter of Dr. Robert B. Ridley and the former Mrs. John F. Kiser, whom he married in 1886. Dr. Ridley had a farm called Clairemont that comprised much of the land in the area and gave its name to the road that passed through his land. The former name of the road was, of course, the Shallowford Trail that was created by Indians. Why Clairemont is spelled without the "e" in some places is still somewhat of a mystery or perhaps simply arbitrary.[722] The change seems to have occurred when the land was divided into plots for development in 1939 and the neighborhood that was established was called "Clairmont Estates" without the "e." Since then, the naming has either been drawn from the original spelling of the farm or from the name of the original subdivision. Clairmont was also called Webster Street and Winn Street at different times in the past.

Clarkston: Was incorporated December 12, 1882 and was named for W.W. Clark.[723]

[718] Swanton, John R. (1922) Early History of the Creek Indians and Their Neighbors; Smithsonian Institution Bureau of American Ethnology; Bulletin 73; Washington Government Printing Office
[719] (1970) Early DeKalb County History, prepared by and Furnished as a service of the DeKalb Chamber of Commerce
[720] Collections of the DeKalb Historical Society, Year Book, 1952
[721] Price, Vivian (1997) History of DeKalb County, Georgia, 1822-1900; Wolfe Pub. Co.
[722] Price, Vivian (1997) History of DeKalb County, Georgia, 1822-1900; Wolfe Pub. Co.

Cone Street: Named for Reuben Cone, one of DeKalb County's first County Commissioners.[724]

Doraville: Was founded December 15, 1871 and was named for Dora Jack, daughter of an official for the Atlanta and Charlotte Airline Railway. Before that, the name of the area was Cross Keys. [725]

Dunwoody: Was named for Major Charles Dunwoody who had owned this land.

East Lake: Was incorporated on August 16, 1910 and was named for the lake located there and the fact it lies on the eastern side of Atlanta. [726]

Edgewood: Was incorporated December 9, 1898 and was so named because it was so close to Atlanta. It was made part of Atlanta in 1909.[727]

Gilmer Street: Named for captain Gilmer who established Fort Peachtree as James Mc. Montgomery's commanding officer.[728]

Kirkwood: Named for James H. Kirkpatrick, a pioneer landowner of Decatur. The area of Kirkpatrick is shown on the map in the 1864 map pictured in this book on page 72. [729]

Marthasville: The Atlanta area was originally just called "Terminus" and was then founded as Marthasville on December 23, 1843. It was called Marthasville for Martha Lumpkin, daughter of Governor Wilson Lumpkin. The name was changed to Atlanta on December 26, 1845.[730][731]

McElroy Road: Named for John Calin McElroy[732]

Montgomery Ferry Drive: Named for the ferry operated by JMC Montgomery on the Chattahoochee River. JMC Montgomery is also the namesake for Montgomery street in downtown Decatur.[733]

Nancy Creek: Most likely named for the widow of Mr. John L. Evins, Nancy Evins nee Baugh. They moved to the area in 1818 and settled on the creek that was named for her. Alternatively, some claim the name of the creek is "Nance" Creek and was named after a chief of the Indians that resided in the area. [734]

[723] Collections of the DeKalb Historical Society, Year Book, 1952
[724] Hoyt, S. B. Hoyt (1886) The Shumate Family; The Story of Some of the Pioneers of DeKalb County; The Atlanta Constitution
[725] Collections of the DeKalb Historical Society, Year Book, 1952
[726] Hudgins, Carl T. (1952) Collection of the DeKalb Historical Society, The Year Book – 1952
[727] Collections of the DeKalb Historical Society, Year Book, 1952
[728] Franklin M. Garrett; (1969) Atlanta and Environs: A Chronicle of Its People and Events, Volume 1; University of Georgia Press
[729] Collections of the DeKalb Historical Society, Year Book, 1952
[730] Collections of the DeKalb Historical Society, Year Book, 1952
[731] Collections of the DeKalb Historical Society, Year Book, 1952
[732] Collections of the DeKalb Historical Society, Year Book, 1952
[733] (1970) Early DeKalb County History, prepared by and Furnished as a service of the DeKalb Chamber of Commerce

Nelson's Ferry Road: Named for the ferry operated by John B. Nelson who also had the misfortune to be the first murder victim in DeKalb County (see section of firsts on previous pages).[735]

Oakhurst: Was incorporated April 19, 1909 and was named for a particularly beautiful forest that was growing on that location.

Redan: Was named for N. M. Reid and John T. Alford's wife, Mrs. Annie Alford by combining the two names into one word. [736]

Rockbridge Road: The origin of the name of Rock Bridge Road is interesting. It identified a point where there was a shoal in the Yellow River where you could cross by stepping from rock to rock, not an actual bridge the way we think of it. I haven't tried yet, but I believe you can go to the river near the point where the road crosses it and identify these rocks where people crossed for thousands of years.[737]

> I believe you can go to the river near the point where the road crosses it and probably identify these rocks where people crossed for thousands of years.

Sandtown: The name of Sandtown probably comes from a group of Hilibi Indians who arrived from a town of the same name in Alabama[738]

Scottdale: Was named for the Mill Village built by the Scott Investment Company built by George W. Scott. [739]

Snapfinger Creek: While DeKalb County was being surveyed in 1821, one of the surveyors fell and broke a finger along this creek. [740]

South River: The original, more accurate name for this river is "The South Fork of the Ocmulgee River". Over time, the part referring to the Ocmulgee River was dropped to just "South River."[741]

Standing Peachtree and Peachtree Road: There is a couple of different stories regarding the possible origin of the name "Peachtree." Both agree that it emanates from the town of Standing Peachtree located at the point of

[734] Garrett; Franklin (1969) Atlanta and Environs: A Chronicle of Its People and Events, Volume 1; Univ. of Georgia Press
[735] Price, Vivian (1997) History of DeKalb County, Georgia, 1822-1900; Wolfe Pub. Co..
[736] Collections of the DeKalb Historical Society, Year Book, 1952
[737] Garrett; Franklin (1969) Atlanta and Environs: A Chronicle of Its People and Events, Volume 1; Univ. of Georgia Press
[738] Price, Vivian (1997) History of DeKalb County, Georgia, 1822-1900; Wolfe Pub. Co.
[739] Collections of the DeKalb Historical Society, Year Book, 1952
[740] (1970) Early DeKalb County History, prepared by and Furnished as a service of the DeKalb Chamber of Commerce
[741] Summary of Remarks by John H. Goff before the DeKalb Historical Society, March 30, 1961

confluence of Peachtree Creek and the Chattahoochee River. One story is that there was an enormous pine tree on the bank near the creek that was blazed so that the local Indians could gather sap from it, also called "Pitch", hence it was the "Pitch Tree." The more likely of the stories is that it was named for an actual peach tree that stood on top of the enormous mound at that location; the "Standing Peachtree."[742] George Washington Collier, who would carry the mail between Decatur and Allatoona in the 1830s would pass the location often in his mail deliveries and attested to this point as a fact.[743] Peaches were initially brought to America by the Spanish in the mid-16th century.[744]

Stone Mountain: Before it was founded, it was identified on maps simply as the "Rock Mountain". Upon its founding in 1839, the original name of Stone Mountain was New Gibraltar. The name was changed in 1847. [745] The Creek name for the Stone Mountain is said to have been "Mountain Knife" because the shape of the mountain resembles a giant granite knife in the style fashioned by the Creeks. [746]

> The name of the Yellow River is a translation of its Muscogee name, which identified it as the primary place one would find the Jerusalem Oak and to make the "yellow water".

Tucker: Was named for a Capt. Tucker who was an official for the Seaboard Airline Railway. [747]

Yellow River: The origins for the name of this river are quite interesting. It is not named for the color of the water or the sand underneath the water as one might think. The name is much more significant. The Creeks harvested the Jerusalem Oak tree to obtain a liquid they called "yellow water" used in many of their ceremonies including the "Green Corn Dance", one of their central rituals. The name of the Yellow River is a translation of the Muscogee name for this river which, identified it as the primary place one would find the Jerusalem Oak and to make the "yellow water".[748]

---

[742] Franklin Garrett (1969) Atlanta and Environs: A Chronicle of Its People and Events, Vol. 1; University of Georgia Press,
[743] Garrett, Frank (1969), Atlanta and Environs: A Chronical of Its People and Events, 1820s – 1870s (vol. 1).
[744] Price, Vivian (1997) History of DeKalb County, Georgia, 1822-1900; Wolfe Pub. Co.
[745] Collections of the DeKalb Historical Society, Year Book, 1952
[746] Summary of Remarks by John H. Goff before the DeKalb Historical Society, March 30, 1961
[747] Collections of the DeKalb Historical Society, Year Book, 1952
[748] Summary of Remarks by John H. Goff before the DeKalb Historical Society, March 30, 1961

CHAPTER 15:
DECATUR AND THE CREEK WAR OF 1836

The last chapter in the saga of the Creek Indians in Georgia directly involved several Decatur residents and the cannon that now sits on the city square. After their land in Georgia had been sold to the United States and issued out through the land lottery system, the first group of Creeks who had supported William McIntosh voluntarily chose to leave Georgia for land at Fort Gibson in Oklahoma (near present day Muscogee Oklahoma) in 1827. They brought 703 Creeks and 86 slaves. About a year later, 400 more left. In 1829, 1,200 more left from Fort Bainbridge and Line Creek in 1829, some by land and many by steamship up the Mississippi River.[749]

Many other Creeks from Georgia tried to avoid removal and sought refuge among the Seminoles, the Chickasaws or, in some rare cases, sympathetic white settlers like the Perkersons in Decatur.

Many other Creeks from Georgia tried to avoid removal and sought refuge among the Seminoles, the Chickasaws or, in some rare cases, sympathetic white settlers like the Perkersons in Decatur.[750]

The last of the voluntary emigrants from Georgia arrived in Oklahoma during the month of September 1829. They immediately had to face a cholera epidemic upon their arrival. They also had to suffer raids from western Indians who had not at all agreed to hand over the land in the West to these new arrivals.[751]

Many of the Creeks who had left voluntarily chose to return to land still owned by the Upper Creeks in Alabama rather than stay in Oklahoma.[752] More groups of Creeks removed themselves from Alabama and left for Oklahoma in 1835 and 1836, but most Creeks chose to stay on the land they still owned in Alabama. However, settlers continued to ignore Creek rights to the land and settled within their borders. The state governments continued to refuse to

[749] Kane, Robert (2016) Second Creek War; Encyclopedia of Alabama
[750] Kane, Robert (2016) Second Creek War; Encyclopedia of Alabama
[751] Kane, Robert (2016) Second Creek War; Encyclopedia of Alabama
[752] Kane, Robert (2016) Second Creek War; Encyclopedia of Alabama

enforce Creek land rights. Several skirmishes broke out among the Creeks and the settlers. [753]

Temporary refuge in Alabama would provide short-lived relief. In 1836, the Creeks in Alabama had had enough and took up their arms against the Americans once again. They were partly inspired by the recent success of their cousins, the Seminoles, to the south. The violence began in Russell County, Alabama with sporadic attacks on intruding settlers.[754]

Creeks from the towns of Chehaw, Yuchi and Hitchiti and other towns attacked squatters on Creek land and burned down their plantations in present day Alabama. [755] The conflict attracted the attention of the Federal Government, and Andrew Jackson traveled south to squash the disruptions in what has come to be called the Second Creek War of 1836.[756]

The first regularly organized military company in the new DeKalb County, as distinguished from the militia, was the "Volunteer Light Infantry," incorporated by Act of the Legislature approved December 22, 1835. It was organized by Ezekiel Calhoun. A profile of the personal history of these two brothers is included in the previous chapter.

When the war crossed the border of Alabama and entered Georgia, a call to arms went out from the Georgia governor on May 15, 1836. On that morning, a force of Creek warriors invaded the little town of Roanoke, Georgia along the Chattahoochee River about 30 miles south of Columbus (the town of Roanoke is now beneath Walter F. George Reservoir). The Creeks burned the little town to the ground and killed 12 of its residents. The surviving townspeople fled into the woods.

In January, another issue went out from the Governor to muster the troops and "be prepared to march at a moment's warning" and the Calhoun brothers both responded eagerly to the call.

While E.N. Calhoun was mustering up his light infantry, his brother James was helping to organize the DeKalb Cavalry although he was not its commanding officer.[757] On January 29, 1836, Charles Parr was captain of the DeKalb Cavalry and its 28 officers and men. He then sent a tally of the available people in his company to Milledgeville. He partially blamed the small size of the company on the fact they had never been issued any arms.

[753] Kane, Robert (2016) Second Creek War; Encyclopedia of Alabama
[754] Haveman, Christopher (2009), Creek Indian Removal, Encyclopedia of Alabama
[755] Kane, Robert (2016) Second Creek War; Encyclopedia of Alabama
[756] Kane, Robert (2016) Second Creek War; Encyclopedia of Alabama
[757] Oakland Cemetery, Oakland Resident Spotlight: James Calhoun

Nevertheless, they seemed eager to serve, though unclear about why they were being mustered. Ezekiel wrote to Milledgeville, "Those who have been paraded today are ready for any service either in Florida or in this state."

> **The Decatur and Dekalb troops lost six soldiers killed and several wounded in the Creek War of 1836.**

There were a few other companies formed for the call in 1836 that also included many of Decatur's well-known residents. The DeKalb Independent Volunteer Rifle Company of DeKalb County was formed with 65 officers and men. Thomas Akins was elected captain of that unit.[758]

Another order was sent out from Milledgeville in June of 1836 for "the voluntary enlistment or draft of every sixth man from the 54th Regiment of the Georgia Militia to form the DeKalb Independent Guards. William Ezzard was elected to become their captain.

Apart from the officers, the soldiers of the DeKalb forces called up to respond to the War of 1836 reflect the names very familiar as the first merchants, judges and other settlers in Decatur, including several Diamonds, Montgomerys, Fowlers, Shumates, Latimers, Akins, Biffles, McElroys and Sprayers.[759]

Ezekiel Calhoun's Infantry left Decatur in July 1836 with 84 strong. On its departure, the ladies of Decatur presented the Company with an American flag to carry into battle.[760]

The DeKalb companies were all sent to the southwestern part of the state near Columbus where fighting was already in progress. After arriving, they were stationed at Fort Macreary in Columbus. The cannon was taken to West Point Georgia by E.N. Calhoun's company.[761]

The Decatur Cavalry Battle in The Second Creek War of 1836
On July 31, 1836, James Calhoun was in command (as a temporary position) of the DeKalb Cavalry when they attacked a band of around 30 Indians who were hiding in a swamp on the plantation of a Mr. Quall near Columbus, Georgia.

[758] Collections of the DeKalb Historical Society, Year Book, 1952 – Excerpt from a story in the AJC by Winifred L. Moore.
[759] Records of the DeKalb Historical Society
[760] Collections of the DeKalb Historical Society, Year Book, 1952 – Excerpt from a story in the AJC by Winifred L. Moore.
[761] Price 76, Hochim, Mrs. Eldred Martin, 1990, DAR Patriot Index, Centennial Edition Part I, National Society of the DAR

An account of the engagement appeared in the Columbus Enquirer after the battle.

"THE WAR NOT YET ENDED.[762]

On Sunday morning last a severe engagement took place as usual, between the Georgians and the Indians, in the neighborhood of Mr. Quall's [Quarles in another article] plantation, above Roanoke. We have not received the particulars of the fight but learned that information was given to the forces stationed at Fort McCrary, that fresh signs of the Indians had been discovered in a swamp in Mr. Quall's plantation; upon which Captain Calhoun, of DeKalb County, with a command of ninety men, were dispatched in pursuit of the enemy. In scouring the place, a fresh trail was found, leading out of the swamp in the direction of Lumpkin. It was followed. In a short time, the party came up with a small gang of Indians, of thirty or more and commenced the fight. The Indians soon fled, leaving seven of their number killed. The whites, after the first skirmish, supposed the Indians whipped and the fight over; but they found that this advance party was a mere decoy, to draw them into the midst of their enemies, by whom they soon found themselves completely flanked on both sides. The battle was renewed, but the ammunition of the whites being exhausted, they were compelled to retreat. In the engagement, the whites lost five soldiers killed and several wounded. Among the slain were, Mr. Colly, (overseer for D.P. Hillhouse, Esq.,) a brave man and much respected; a Mr. Willis and Dr. Orr, of DeKalb -- the names of the others are not yet known to us. It is said that the whites had only three rounds of cartridges apiece when the fight first commenced -- a very unfortunate oversight, indeed, and if true, wholly unpardonable in the commanding officer. Something of this sort was surely the matter or the DeKalb boys would never have turned their backs upon their enemy, although they may have outnumbered them three to one."

The two other men lost were John Willis, son of James Willis of Snapfinger and Matthew J. Orr, son of Robert Orr, of Sandtown. Robert Billups was also killed in a separate battle during the war[763]

In defense of Captain Calhoun, the indictment leveled against his preparation of his soldiers in the article above is very probably unfounded. The supplies given to the troops mustered out of DeKalb County had been an issue from

---

[762] The War Not Yet Ended; Columbus Sentinel; 2 Aug 1836,
[763] Collections of the DeKalb Historical Society, Year Book, 1952

The Decatur Cavalry Battle in the Creek War of 1836[764]

the beginning. The Calhouns were clearly very intelligent and forthright people and I find it much easier to believe that Capt. Calhoun agreed to follow his orders and do his duty while making clear to his commanding officers that he was not well provisioned with ammunition rather than that he was negligent and endangered his neighbors from back home.

On January 22, 1836, long before the engagement, James' brother, Ezekiel had written to Col. Robinson at the capital in Milledgeville with an ardent complaint about the supplies being sent to the DeKalb troops, saying in part…

"…Their uniform is citizens' clothing. They have around 44 guns between them. I have called for a company muster on the 27th. The muskets and uniforms and accouterment we received from Milledgeville were in such a bad state of repair that they seemed to have been through not only the last Indian war but also the revolutionary war. They also have no music. I hope I will be effectual in rousing immediately a necessary degree of military feeling."[765]

The Battle of Jarman's Troops and the Death of Robert Billups

The fighting in which Robert Billups was killed was more deadly and brutal than the battle involving James Calhoun's cavalry. It's not clear how it came about, but Billups somehow ended up in a company that wasn't from DeKalb County. He served in the company of a Captain Jarman from Mississippi. While encamped (specific date unclear), they were attacked by a group of Creeks near Fort Mitchell. The Creeks were patient and waited silently in the surrounding woods while the company spent several hours settling into their camp, ate their meals and began to relax. As evening was setting in, a war whoop sounded, and the Creeks suddenly attacked from all sides. The soldiers were caught completely unprepared. Most were not able to even reach their weapons. The Creeks very nearly killed every member of the company. There were only two known survivors of the battle. Among the Americans, one was a traveler named John Landrum who had come across the company and joined them to share their campfire. Landrum became the teller of the grim tale.

The other survivor was a lone soldier from Jarman's company who said that, unlike all the other soldiers, he had galloped his horse straight toward the attacking Creeks and perhaps thanks to the Creek's sheer surprise at his maneuver, was able to break through their line and escape to their backs before any had a chance to turn and fire. We unfortunately do not know the name of this other survivor.

---

[765] Report from the DeKalb light infantry, E.N. Calhoun Captain (37 officers and men) to Col. Bolling H. Robinson, Aide de Camp

DeKalb resident Robert Billups was shot out of his saddle as he tried to escape the scene. John Landrum was then able to ride away on Billup's horse after his own had been shot out from under him. There were around 49 soldiers killed.

In the days following the battle, Landrum and several other soldiers traveled from Columbus to bury the dead. Former Decatur resident Robert Billups is buried somewhere down there on the east bank of the Chattahoochee in an unmarked grave with his comrades.[766]

Creek Removal and The Departure of Menawa

Following the war of 1836, all Creeks were finally forcibly removed from both Georgia and Alabama. Most were put on steamboats out of Mobile and New Orleans and then marched to Fort Gibson in Oklahoma. Remaining "friendly" Creeks were rounded up and sent along behind them in August and September of 1836.[767]

The government forced removals continued all the way into 1837 and 1838. Voluntary removals from Alabama continued through the 1840s and 1850s and some Creeks still remained behind.[768] A small number of them were able to stay in their homeland and avoid the US government. They formed the Poarch Band of Creeks that still resides in Southern Alabama.[769]

"They do not know me who suppose I can be influenced by fear. I desire peace but would not turn my back on danger. I know there will be blood shed, but I am not afraid. I have been a man of blood all my life. Now I am old and wish for peace."
~ Menawa (1836)

In all, the Creek Removals from the Southeast to Oklahoma accounted for around 23,000 Creek people.[770]

Menawa, the Upper Creek chief who had led much of the Red Stick War and the Battle of Horseshoe Bend, participated in the Creek War of 1836 alongside the Americans. He felt it was his duty to be true to the promises he had made in the Treaty of Washington.

[766] Documentation from the DeKalb Historical Society
[767] Kane, Robert (2016) Second Creek War; Encyclopedia of Alabama
[768] Kane, Robert (2016) Second Creek War; Encyclopedia of Alabama
[769] Etheridge, Robbie; (2003) Creek Country, University of Carolina Press
[770] Kane, Robert (2016) Second Creek War; Encyclopedia of Alabama

The chief they called Great Warrior was old now. He had only one wish for which he strenuously argued with the Americans. This was that he be allowed to remain in his homeland and abide by the laws of the United States. At first, he was granted this consideration for the help he had given them. But for some reason, the permission was later rescinded, and he was ordered to leave with all the others. [771]

After Menawa was informed that he would have to leave, he grew quiet and morose. He avoided questions about when he would go and seemed to avoid establishing a final day of departure. It was suggested to him at one point that part of his reluctance may have been out of fear of meeting up with the followers of McIntosh who were already waiting there in Oklahoma.

In reply, he said, "They do not know me who suppose I can be influenced by fear. I desire peace, but would not turn my back on danger. I know there will be bloodshed, but I am not afraid. I have been a man of blood all my life. Now I am old and wish for peace."[772]

Before he took his final leave, he spent a last night in Oakfuskee where he had grown up and become chief. He stayed there one night and began the journey to Oklahoma on foot the next morning. After crossing the Tallapoosa River, he seemed as if he had forgotten something and was asked if he'd like to return for it. In response, he said

After his departure from the Southeast, the story of Menawa passes into history and legend. It is not known if he ever reached the Creek Reservation in Oklahoma.

"No! Last evening, I saw the sunset for the last time, and its light shines upon the tree tops and the land and the water, that I am never to look upon again. No other evening will come, bringing to Menawa's eyes the rays of the setting sun upon the home he has left forever!"[773]

From there, the story of Menawa passes into history and legend. It is not known if he ever reached Oklahoma.

[771] McKenny, Thomas & Hall, James & Todd, Hatherly & Todd, Joseph. (1872) History of the Indian tribes of North America: with biographical sketches and anecdotes of the principal chiefs., Philadelphia: D. Rice & Co.
[772] McKenny, Thomas & Hall, James & Todd, Hatherly & Todd, Joseph. (1872) History of the Indian tribes of North America: with biographical sketches and anecdotes of the principal chiefs. Philadelphia: D. Rice & Co.
[773] McKenny, Thomas & Hall, James & Todd, Hatherly & Todd, Joseph. (1872) History of the Indian tribes of North America: with biographical sketches and anecdotes of the principal chiefs., Philadelphia: D. Rice & Co.

Portrait of Menawa[774]

EPILOGUE

Last Living Witnesses to Decatur's Pioneer Days

I had the great fortune to visit Jerusalem as a child about 40 years ago. I was about 10 years old but not too young to appreciate how accessible the ancient history of that city is. We walked on the road where Jesus had dragged His cross to crucifixion, and it had not been repaved. These were the same stones. I didn't expect that. I was astonished.

The place that made the most indelible impression on me wasn't a temple or church. It was a garden, the Garden of Gesthemane. Jesus and His disciples slept here, and He preached to them on the night before His crucifixion. In that garden, the same olive trees that were growing there that night still grace the garden today. It has been proven that olive trees can live for more than 2,000 years, and if they are cared for the way these ones have been, they can live much longer.

These are living things here on Earth that were present to witness a sermon given by Jesus. Whether you are Christian or not, we know this to have been a true event that had an impact on world history. The opportunity to touch a tree that was alive then and is still living now set my imagination on fire. I'm not a Druid. I don't feel trees are conscious beings. However, I do feel there is a difference between a rock and a living, growing thing. To this day, I find the fact these trees were there alive at that time very fascinating and moving.

In Decatur, it's not quite so dramatic as that, but the area has its own American versions of the Garden of Gesthemane. There are trees in town that witnessed some of the most dramatic scenes in the area's history and were present with the people we are disconnected from today.

Trail Trees

One of the most significant and exciting relics of the days before Decatur settlement are trail trees. They can be found in unexpected places and it's extremely exciting to come upon one still alive. Trail trees are trees that were bent over by Indians when the trees were still young to mark or point to a significant spot. Many of them marked trails passing through the thick forest that covered the entire South in those days, hence the name. Others, as we are told by Native Americans, marked important places where someone is buried or where an important event such as a battle occurred. There has been a lot of interest during recent years in identifying and protecting the Indian trail trees that litter the landscape of America, particularly in the South.

There are several trail trees in the general Decatur area and in Stone Mountain. The closest one I know of is four miles from the old courthouse on Indian Creek Drive on the grounds of the Indian Creek Lodge owned by Georgia State University. It is enormous, still in excellent health and very beautiful.

The existence of these old trees that clearly were modified long ago also provides additional support for a point I've been eager to prove as best I can. This is that I believe there was a significant number of Creek and Cherokee Indians living in the Decatur area continuously all the way up to the forced removals. The tree pictured on page 242 is clearly a trail tree and clearly very old. On the outside, I think it is unlikely that it's older than 300 years, which would mean it had to be made into a trail tree somewhere around 1750 when Decatur was only part of the backcountry.

The Deepdene Revolutionary Oak
The oldest, documented tree I'm aware of that is still living in Decatur is a massive White Oak in Deepdene Park. It has been confirmed through core samples to pre-date the Revolutionary War that began in 1775, 248 years ago in 2018 as I write this. Thankfully, it survived Hurricane Irma that took down hundreds of trees around Decatur and still looks very strong and healthy.

It has been standing there on a hill overlooking the creek since the only people passing by were Creeks and all the way through the years when Decatur was backcountry claimed by Indians and through the founding of the town to now.

Mark Pifer

The Trail Tree on Indian Creek Drive[775]

The Standing Peachtree Oak

The oak tree pictured here is not a peach tree (that would be exciting), but it is a very old oak that I found at the site of Fort Peachtree near the Atlanta pumping station on the Chattahoochee. I show it only to point out its age. I counted the rings, and this tree was 201 years old when it fell. That means it was growing there in 1817 when this was still a thriving Indian settlement and when James Mc. Montgomery and George Gilmer arrived to

build Fort Peachtree. There are many more trees of greater size than this one that are healthy and still growing in the area. These trees were there when the Cherokee returned to celebrate their victory at Horseshoe Bend and routed the Red Sticks out of the Tallapoosa and broke the Creek resistance which, led to the ceding of the land on which they grow and eventually the founding of Decatur.

Other Significant Old Trees of Decatur

The Significant Trees of Georgia Project is an effort to document the most historical and horticulturally significant trees in Georgia that are part of public or private landscapes. It's not an effort to find Champion Trees, the biggest overall tree in the state, though many of these trees are certainly large. It is organized by Dr. Tim Smalley of the Horticultural Dept. at the University of Georgia. Decatur boasts several trees that have made it onto the list.

Professor Dieckmann's Magnolias[776]

This grove of big Southern Magnolias was added to the list of Atlanta and Georgia Urban Forest Council Landmark & Historic Tree Register in 1996. They are located on the campus of Agnes Scott College in front of Rebekah Scott Hall. Professor Dieckmann was a professor of music at Agnes Scott College from 1905 to around 1942 and would frequently go for Sunday afternoon walks with Dr. J.D.M. Armistead of the English department through the woods along South Candler Street. On one of these walks in 1905, he took and opened a batch of Magnolia cones and removed the seeds with his pocket knife. He then planted the seeds in front of Rebekah Scott Hall where the trees

---

[776] Atlanta and Georgia Urban Forest Council Landmark & Historic Tree Register

grow today. The biggest of these magnolias was last measured in 2006 when it was 56 feet high, 28 inches around at the base and 65 feet around at the crown.[777]

The "Battle of Decatur" White Ash[778]
This tree was awarded to the list of Georgia Landmark and Historic trees in 1996 and placed on the Significant Trees of Georgia list in 2006. It is located on the campus of Agnes Scott College on Milton Candler Drive. The tree dates to 1854 and the Battle of Decatur. The Eastern front of the Battle of Decatur was right there with this old tree bearing witness to the carnage. When last measured in 2006, it was 67 feet high, 56 inches around at the base and 77 feet around at the crown.[779]

The Magnolia Room[780]
This beautiful little grove is located in front of the Rec Center (231 Sycamore Street) and may have been planted by Col. George Washington Scott in the late 1800s like the Horse Chestnut discussed below. They are Southern Magnolias whose limbs have spread out to a diameter of about 40 feet, sprawling out and down into the ground again. They are so large that they make a kind of dome that some call "The Magnolia Room." When last measured in 2006, the trees were 65 feet high, one of them was 26 inches around and another one 35 inches at the base and 72 feet around at the crown. Just about every day of the year you can find children visiting to climb the low spreading limbs of this beautiful old tree including my own children Ava and Sasha.

The Champion Rec Center Horse Chestnut[781]
The Horse Chestnut in front of the Decatur Recreation Center (231 Sycamore Street) is not only one of the "Significant Trees of Georgia", but it is also the largest known tree of this species in the state. At the time it was last measured in 2010, it was 60 feet tall, 66 inches around at the base and 53 feet around at the crown. The grounds of the Rec Center were once the home of Col. George Washington Scott, the benefactor of the Agnes Scott College (the school is named after his mother) who resided there from 1877 to 1902. Both the old Horse Chestnut and the Magnolias could have been planted at that time. Col.

[777] Significant Trees of Georgia Project – University of Georgia
[778] Atlanta and Georgia Urban Forest Council Landmark & Historic Tree Register
[779] Significant Trees of Georgia Project – University of Georgia
[780] Significant Trees of Georgia Project – University of Georgia
[781] Significant Trees of Georgia Project – University of Georgia

The Younger Pifer Ladies at the Magnolia Room

Scott's daughter donated the land in the 1950s. The Recreation Center replaced the Scott-Cooper home in 1958.[782]

The Mystery Incense Cedar[783]

Another tree on the Atlanta and Georgia Urban Forest Council Landmark & Historic Tree Register was nominated by Victoria Lambert and Mary Zimnik in 1996. The Mystery Incense Cedar is located on the campus of Agnes Scott College along South Candler Street by the Walters parking lot. It is believed to be around 200 years old. How the tree came to be there is the mystery because of its age and the fact it cannot be native to the area. An Incense Cedar would have been a very unusual tree to find in the area at the time this one came to be here. Incense Cedars are native to West Coast of North America.[784]

There are two plausible theories for how it got here. It is already known that there was an Antebellum home on the land where Agnes Scott College is now located. The boxwood hedge of this now disappeared old home is still present about 170 feet north of the tree. A wealthy landowner from this time could have purchased the seed of an Incense Cedar from a ship in Savannah or Charles Town.

Another theory is that this is one of the trees imported to the Eastern US in the early 1800s as an experiment to see if they could adapt to the climate and become a good resource for the manufacture of pencils. The Red Cedar eventually became the preferred species from which pencils were made but incense cedars were another candidate considered. Perhaps this incense cedar is a surviving one of these test subjects.

---

[782] Georgia Champion Tree Program
[783] Atlanta and Georgia Urban Forest Council Landmark & Historic Tree Register
[784] Significant Trees of Georgia Project – University of Georgia

FINAL THOUGHTS ON DECATUR HISTORY

Decatur History

Decatur is a beautiful place. It's also quite an old place with many, many layers underneath it. The land where the town now sits has been high in the mountains for much of its history, and it has been beneath the ocean longer than that.

If you dig anywhere in town you will soon get to things that are hundreds of millions of years old, formed when the ground was joined with the continent of Africa.

Water has been flowing down the hills and into the creeks and rivers in Decatur, then on into the South longer than any animal or insect has been alive on Earth.

Dinosaurs lived here. So, did wooly mammoths, saber-toothed tigers, giant chipmunks and colossal bears that dwarfed the biggest predators walking the planet today.

When people arrived, they found a haven between ice and ocean and they stayed. People have continuously lived in Decatur for several thousand years shaping the land and leaving things behind to let you know they were there.

The places some of those earliest residents made and the tools they used have remained undisturbed on the ground during all that time. We put our community buildings on the same spots they chose to meet. We drive our cars on the paths they created.

Over the thousands of years this place has forming, changing and hosting countless lives, it has been called Decatur for only about 200 years.

It's a very special place and has been for a very long time.

Anyone who happens upon it and gets to call it home for a while, like so many have before, should feel very lucky indeed.

Next Steps and Additional Work to be Done

Decatur is growing very rapidly. There is a lot of construction and lot of new apartment buildings going up every year and that will continue indefinitely. This construction is also rapidly moving into places that are rich in history but have been able to avoid overzealous development. I'm referring to places like Unincorporated Decatur, Panthersville and the Indian Creek area. We still have a great opportunity to identify, examine and hopefully preserve remaining important sites before they are bulldozed over. Further research and sharing of information is needed to identify these places so that a plan can be formulated to study and preserve them.

There are two specific groups of people for whom I think there is an enormous and urgent need for work to recover much of their missing history before more of it is lost.

Local Indian Sites

The first of these is the local Indian history. The story of what happened to the Creeks and how they ended up leaving the Southeast is well understood. The specific local history of the people who lived in Decatur before Americans did is very incomplete.

I love that there are parts of Soapstone Ridge where anyone can visit and see the old quarries, but it also reflects a lack of value being put in these historic places. Construction has been restricted in some key areas of Soapstone Ridge and the County has taken ownership of some of the most important historical areas, but huge, understudied swaths of Soapstone Ridge have already been destroyed by development. More are being lost every year.

There are also sites along the South River, Peachtree Creek and around the former locations of Standing Peachtree and Sandtown that desperately need more study before the next major piece of construction comes along.

Decatur Black History

The second group of people whose history needs additional work is Decatur's black pioneers. Even though most of the earliest records about Decatur were burned in a fire that destroyed the courthouse in 1842, there is much known about half of Decatur's pioneers, the white half (the white male half for the most part). There is comparatively very little known about Decatur's black pioneers. That doesn't mean that knowledge is lost to history. I believe there is very much we can still do to collect and document their stories, records and remaining sites and artifacts.

Early Decatur

Lastly, there are sites still in town that can be identified and studied before they are lost. I have found a great number of interesting pieces of very old porcelain, glass and clayware while tramping in the local creeks. A mark I was able to read on one of the pieces from a broken teapot has a readable mark for "Alfred Meakin", a label I have found to have operated in Tunstall, England between 1875 and 1897 (In 1897, the name changed to Alfred Meakin Limited but the "Ltd." is omitted on the mark I found.).[785]

Early Decatur Artifacts Recovered from Glenn Creek

In 1976 – 1978 there were several archaeological digs in Atlanta associated with the development of MARTA stations including the one in Decatur. One of the major finds from these excavations was a neighborhood garbage dump at the corner of Clifton Road and DeKalb avenue that dated to between 1890 and 1910. The excavation produced more than 20,000 artifacts that are now housed and still being examined and catalogued at Georgia State University.[786]

I believe these shards of 19th century porcelain and dinnerware are from a similar, probably older garbage dump close to the city center of Decatur. All the pieces I found are just fragments. If we can figure out exactly where it is (I think I have a fairly good idea), there is probably an enormous wealth of new

[785] Birks, Steve; A-Z of Stoke-On-Trent Potters, The Local Histories of Stoke-On-Trent, England.
[786] Records of the DeKalb Historic Society

discoveries we still could retrieve that can give us a lot of new information about the town's earliest residents.

EXHIBITS

Exhibit: Historic Fish Weirs in the Chattahoochee[787]

Bowman's Island Fish Weir (9GW344, also known as Site 140) is located below Bowman's Island and consists of a W- shaped line of rocks (18- 36" in diameter) and logs. (9) Not readily apparent in the aerial photographs, it is reported to zigzag about 200 feet across a broad, shallow part of the river at the southern end of a long set of shoals. It is most likely of historic Indian or Euro- American origin predating 1820. (10) It was in poor condition in 1996 but its construction, consisting of logs incorporated within the rock walls and at the apex of the Vs, was clearly visible. (11) This weir is the first to catch the full force of the water each time it is released from Buford Dam.

Settle's Bridge Fish Weir (9GW197, also known as Site 108) lies just below Settles Bridge and consists of a W- shaped line of rocks (18- 36" in diameter) most likely of historic Indian or Euro- American origin. (12) It was probably built circa 1810 by Cherokee Indians but could have been constructed as late as 1820, when Gwinnett County passed a law forbidding the obstruction of more than one-third of the river by dams, fish traps, or other constructions in order to allow free passage of boats and fish. (13) Although this weir is not apparent in aerial photographs, it was described as "a wooden fish dam" that was observed during a dredging operation in 1993. It ran bank to bank and was made of stones and six or eight timbers, 30' long with a gap in the center of the weir. (14)

Berkeley Lake Fish Weir (also known as the Atlanta Athletic Club/Hermitage Plantation weir) (9GW318) above Medlock Bridge Unit, is located behind a residence in Duluth in 1994. It has not been described but is clearly visible in aerial photographs.

Jones Bridge Fish Weir, Jones Bridge Unit, has been located in Gwinnett County on the east side of Jones Bridge Road off Medlock Bridge Road. No other information is available.

Holcomb Bridge Fish Weir #1 (9GW141; also known as 9GW62), in the Holcomb Bridge Unit, is a V- shaped trap located a bit upstream from the Holcomb Bridge Road crossing, in Fulton County. It is approximately 65' on one side, slanting to the V- notch, which is 8' wide, running another 100' to the opposite river bank. This site was first reported in 1976 by professional archeologists (15), and Frazier located the site in 1995. (16)

Holcomb Bridge Fish Weir #2 or Simpson Woods Retreat Fish Dam (9GW 172, also known as 9GW63), Holcomb Bridge Unit, is located just downstream of Holcomb Bridge Fish Weir #1. No condition assessment is available.

---

[787] Reprinted from Chattahoochee River National Recreation Area; Historic Resource Study (February 2007)written by Marti Gerdes and Scott Messer; additional material by Tommy Jones; edited by Jody Cook and Tommy Jones

The so-called Isham's Fish Dam lies about a half mile above the mouth of Sope Creek, just northeast of the Atlanta Country Club. It is also known as Heard's Fish Trap/Heard's Ferry Fish Dam and as Isom's Fish Dam, although the pioneer whose name was given to the nearby ford in the river was Isham. It and the Settles Bridge weir are the only of the study area's fish weirs that are W- shaped rather than V- shaped. This "fish dam" is the one noted in the Official Records (17) as the route of Cameron's Brigade (23rd Corps, 8th McCook's Cavalry) when they crossed the river on July 9, 1864, as an advance guard to cover Schofield's Army of the Ohio, which crossed the river on a pontoon bridge built that same day just below the mouth of Sope Creek. This may be the same fish dam that was illustrated in Harper's Weekly in August 1864. (18) This weir was not located in 1997, the most recently documented attempt to find it, but it is apparent in aerial photographs.

Mulberry Creek Fish Weir (9C0142), Johnson's Ferry Unit. This structure is located at the mouth of Mulberry Creek, about three-quarters of a mile south-southwest of the George Power House. The late J.C. Hyde, whose farm lies nearby, said George Power's brother Pinkney Power (19) had a fish dam in the Chattahoochee River below what is now Morgan Falls Dam between 1880-1890, and this may be that trap. (20)

Cochran's Fish Dam (or Cochran's Fish Trap) (9C078), is located in the Cochran Shoals unit a little less than a mile above the Powers Ferry bridge, near the south end of the unit's jogging trail. Not located during surveys in 1994 and 1997, but it is described as of timber construction in a 1972 assessment. It is clearly visible in aerial photographs. Fish weirs not located for this study but noted in previous documentation include *Stricklins* (sic) Fish Trap on Suwanee Creek. Frazier was not able to locate this weir but noted that it was mentioned in Gwinnett County Inferior Court Records, 1832, page 339.21 Pace's Ferry Fish Weir has also been documented as having existed between river miles 302 and 303.

Mark Pifer

Exhibit: Brief Overview of Geologic Periods in Decatur and Georgia

		LAND FORMATION IN GEORGIA & DECATUR	ANIMAL LIFE
PRECAMBRIAN (undefined to 542 million years ago)	Archean (undefined to 2,500 million years ago)		None
	Proterozoic (2,500-542 mya)	• 1 billion YA: Proto-North America collides with to for the ancient supercontinent Rodinia. An enormous mountain range is thrown up as a result that spans from Labrador to Mexico and over into what is now Scotland. • The mountains were called the Grenville range and remnants of it can be found near Cartersville Ga., on the east side of I-75 and Route 20/Canton Hwy. • The Grenville event (orogeny) also created other igneous rocks like Granite. • 630 – 700MM YA: The continents begin to separate. The Lapetus (proto-Atlantic) ocean forms. • The Grenville mountains are worn down and transported to sea (which covers much of Georgia). Separation of the continents creates the Ocoee Basin – an area of lower elevation spanning the Western Carolinas, east Tennessee and north Georgia. The basin was eventually filled in by sediment deposited from the erosion of the mountains • Volcanic islands form in the Lapetus sea covering Virginia, the Carolinas, and Georgia. Mineral-rich hot water passing through the rocks created by these volcanic islands creates gold found in Dahlonega.	During the late Cambrian, trilobites, Sponges, Brachiopods and worms flourish in the shallow Lapetus sea that covers Georgia.
PALEOZOIC (542-251 million years ago)	Cambrian (542-488 million years ago)	• The northern part of Georgia and Decatur is still covered by the shallow Lapetus sea. • The environment of Georgia is very tropical. • Sandstone, dolostone, and shale are deposited on the new coast created by the separation of supercontinent Rodinia.	First life is appearing in present-day Georgia and Decatur. The Lapetus Sea is abundant with life including corals, brachiopods, snails, nautiloid cephalopods, crinoids, trilobites and bryozoans mainly found in North Georgia.

	LAND FORMATION IN GEORGIA & DECATUR	ANIMAL LIFE
Ordovician (488-444 mya)	• The Lapetus Sea begins to close but Georgia and Decatur are still submerged. As another tectonic plate moves toward the East Coast, the floor of the Lapetus Sea is pushed downward and New volcanoes and islands are formed in the shrinking Lapetus sea. • Volcanoes stretched across north Georgia and as far west as the Mississippi. • Beds of volcanic ash can be found within the limestone in northwest Georgia.	Conditions for life are like the Cambrian period. The state remains submerged under the Lapetus Sea. Tidal flats form at the coast.
Silurian (444-416 mya)	• The Lapetus Sea still covers Georgia. Decatur is submerged. • Late Ordovician and Silurian: Volcanic islands and possibly a small continent collides with Georgia creating a new belt of mountains called the Taconic range • Glacial ice is building at the South Pole.	Georgia and Decatur are still submerged under a shallow sea that contains deep water. This sea contains animals like Archimedes bryozoans, blastoids,
Devonian (416-359 mya)	• A large continent called Baltica (Europe) collides with North America including Georgia. Volcanic islands form and new mountains are thrown up once again called the Acadian Highlands (not the same ones that exist today). Sea levels are still generally dropping.	Sea levels rise and Georgia/Decatur are covered by relatively marshy river systems. Late Mississippian: The marshy river complexes that formed became
Mississippian (359-318 mya) (Early Carboniferous)	• Seas are withdrawing as glaciation is beginning again. Water in the state becomes shallower.	Higher elevations of Georgia became vast, during the middle Pennsylvanian and Permian periods has been lost in Georgia due to erosion during that time.
Pennsylvanian (318-299 mya)	• Late Mississippian through the Pennsylvanian and into the Permian: Africa (as part of the ancient supercontinent Gondwana) is colliding with North America. • New mountains form called the Alleghenian which will become Appalachian range. • The Lapetus Sea completely closes and the supercontinent of Pangaea has formed. All the continents we	The fossil record during the middle Pennsylvanian and Permian periods has been lost in Georgia due to erosion during that time.

	LAND FORMATION IN GEORGIA & DECATUR	ANIMAL LIFE
Permian (299-251 mya) (Late Carboniferous)	• Decatur is located high up in the Alleghenian/Appalachian mountain range which soars up 2.5 to 4.5 miles above sea level, rivaling the size of the present-day Himalayas. • To the east and south of the mountains where the Iapetus sea once was are vast, swampy forests filled with giant ferns, huge insects and amphibians. • Sea levels frequently rose and fell. Sandstone deposited by runoff from these mountains can be found on Lookout Mountain. Throughout the Permian, the Alleghenian mountains are being worn down.	The fossil record is sparse during this period because it is a time of erosion where rocks and fossils are being melted away.
Triassic (251-200 mya) (MESOZOIC (251-65.5 mya))	• Africa begins to split away from North America and Georgia. As the rift opens, the Atlantic Ocean forms. • As the continents separate, a piece of Africa is left behind which we now know as South Georgia, Southern Alabama, Florida and possibly the Bahamas and other parts of the Caribbean. As pressure is relieved, cracks open in the preexisting rocks that are filled by magma from underneath and forms into the igneous rock diabase. Diabase deposits from this period can be seen in Stone Mountain. These diabase deposits range from 180MM to 230MM years old. • Sedimentary rocks from the late Triassic and Jurassic periods can be found in the coastal plain of Georgia buried beneath younger sedimentary rocks.	The fossil record is sparse during this period because it is a time of erosion where rocks and fossils are being melted away. Unfortunately, the fossil record in Georgia from this time was erased due to the continued metamorphosis of rocks in our area.
Jurassic (200-145 mya)	• The Alleghenian mountains are eroded down and deposited into the Atlantic and Gulf of Mexico.	Late Cretaceous: Dinosaurs become extinct. Mammals, reptiles and birds inherit the Earth.
Cretaceous (145.5-65.5 million years ago)	• The Alleghenian mountains are eroded down and deposited into the Atlantic and Gulf of Mexico. • Sea levels are very high. Most of Georgia is covered by the Atlantic Ocean. Macon, Columbus and Augusta are under water. Decatur is about 80 miles from the coast. • Cretaceous sedimentary rocks that overlap older ones in the fall line of Georgia have been uncovered by water flowing into the coastal plain forming many of the shoals in Georgia rivers. These rocks are part of a band of rocks where Cretaceous dinosaurs have been found in Georgia.	The climate was much warmer than today and Georgia is very tropical. Dinosaurs are roaming in Georgia near the water including Hadrosaurs, Ornithomimids and Albertosaurus. Pterosaurs and mosasaurs have also been identified in Georgia.

Mark Pifer

		LAND FORMATION IN GEORGIA & DECATUR		ANIMAL LIFE
CENOZOIC (65.5 mya to present)	Paleogene (65.5-23 mya)			The dinosaurs perished in a mass extinction caused by the impact of an enormous asteroid.
		Another gigantic comet or asteroid slams Virginia and Maryland creating the Chesapeake Bay and sending debris for hundreds of miles and raining down on Georgia. Pieces of this cataclysm, called Georgialites, can be found scattered throughout the state today. Late Eocene: The climate dramatically cools. Sea levels drop. Glaciers begin crawling from the poles once again. Georgia becomes dry land.	Similar conditions to the Eocene	Georgiacetus, an ancestor of modern whales, 12 feet long with legs is crawling and swimming around in the shallow Atlantic over present day. Georgia and undoubtedly being hunted by the 25-foot crocodiles and Megladons (50-foot-long sharks) that also prowl the shallow Atlantic. 35MM YA
			Similar conditions to the Oligocene	Similar conditions to the Eocene
	Neogene (23 mya to the present)		Similar conditions to the Oligocene	
		Glaciers build and recede. Georgia remains Ice free. Seas deepen and recede. Seas were sometimes 120 meters shallower than today. Other times they were about 50 meters deeper than today. Most of Georgia is covered by forest and grassland. Beach ridges mark the past sea level highs. The climate was sometimes arid. Some rivers dried up and wind from the west blew giant sand dunes off the river beds which can be seen along the Flint River, Ohoopee and Canoochee.		As glaciers grow and recede throughout the Pleistocene and ocean levels rise and fall and the Alleghanian/Appalachian Mountains have been worn down, the area of Decatur would have become a haven and a paradise for animal life, and particularly for mammals. As a result, fossils show an enormous diversity animals and evidence from near Cartersville, Ga., (which would have had the same climate and landscape as Decatur) has been well documented.

Sources

o An Aphelaspis Zone (Upper Cambrian, Paibian) Trilobite Faunule in the Central Conasauga River Valley, North Georgia USA. David R Schwimmer and William M. Montante. Southeastern Geology, V. 49, No. 1, June 2012, p. 31-41Geology of the Greater Atlanta Area, Keith McConnell, Keith and Abrams, Charlotte; (1984), Geology of the Greater Atlanta Area, Department of Natural Resources Environmental Protection Division; Georgia Geologic Survey

o Geologic Guide to Stone Mountain Park, Robert L. Atkins and Lisa G. Joyce, Georgia Department of Natural Resources, Environmental Protection Division and Georgia Geologic Survey; 1980

o Geologic History of the Southern Appalachians

o Geology of the Greater Atlanta Area, Keith McConnell, Keith and Abrams, Charlotte; (1984), Geology of the Greater Atlanta Area, Department of Natural Resources Environmental Protection Division; Georgia Geologic Survey

o Gore, Pamela J. W. (2006), Geologic "History of Georgia: Overview" New Georgia Encyclopedia

o John Schlee,"Our Changing Continent", USGS

o Oskin, Becky (2014), Weird Magnetic Anomaly Reveals Ancient Tectonic Crash, Live Science

o Ray, C. E. 1965. A new chipmunk, Tamias aristus, from the Pleistocene of Georgia. Journal of Paleontology **39**(5):1016-1022.)

o USGS Mineral Resources On-Line Spatial Data

Exhibit: A Summary of Georgia's Cultural Sequence[788]

Period	Time	Subsistence Pattern	Development Pattern in Georgia and Decatur	Settlement Pattern	Identifying Features
European colonization	1632 to 1775	Farming, trading, pioneering, military service, exporting-importing	• The Yamasee War • Deer trade replaces slave trade as a primary source of Indian livelihood. • Importing of African slaves became more profitable than continuing to trade in Indian slaves.	Family farmsteads, port towns, pioneer settlements and Indian villages to non-ceded lands	Horses European tools replace Indian tools
European contact and exploration	1541 to 1632	Farming, trading, hunting, trapping, factoring, exploring	• Wide scale death from disease Mound construction ceases as well as Remaining Indians organize into larger groups • Local Indians were part of the Coweta group that joined the Creek Confederacy – part of the Lower Creeks that lived along the Chattahoochee. Local Indians gather along the Chattahoochee in the South or in Sandtown and Standing Peachtree.	Trading outposts, missions, forts, cantonments and smaller Indian villages	
Mississippian	900 to 1541	Intensive agriculture supplemented by gathering and hunting	• Chiefdoms that link together several towns.[789] • Villages became larger and less dispersed. • The Etowah site is the largest known Mississippian site that is still intact.[790] • The vicinity of Sandtown became larger and may have had many mounds. • Apart from Sandtown and the Shallowford area, the rest of the area is sparsely occupied by around 1100.[791] • Europeans were more present at the end of the Mississippian.[792]	Large permanent fortified towns with many forms of public architecture, smaller communities, separate homesteads, extensive network of foot trails	Temple mounds, plazas, ditches, Corn, beans, squash, small triangular projectile points

[788] Society for Georgia Archaeology
[789] New Georgia Encyclopedia
[790] New Georgia Encyclopedia
[791] Price, Vivian (1997) History of DeKalb County, Georgia, 1822-1900; Wolfe Pub. Co.
[792] New Georgia Encyclopedia; Woodland Period: Overview

Period	Time	Subsistence Pattern	Development Pattern in Georgia and Decatur	Settlement Pattern	Identifying Features
Woodland	3000 ya to 1,100 ya	Gathering and hunting supplemented by horticulture	• Pottery replaces soapstone bowls • Indians move to larger villages. Some of these are located around Stone Mountain, Nancy Creek, in the crook of the North and South Forks of Peachtree Creek and at the location of Sandtown where Six Flags Over Georgia is today. • Tribes may have engaged in warfare with one another. Fortifications appeared around towns for the first time.[793]	Small, widely-dispersed villages inhabited most of the time occupying floodplains and clearing for gardens.	Bow & arrow, decorated pottery, food storage pits, stone/earth burial mounds, sturdy homes
Archaic	10,000 ya to 3,000 ya	Gathering and hunting of wild plants and animals; clearing areas in forest to attract game to new plants	• Settlements near North/South Forks of Peachtree Creek, Stone Mountain, Snapfinger Creek, Sugar Creek and the South River.[794] • Soapstone Ridge is a major area of activity. Soapstone slabs traded through extensive network • Frequent trade using rivers and trails.	Larger seasonally occupied camps	Atlatl, soapstone vessels and ornaments, stone grinding tools
Paleoindian	>12,000 ya to 10,000 ya	Small game hunting; fishing, foraging and gathering of various plants; hunting of large game extinct today: mastodon, mammoth, giant beaver, ground sloth, musk oxen	• Seasonal bands passed through the area of Decatur depending upon the season and the availability of game.	Small seasonally occupied camps	Clovis projectile points

---

[793] New Georgia Encyclopedia; Woodland Period: Overview
[794] Price, Vivian (1997) History of DeKalb County, Georgia, 1822-1900; Wolfe Pub. Co. , 1986

Mark Pifer

Exhibit: Long List of Georgia's Pleistocene Fossils[795]
Vertebrates from various sources (This should not be considered a complete list.)
Georgia's Pleistocene Fossil Reports
Smithsonian National Museum of Natural History

Fish

Genus & Species	Common Name	Specimens	Location
Carcharodon carcharias	Great White	Tooth	Georgia

Amphibians

Genus & Species	Common Name	Specimens	Location
Gastrophryne carolinensis	Narrowmouth Toad	Skeletal parts	Bartow 1969
Gyrinophilus	Salamander	Vertebra	Bartow

Retiles

Genus & Species	Common Name	Specimens	Location
Crotalus (Species?)	Timber Rattlesnake	54 Vertebra	Bartow
Diadophis punctatus	Ringneck Snake	19 Vertebra	Bartow
Geochelone crassiscutata	Tortoise (Juvenile)	Partial shell	Bartow 1968
Geochelone crassiscutata	Tortoise (Adult)	Various	Bartow
Kinosternon subrubrum	Eastern mud turtle	Partial shell	Bartow
Lampropeltis Triangulum	Milk snake	4 Vertebra	Bartow
Nerodia sipedon	North Water snake	Vertebra	Bartow
Pseudemys concinna	River cooter turtle	Partial carapace	Bartow
Sceloporus undulates	East fence lizard	Skull/teeth	Bartow 1963
Storeria (Species?)	Red belly snake	Vertebra	Bartow
Terrapene canaliculata	Box Turtle	Carapace frag.	Georgia
Terrapene carolina	Eastern Box Turtle	Multiple Skeletal	Bartow 1968
Thamnophis sirtalis	Garter snake	Vertebra	Bartow

Birds

Genus & Species	Common Name	Specimens	Location
Class: Aves	Owl	Partial Skull	Bartow
Anas rubripes	Black Duck	Humerus	Bartow
Canachites canadensis	Spruce Grouse	Humerus	Bartow
Ectopistes migratorius	Passenger Pigeon	Hunerous	Bartow
Meleagris gallopavo	Wild Turkey	Skeletal Parts	Bartow

Mammals

Genus & Species	Common Name	Specimens	Location
Family: Delphinidae	Dolphin	8 Skull bones	Georgia
Family: Physeteridae	Sperm Whale	Tooth	Georgia
Family: Physeteridae	Sperm Whale	25 Skull bones	Georgia
Physeter vetus	Sperm Whale	Tooth	Georgia 1929
Castoroides (species?)	Giant Beaver	2 Teeth	Glynn
Equus leidyi	Horse	Tooth	Glynn
Equus leidyi	Horse	Partial skull	Glynn
Equus (Species?)	Horse	Multiple	Glynn

[795] Georgia's Pleistocene Fossil Reports; Smithsonian National Museum of Natural History; Online Collections Catalog; Georgia Specimens; Quaternary Period, Downloaded 7/April/2013

Scientific Name	Common Name	Description	Location
Eremotherium (species?)	Giant Ground	SlothMulti. Teeth	Glynn
Megatherium mirabile	Giant Sloth	15 Assorted	Georgia 1823
Mammut americanum	American Mastodon	Tooth	Georgia 1950
Mammut americanum	American Mastodon	Tooth	Coffee
Mammuthus columbi	Columb. Mammoth	Tooth	Coffee
Neochoerus (Species?)	Capybara	Tooth	Glynn
Neochoerus (Species?)	Capybara	2 Teeth	Georgia
Neotoma (Species?)	Packrat	Lower Jaw	Bartow 1885
Tamias aristus	Chipmunk	Partial skull	Bartow 1964
Tapirus veroensis	Tapir	Partial Skull/Teeth	Georgia

Ladds Cave; Bartow County

Most of these Bartow County reports originated with research in Ladds Cave and quarry operations in that immediate area. This site is popular with rock clubs as it produces very attractive cave onyx.

Age of fossils from the Ladds Area:

The Ladds Quarry site yielded dates of 10,290 (+or-100) years ago and 10,940 (+ or - 210) years ago. Kingston Saltpeter Cave yielded dates of 10,300 (+or-130) years ago. Yarborough Cave yielded dates of 14,315 (+or- 755) years ago, 16,500 (+or-1,250) years ago, 18,610 (+or-960) years ago and 23,880 (+or-200) years ago. (30)

Land Mammals Carnivores listed first with herbivores listed below.

(Smaller rodents such as mice have been omitted.)

Scientific Name	Common Name
Carnivores	
Canis lupus	Gray Wolf
Conepatus leuconotus	American Hog-nosed Skunk
Didelphis virginiana	Virginia Opossum (Marsupial & omnivore)
Leopardus sp	Ocelot or Margay
Lutra canadensis	North American River Otter
Lynx Rufus	Bobcat
Martes pennanti	Fisher Cat
Mephitis	Striped Skunk
Mustela frenata	Long Tailed Weasel
Panthera onca	Jaguar
Puma concolor	Cougar
Procyon lotor	Raccoon
Urocyon cinereoargenteus	Gray Fox
Ursus americanus	American Black Bear
Spilogale putorius	Eastern Spotted Skunk
Tremarctos floridanus	Extinct Florida Cave Bear

Land Mammals, Herbivores/Omnivores

Scientific Name	Common Name
Bison sp?	Bison (Species?)
Bison Latifrons	Giant Bison
Castor canadensis	Beaver
Castoroides ohioensis	Extinct Giant Beaver
Dasypus bellus	Large Armadillo
Equus	Horse -
Eremotherium laurillardi	Largest Giant Ground Sloth

Glaucomys volans	Southern Flying Squirrel
Holmesina septentrionalis	Giant armadillo
Hydrochaeris holmesi	Extinct Holmes Capybara
Mammut americanum	American Mastodon
Mammuthis columbi	Columbian Mammoth
Megalonyx sp?	Giant Ground Sloth
Mylohyus fossilis	Extinct Peccary
Neochoerus pinckneyi	Extinct Giant Capybara
Odocoileus virginianus	White Tail Deer
Palaeolama mirifica	Extinct Stout Legged Llama
Paramylodon harlani	Ground Sloth
Platygonus compressus	Extinct Flat Headed Peccary
Rangifer tarandus	Reindeer/Caribou
Sciurus caolinensis	Eastern Gray Squirrel
Spermophilus sp?	Ground Squirrel
Sylvilagus floridanus	Cottontail Rabbit
Sylvilagus palustris	Marsh Rabbit
Tapirus veroensis	Extinct Tapir

Mammals; Bats

Scientific Name	Common Name
Eptesicus fuscus	Big Brown Bat
Myotis grisescens	Gray Bat
Myotis lucifugus	Little Brown Bat
Pipistrellus subflavus	Eastern Pipistrelle Bat

Reptiles; Turtle/Tortoise

Scientific Name	Common Name
Apalone ferox	Florida Soft-shelled Turtle
Chelydra serpentina	Common Snapping Turtle
Chrysemys picta	Painted Turtle
Clemmys insculpta	Wood Turtle
Clemmys muhlenbergii	Bog Turtle
Deirochelys reticularia	Chicken Turtle
Gopherus polyphemus	Gopher Tortoise
Hesperotestudo crassiscutata	Extinct Giant Land Tortoise
Hesperotestudo incisa	Extinct Land Tortoise
Kinosternon subrubrum	Eastern Mud Turtle
Kinosternon sp?	Mud Turtle
Pseudemys concinna	Eastern River Cooter
Pseudemys nelsoni	Florida Redbelly Turtle
Sternotherus sp?	Musk Turtle
Terrapene carolina	Eastern Box Turtle
Trachemys scripta	Pond Slider

Reptiles; Snakes

Scientific Name	Common Name
Agkistrodon contortrix	Southern Copperhead
Agkistrodon piscivorus	Eastern Cottonmouth
Carphophis amoenus	Eastern Worm Snake
Coluber constrictor	Eastern Racer
Crotalus horridus	Timber Rattlesnake

Crotalus sp?	Rattlesnake
Diadophis punctatus	Ringneck Snake
Elaphe guttata	Corn Snake
Elaphe obseleta	Black Rat Snake
Elaphe vulpina	Eastern Fox Snake
Heterodon platyrhinos	Eastern Hognose snake
Heterodon sp?	Hognose snake
Lampropeltis calligaster	Mole Kingsnake
Lampropeltis getulus	Eastern Kingsnake
Lampropeltis triangulum	Milk Snake
Nerodia fasciata	Southern Water Snake
Nerodia sipedon	northern Water Snake
Opheodrys aestivus	Rough Green Snake
Pituophis melanoleucus	Pine Snake
Regina sp?	Colubrid family of snakes
Storeria dekayi	Brown Snake
Thamnophis sauritus	Ribbon Snake
Thamnophis sirtalis	Common Garter Snake
Virginia striatula	Rough Earth Snake
Virginia valeriae	Smooth Earth Snake

Reptiles: Crocodilian

Scientific Name	Common Name
Alligator mississippiensis	Modern American Alligator

Below are lists of animals whose fossils haven't been seen in Georgia but are expected to be present as they're known from surrounding states. In many cases, this is simply a matter of research. Many surrounding states, especially Florida, have conducted extensive research in this area where Georgia has not.

Inferred Megafauna Mammals with confirmed locations

Scientific Names	Common Name	Known Ranges
Bootherium bombifrons	Marlan's Muskox	Florida & north Carolina
Bison antiquus	Ancient Bison	Florida (N. America)
Equus alaskae	Small Yukon Horse	Florida (known in Alaska)
Equus fraternus	Short Legged Horse	Florida & Virginia
Equus laurentius	Western Horse	Florida (also California)
Glyptotherium floridanum	Glyptodont	Florida & South Carolina
Hemiauchenia macrocephala	Large Headed Llama	Florida (Once widespread)

Inferred Carnivore Mammals with confirmed locations

Scientific Names	Common Name	Known Ranges
Canis dirus	Extinct Dire Wolf	FL & Virginia (Across NA)
Canis latrans	Coyote	Florida & Virginia (In GA today)
Canis rufus	Red Wolf	Florida (Across Southeast)
Dinobastis serus	Extinct Sabertooth Cat	Florida (Once widespread)
Leopardus amnicola	Margay	Florida (Once widespread)
Leopardus pardalis	Ocelot	Florida (Once widespread)
Panthera atrox	Extinct American Lion	Florida & Virginia (Across NA)
Smilodon fatalis	True Saber-tooth Tiger	Florida & S. Carolina (Common)
Ursus arctos	Brown Bear	Florida (Once widespread)

Made in the USA
Columbia, SC
28 December 2020